SUPERMARKETING

FRANK J. CHARVAT, Ph.D.
Associate Professor of Marketing
School of Business Administration, Emory University

THE MACMILLAN COMPANY　　NEW YORK

© Frank J. Charvat 1961

First Printing

Library of Congress catalog card number: 60-14467

The Macmillan Company, New York
Brett-Macmillan Ltd., Galt, Ontario

Printed in the United States of America

PREFACE

The supermarket today is regarded as an established institution, yet only thirty years ago it was but an embryonic idea. Already, this marketing innovation has left an indelible imprint on most aspects of food manufacturing, processing, wholesaling, and retailing. The lack of a text devoted to a comprehensive appraisal and analytical study of the industry has prompted the writing of this book.

Directed toward a broad audience, *Supermarketing* is intended as an aid to food and related-industry entrepreneurs, executives, key employees and those aspiring to positions of responsibility, and marketing students at the university level. It is hoped that all will find something helpful here. Top executives, for example, who must be well informed about all the many facets of supermarket operation, will find of particular interest the chapters on financial considerations, the impact of the supermarket on the food industry, and managerial policy and practice. Superette managers who want to attain supermarket status for their enterprises will find of value the store-operation sections and the appendix. Food brokers, manufacturers' salesmen, processors, and wholesalers will be interested in the entire text, especially the sections on buying operations and the supermarket's impact on the industry. Executives of retailing operations affected by the supermarket may find information relevant to the increasing competition they face from the supermarkets. Finally, students of marketing at universities, particularly in the areas of retailing, can learn principles and practices which will be of value

iii

in their future business careers. The book may also be of use as a supplement in many different courses in marketing.

The author owes a debt of gratitude to the library of the Super Market Institute for the use of its excellent research facilities. Research there was facilitated by the cheerful cooperation of the librarian, Catherine McAndrews. Other invaluable aid in the gathering of pertinent data was rendered by the Institute's Research Department, directed by Curt Kornblau. The book has benefited greatly from the counsel of Dr. Richard M. Clewett, Professor of Marketing at Northwestern University. The analytical criticism of Dr. W. Tate Whitman, Professor of Economics at Emory University, has been equally helpful. Dr. Patrick Kemp, also of Emory University, edited the sections on financing, operations, and managerial policy and perspective. Facilities for research and the mechanical work of compiling the text were provided by Emory University's School of Business through the assistance of Dean Guy W. Trump and the late Dean Gordon Siefkin. Thanks go also to all the other university colleagues and business associates who were so helpful.

Above all, credit is due my wife, Theodora, for her help with the editing and other intricate details and for her encouragement and inspiration. Nor do I forget my son, Jimmy, who always wanted to help.

FRANK J. CHARVAT

Atlanta, Georgia

CONTENTS

1. **INTRODUCTION**   1

Significance of the supermarket industry • Composition of the industry in 1958 • Approach of the book to study of the supermarket industry • Scope of the study

2. **DEVELOPMENT OF THE SUPERMARKET**   11

Introduction • Large markets prior to 1930 • Era of the "cheapy" supermarket, 1930 to 1935 • Period of experimental growth and development, 1935 to 1946 • Postwar period of modern supermarket expansion • Summary

3. **EXTERNAL FACTORS THAT INFLUENCED THE GROWTH OF THE SUPERMARKET INDUSTRY**   30

Introduction • Changes in personal disposable income and personal consumption expenditures • Shifts in upper income shares • Changes in the pattern of food consumption • Changes in expenditures in food stores • Technological developments and their adoption • Population growth and shift to the suburbs • Retail trend toward decentralization • Shift in consumer buying habits, including one-stop shopping and scrambled merchandising • Additional external factors that influenced the supermarket development • Market of the 1960's • Summary

4. **SELLING OPERATIONS**   53

Introduction • Volume—a supermarket necessity • Sales practices of supermarkets • Summary

J.W.D.
X
X

5. BUYING OPERATIONS AND MARGINS   75

Introduction · Cost of goods sold · Gross margin · Summary

6. EXPENSES AND PROFITS   99

Introduction · Operating expenses · Profit · Summary

7. FINANCIAL FACTORS   121

Introduction · General asset structure of a supermarket · Development of a representative supermarket balance sheet · Current assets · Equipment needs in a supermarket · Land and
building · Intangible assets · Leasing of fixed assets · Sources
of capital—debt · Sources of capital—ownership · Profits on
equity capital · Results of the analysis of certain financial statements of supermarket chains · Summary

8. EARLY SUPERMARKET IMPACT ON THE FOOD
   STORE INDUSTRY   152

Introduction · Los Angeles area supermarkets · Invasion of the
East by the "cheapy" supermarket · The small independent
grocer versus the "cheapy" supermarket · Food chains versus
the "cheapy" supermarket · The case of the Great Atlantic &
Pacific Tea Company · Supermarket advantages for large food
chains · Summary

9. SUPERMARKETS BECOME BIG BUSINESS—
   INTEGRATION   168

Introduction · Chains dominate supermarket industry · Integration · Concentration among major food chains · Food chain
dilemma—acquire or expire · Voluntary chain growth · Summary

10. CHANGES IN NUMBER OF FOOD STORES AND
    THEIR SALES VOLUME   188

Introduction · Changes in the number of food stores · Changes
in the sales by type of food store · Conclusions on changes in
the number of food stores and their sales volume · Summary

11. CHANGES IN THE SALES OF MAJOR PRODUCT
    LINES BY TYPES OF FOOD STORE OUTLETS   199

Introduction · Sales of major product classes in supermarkets · Sales of meat products, poultry, and seafood by type of
food store · Sales of fresh fruit and vegetables by type of food

11. CHANGES IN THE SALES OF MAJOR PRODUCT
LINES (Continued)

store · Sales of confectionery products by type of food store ·
Sales of bakery products by type of food store · Sales of canned
goods and grocery items by grocery stores and combination
markets · Sales of nonfood products in grocery stores and combination markets · Summary

12. MANAGERIAL POLICY AND PERSPECTIVE   221

Introduction · Dynamic nature of the supermarket · Position in
its growth cycle · Supermarket trend toward "bigness" · Organization concepts · Science of decision making in management · Use of research · Relationship of profit to volume, fixed
expense, and promotion · Merchandising policies · Store operations · Financing growth · Deterrents to supermarket growth ·
The illusiveness of good will

APPENDIX A   253

BIBLIOGRAPHY   265

INDEX   271

J.W.D.

TABLES

1-1 Total Sales by Selected Types of Retail Outlets for the Year 1958   2

1-2 Number of Supermarkets in the United States, Estimated Sales Volume and Per Cent of Grocery Store Sales and of Food Store Sales Transacted by Supermarkets for the Years 1935 to 1958   3

1-3 Ownership of Supermarkets Classified by Size of Organization for the Year 1958   4

1-4 Number and Sales of Supermarkets Classified by Dollar Volume for the Year 1958   5

2-1 National Income and Employment in the United States for the Years 1929 to 1936   20

2-2 Profit and Loss Statement for the Average Grocery Store in the Louisville Survey as a Percentage of Sales for the Year 1929   22

2-3 Condensed Profit and Loss Statement of the Retail Store Operation of the Great A & P Tea Company as a Percentage of Sales for the Years 1929 to 1935   23

2-4 Operating Statement of the Big Bear, Elizabeth, New Jersey, for the Year 1933   24

2-5 Operating Statement of an Average Independent Combination Market as a Percentage of Sales for the Year 1935   26

2-6 Number of A & P Supermarkets and Small Economy Stores for the Years 1936 to 1943   27

3-1 Total Disposable Personal Income, Total and Per Capita Personal Consumption Expenditure, and the Cost of Living Index in the United States for the Years 1935 to 1958   32

3-2 Yearly Consumption of Food Products per Capita, Retail-Weight Equivalent (in pounds) by Major Food Groups for the Years 1929, 1948, and 1954   34

3-3 Total Food Store Sales, Per Capita Food Store Sales, and Retail Food Price Index for the Years 1935 to 1958   36

3-4 Percentage of Personal Income Expenditures Spent in Food Stores   37

3-5 Motor Vehicle Registrations (in thousands) in the United States for the Years 1915 to 1958   38

3-6 Manufacturers' Sales by Number of Units of Refrigerators and Home Freezers for the Years 1926 to 1956   39

3-7 Shift in Population in 140 Central Cities of the United States with 50,000 Population and Over for the Years 1930 and 1940   42

3-8 Shift in Population in 168 Central Cities of the United States with 50,000 Population and Over for the Years 1940 and 1950   43

3-9 Retail Trade by City Size for the Years 1954, 1948, and 1939   44

3-10 Number of Supermarkets in the United States by Size of the Community for the Years 1940, 1950, and 1954, and the Percentage that Each Community is to the Total   46

3-11 Findings from McCall's Magazine Consumer Diary Study of Food Purchases Made by 1,090 Families for One Week in the Year 1956   48

4-1 Sales of Certain Classes of Retail Stores and Total Retail Sales in the United States for the Years 1929, 1939, 1948, and 1954 (in billions of dollars)   54

4-2 Operating Statistics of Selected Food Chains Expressed as a Percentage of Sales for the Years 1955 to 1958   55

4-3 Operating Statistics of Wilt's Supermarket, Elkhart, Indiana, Expressed as a Percentage of Sales for the Year 1956   56

4-4 Maximum Trading Area Radius for a $500,000 Yearly Volume (and over) Supermarket by Size of Community   65

4-5 Annual Inventory Turnover of Selected Supermarket Chains for the Year 1956   70

4-6 Annual Inventory Turnover of Various Lines of Retailing for the Year 1954   71

4-7 Source of Nonfood Products in Supermarkets Expressed as a Percentage of Stores Using the Source   72

5-1 Grocery Promotion and New Item Fact Sheet   81

5-2 Gross Margin, Expense and New Profit (before taxes) as a Percentage of Sales for Selected Supermarket Chains for the Year 1956   91

5-3 Gross Margins in Supermarkets by Major Product Lines   92

5-4 Gross Margin for Various Kinds of Retail Establishments for the Year 1954   94

6-1   Operating Statistics of Selected Super Market Institute Members as a Percentage of Sales for the Years 1954 to 1958   100

6-2   Operating Expenses as a Percentage of Sales for Various Types of Retail Stores for the Year 1954   102

6-3   Major Operating Expenses as a Percentage of Sales for Certain Types of Retail Outlets   103

6-4   Advertising Expenditures by Media for the Supermarket Industry as a Percentage of Total Dollar Ad Expenditures for the Year 1956   105

6-5   How Stamps Affect Supermarket Sales   107

6-6   Functional Expense Analysis of Selected Food Chains as a Percentage of Sales for the Years 1950 to 1958   110

6-7   Itemized Expenses Classified by Functions for Selected Food Chains for the Year 1958   111

6-8   Net Profit as a Percentage of Sales for Various Types of Retail Stores for the Year 1954   119

7-1   Balance Sheet and Yearly Operating Statement of a Representative Supermarket   124

7-2   Sources of Capital for the Supermarket Industry   138

7-3   Sales, Cost, and Profit Relationships for the Representative Supermarket at Various Levels of Volume   146

7-4   Results of Financial Ratio Analysis of Certain Major Supermarket Chains for the Years 1950 and 1956   150

8-1   Statistics on the Number and Volume of Sales of Large Combination Markets in the United States for the Years 1929 and 1935 (in thousands)   156

8-2   Number of Stores in the Five Largest Food Chains for the Years 1934 to 1940   159

8-3   Sales for the Five Largest Volume Food Chains for the Years 1934, 1937, and 1940 (in millions)   159

8-4   The Total Number of Stores and Number of Unprofitable Units of the A & P Co. for the Years 1933 to 1941   161

8-5   Total Sales of A & P, All Grocery and Combination Markets and All Food Stores for the Years 1929 to 1943   163

8-6   Statistics on Total Number of A & P Stores, Number of Supermarkets, Total Sales and Supermarket Sales for the Years 1936 to 1943 (sales in millions of dollars)   164

8-7 Operating Results of the A & P, Detailed into Economy Stores and Supermarkets for the Year 1941 (sales in thousands)   166

9-1 Number of Food Manufacturing Plants Operated by 62 Major Food Chains and the Value of Shipments from these Establishments for the Years 1954 and 1958   171

9-2 Dollar Sales of Ten of the Largest Food Store Chains for the Years 1945 and 1958 (in millions)   173

9-3 Sales of Ten Major Supermarket Chains and Total Food Store Sales for the Years 1945 and 1958 (in millions)   173

9-4 Number of Stores, Sales per Store, and Net Income per Store for American Stores Company for the Years 1945 to 1958   174

9-5 Number and Volume of Food Stores That Were Acquired by Food Chains for the Years 1949 to 1958   176

9-6 Chain Grocery Store Sales Classified by Volume, Expressed in Dollars and as a Percentage of Total Chain Grocery Sales for the Years 1951 and 1957   177

9-7 Number and Volume of Food Stores That Were Acquired by Ten Major Food Chains for the Years 1949 to 1958   179

9-8 Wholesale Sales of Certain Voluntary Food Chain Groups in the United States for the Years 1948, 1954, and 1958 (in millions)   186

10-1 Number of Food Stores in the United States by Type of Store for the Years 1929, 1954, and 1958   189

10-2 Food Store Sales in the United States by Type of Store for the Years 1929, 1954, and 1958   192

11-1 Results of Three Recent Studies on the Percentage of Sales of Major Product Classes Transacted by Supermarkets   200

11-2 How an Average Customer Spends Her Supermarket Dollars for Grocery Products and the Percentage Gross Margin on Sales of these Items   201

11-3 Estimated Meat, Poultry, and Seafood Sales by Major Type of Food Store Outlet for the Years 1929 and 1954   203

11-4 Estimated Fresh Fruit and Vegetable Sales by Major Type of Food Store Outlet for 1929 and 1954   205

11-5 Sales of Confections by Certain Major Retail Outlets for the Years 1929 and 1954   208

11-6   Estimated Bakery Product Sales by Major Type of Food
       Store Outlet for the Years 1929 and 1954   210

11-7   Sales of Grocery Product Items by Major Food Store Outlets
       for 1929 and 1958   212

11-8   Estimated Percentages of Supermarkets That Handle Non-
       food Lines Together with Major Source of Supply for the
       Year 1958   215

11-9   Sales of Nonfood Items in Grocery Stores and Combination
       Markets in Dollars and as a Percentage of Total Consump-
       tion for the Year 1958   216

1 | INTRODUCTION

SIGNIFICANCE OF THE SUPERMARKET INDUSTRY

The supermarket, which is a relatively new institution, already transacts more dollar volume per year than all department, variety, and drugstores combined. Furthermore, as comparative statistics in Table 1-1 indicate, the supermarket industry has surpassed volume-wise all other types of nondurable-goods stores and now ranks as "volume king" of traditional retailing.[1] Only the automobile dealers —durable-goods outlets with large dollar-unit sales—exceeded the supermarket industry in 1958 on a dollar-volume basis. But consumers basically do not envisage an automobile dealer as a retailer.

The 20,413 supermarkets, supermarts, or supers in the United States in 1958 transacted an estimated volume of $28.7 billion. This phenomenal $28.7 billion volume, averaging more than $1,404,000 per supermarket, represented 64 per cent of all grocery store sales and 57 per cent of the total food store sales in the country.

Yet, 30 years ago, the supermarket industry was comprised of only a few hundred stores scattered throughout the Far West and the Southwest. Statistics in Table 1-2 evidence the phenomenal growth of this industry, which literally has leaped into national prominence. However, statistics in Table 1-2 do not show the complete extent of food sales in large markets inasmuch as the volume prerequisite for admission to the "charmed circle" was changed twice in the past nine years. Prior to 1951, a qualifying super needed to transact a yearly volume of $250,000. In 1951, the standard was raised to

---

[1] The term *traditional retailing* includes bakery, clothing, confectionery, delicatessen, department, drug, furniture and appliances, grocery, hardware, shoe, variety, and vegetable and fruit stores, and service stations.

1

TABLE 1-1 *

Total Sales by Selected Types of Retail Outlets for the Year 1958.

Type of outlet	Sales (in billions)
Automobile dealers	$31.63
Supermarkets †	28.66
Gasoline service stations	15.73
Department stores	12.50
Furniture and appliance stores	10.32
Drug stores	6.59
Variety stores	3.59

* U.S. Bureau of the Census, *Survey of Current Business,* Government Printing Office, Washington, D.C., March, 1959, p. s–9.

† "Industry Survey," *Super Market Merchandising,* XXIV, no. 3, April, 1959, p. 42.

$375,000; and in 1954, the volume requirement was lifted to $500,000 per year. Under the $375,000 requirement, the number of supermarkets in 1956 was 22,567, with sales of $23.2 billion.[2]

COMPOSITION OF THE INDUSTRY IN 1958

It is difficult to visualize an American who hasn't shopped in a supermarket. Supers seem to abound everywhere. Yet, what is the current status as to components of this industry that literally revolutionized not only food distribution but the entire retailing system?

Data in Table 1-3 indicate 20.7 per cent or 4,236 of the supermarkets are individual units as far as ownership and operation are concerned. Many started as small stores. Whatever profits were made have gone into building up the store into a sizable venture, inasmuch as more facilities are needed constantly. An individual super can require ownership capital of several hundred thousand dollars invested at one location. Obviously, close supervision is needed to manage a business of this scope, which averages over $1,000,000 volume per year. However, an additional 6.6 per cent, or 1,343 of the supers, have branched out into two- and three-unit

[2] "Super Market Boom Rides out Another Year," *Super Market Merchandising,* XXII, no. 4, April, 1957, p. 104.

Introduction

TABLE 1-2

Number of Supermarkets in the U.S., Estimated Sales Volume, and Per Cent of Grocery Store Sales and of Food Store Sales Transacted by Supermarkets for the Years 1935 to 1958.

Year	Number of supermarkets *	Estimated supermarket sales * (in millions)	Supermarket sales as a per cent of grocery store sales †	Supermarket sales as a per cent of food store sales †
1935	300	$ 150	—	1.7
1936	1,200	500	—	5.6
1937	3,066	800	—	8.2
1938	3,700	1,000	—	10.5
1939	4,982	1,500	19.4	14.7
1940	6,175	2,000	24.0	18.3
1941	8,175	2,500	26.0	19.8
1942	9,011	3,000	24.7	19.0
1943	9,100	3,500	26.4	20.0
1944	9,460	3,600	26.4	18.9
1945	9,575	4,500	31.4	22.7
1946	10,057	5,500	29.8	22.7
1947	10,846	7,000	31.3	24.6
1948	11,970	7,780	32.3	25.1
1949	13,089	8,507	35.2	27.4
1950	14,217	10,250	40.3	31.3
1951 ‡	15,383	12,356	40.7	32.9
1952	16,501	14,096	43.7	35.4
1953	17,550	16,092	47.9	39.4
1954 ‡	13,598	15,980	45.8	38.5
1955	15,153	18,644	50.5	42.7
1956	17,024	21,797	55.7	47.4
1957	18,843	25,235	59.5	52.8
1958	20,413	28,664	64.3	56.9

* Yearly surveys published in April editions, *Super Market Merchandising*.

† Calculated by dividing supermarket sales by total grocery store sales and total food store sales, obtained from U.S. Department of Commerce, *Survey of Current Business*, Government Printing Office, Washington, D.C., March editions.

‡ Statistics for the years prior to 1951 were for stores with a minimum volume of $250,000. Data for the years 1951 through 1953 were for stores with a minimum volume of $375,000. Since 1954, data include stores with a minimum volume of $500,000.

TABLE 1-3 *

Ownership of Supermarkets Classified by
Size of Organization for the Year 1958.

Size of organization	Number of stores	% of stores	$ Sales (in millions)	% of sales
1 store	4,236	20.7	5,224	18.2
2–3 stores	1,343	6.6	1,813	6.3
4–10 stores	1,244	6.1	1,835	6.4
11 or more stores . .	13,590	66.6	19,792	69.1
	20,413	100.0	28,664	100.0

* "True Look at the Super Market Industry," *Super Market Merchandising,* XXIV, no. 4, April, 1959, p. 102.

operations in an effort to increase earnings, to diversify risk, and to afford a source for reinvestment of earnings. An additional 1,244 stores, or 6.1 per cent of the supers, have grown into larger operations of from four to ten units in a given community or region. Consumers frequently refer to these as *chains.* However, by definition, a chain must contain eleven or more units. Most of the concerns in this four- to ten-unit group are the result of expansion from one store. And, over the years, through opening new stores and acquiring existing ones by exchange of stock or outright purchase, the corporate chain has become the dominant force in the industry, with 66.6 per cent of the stores and 69.1 per cent of the volume. Chains tend to operate the larger stores.

While 33 per cent, or 6,813, of the supers are listed as nonchains or independents, the bulk of these (more than 70 per cent) are members of wholesale- or retail-sponsored voluntary chains.[3] These voluntaries, exemplified by the Independent Grocers Alliance of America and the Red and White Corporation, operate primarily as buying organizations for their members, although they also offer

[3] *Facts in Grocery Distribution* (New York: Progressive Grocer, 1958), p. F–15.

merchandising, advertising, and promotional services. Thus the buying power in supermarts tends to be concentrated.

Statistics in Table 1-4 reveal that 9,223, or about 45 per cent, of the supers transacted a yearly volume of from $500,000 to $1,000,-000. The markets transacting between $1,000,000 and $2,000,000 yearly represented only 39.9 per cent of the supers but were the major class volumewise. If $110 per square foot of space in a super

TABLE 1-4 *

Number and Sales of Supermarkets Classified by Dollar Volume for the Year 1958.

$ Volume	Number of markets	% of markets	$ Sales (in millions)	% of sales
500,000– 999,000	9,223	45.2	$ 6,641	23.2
1,000,000–1,999,000	8,139	39.9	12,045	42.0
2,000,000–4,999,000	2,869	14.1	8,492	29.6
5,000,000–and over	182	0.8	1,485	5.2

* "True Look at the Super Market Industry," *Super Market Merchandising,* XXIV, no. 4, April, 1959, p. 102.

is used as an approximate standard, the latter market would range from 11,000 sq ft to 22,000 sq ft of space, exclusive of any outside facilities.[4] The colossuses with sales of over $5,000,000 are insignificant numerically but transact 5 per cent of supermarket sales.

Where are the supers located geographically? Although supermarkets are found in every state, plus the District of Columbia, they have tended to concentrate (obtain a larger share of the food business) in the newer growing areas. Supermarts transacted more than 70 per cent of the grocery store sales in Arizona, California, Colorado, Florida, Louisiana, and Nevada.[5] Texas has also been a mecca for supermarkets. In Florida alone, supers transacted 87 per cent of the grocery sales. Supermarkets also are especially dominant in New

[4] "Super Market Boom Rides out Another Year," *Super Market Merchandising, op. cit.*
[5] *Ibid.*

Jersey and Michigan, two original "hot beds" of supers in the early 1930's.

The 1958 supermarket had 23.6 full-time and 6.7 part-time employees per store.[6] These data include central office and warehouse personnel as well as store employees. Roughly projecting these statistics to a total industry basis would indicate 400,000 to 500,000 full-time and 125,000 part-time workers.

APPROACH OF THE BOOK TO STUDY OF THE SUPERMARKET INDUSTRY

The size, significance, and composition of the industry have been presented to show the importance of the supermarket in the area of distribution. This is a field in which firms are big business. In tracing the development of the supermarket to its present status, it is necessary to examine certain issues: What is a supermarket? Why did the industry start? Why did the industry develop so rapidly? What practices and policies did supermart management adopt to generate expansion? Furthermore, since such rapid growth was certain to have its impact upon the existing marketing order, what changes in the food store sales pattern resulted? What shifts occurred in the sales and major product lines of other types of stores that were encroached upon by the invading supermarket? An examination of these issues forms the core of this text.

Definition of a Supermarket

First consider the term *supermarket,* which did not appear in Webster's Unabridged New International Dictionary until 1956.[7] Basically the definition evolves around the two terms *super* and *market.*

Super means "above," "over beyond," "that which surpasses."

---

[6] "True Look at the Super Market Industry," *Super Market Merchandising,* XXIV, no. 4, April, 1959, p. 102.

[7] Certain organizations and authorities who pioneered in this field employed the term *super market* as two words instead of one, as Webster lists it. As a result of usage over the years, this spelling also has found wide support in the industry.

Market refers to a "place" where merchandise is displayed or available for sale. Marketing can be considered the act of selling or purchasing in, or as in, a market. Therefore, in a broad sense, supermarketing can be considered the act of marketing on a large scale or in a manner that surpasses ordinary marketing.

However, the term *supermarket* first became associated with the large food stores that developed in the Far West in the 1920's, and through usage the term became synonymous with this type of food retailing. It is in this sense that the term "supermarketing" is used in this text; namely, it describes the marketing activity in the large type of retail food store known as a supermarket.

Next, the specific definition of a supermarket must be considered. This is imperative in order to gather statistical material and to analyze the industry. Literally scores of definitions have been formulated over the years. These have been subject to changes because of wide diversity and extremely rapid growth. Diversity has existed in (1) number of stores by owners, (2) sales volume per unit, (3) product lines handled, and (4) regional features. In this book the accepted definition is:

A supermarket is a departmentalized retail food store having four basic food departments—self-service groceries, meat, produce, and dairy—plus any number of other departments, with the establishment doing a minimum yearly volume of $500,000.[8]

Innovation

The question of definition was answered at the start. Next, what brought about the advent of the supermarket? In the 1920's the food

[8] Authorities in the field have differed as to what the minimum volume of a supermarket should be. Prior to 1951, the two major sources of statistical information in the industry—the magazine, *Super Market Merchandising*, and the trade association, Super Market Institute—were in accord on the $250,000 minimum volume. In order to make adjustment for the change in the rising level of food prices and for the trend toward larger stores, both raised their minimum volume in 1951. The $375,000 volume was selected by *Super Market Merchandising* because it corresponded to the O.P.S. classification for Type 4 stores. The Super Market Institute in 1951 raised its minimum volume to $500,000. In 1954 *Super Market Merchandising* did likewise, and both sources once again were in agreement as to volume.

store industry was composed of many single- or limited-line outlets such as dairy stores, grocery stores without meat, meat markets, confectioners, and delicatessens. The movement toward multi-line operation, however, in the form of the combination market had started. The two major outlets were the grocery store without meat and the combination market. Whether independently owned or members of chains, these were generally small, were located close to the consumer, and offered a variety of services such as credit and delivery.

A marketing innovation, the supermarket, appeared in California in the late 1920's and several years later in the East. The underlying forces behind each of these movements were different. Even the stores were not the same, but each offered a key to the growing importance of the supermarket movement and to changes in the pattern of retail sales. This subject of development is discussed comprehensively in Chapter 2.

Internal and External Factors

The growth of the supermarket industry occurred in an era in which a maze of particular external influences were present that had a bearing on its development. Consumer buying habits changed. A desire for one-stop shopping came into vogue. The automobile came into wider use for everyday living; refrigeration became a "must" for most homes. From the depths of a depression, personal disposable income rose to an unprecedented height by 1958. These and other factors are presented in Chapter 3 to ascertain what influence they had on the development of the supermarket industry.

How did the food store industry as a group fare in this economic, technological, and psychological setting? Did the supermarket gain more in volume than other types of food stores? It was found that it did. Therefore internal features are examined to discern what practices the supermarket operators adopted that attracted customers to them. These techniques are grouped under operational and financial factors and are given close scrutiny in Chapters 4 through 7. Such features as buying practices, selling techniques, pricing, expense control, profit relationships, and investment requirements are highlighted. These chapters, which basically contain the principles of supermarketing, are of special interest to management, owners, and students.

Impact on Pattern of Food Store Sales

Specifically, what changes occurred in the pattern of food store sales by 1958 compared with those of 1929 when supermarkets were for practical purposes nonexistent? An answer to this requires a detailed statistical study of (1) the number of different kinds of food stores, (2) sales by type of food stores, and (3) sales of major product lines transacted by types of food stores. These three constitute the pattern of food store sales as defined in this book. The impact of the supermarket is examined in Chapters 8 through 11. The final chapter, 12, is devoted to industry trends and conclusions of this study, written from a management point of view so as to aid present and future policy and decisions. This final chapter is entitled, "Managerial Policy and Perspective."

SCOPE OF THE STUDY

The growth of the supermarket industry influenced other phases of food and nonfood distribution besides the food sales pattern. The supermarket's successful exploitation of self-service influenced other forms of retailers to review their selling techniques and possibly to adopt this principle. The addition of nonfood lines by supermarkets tended to shift the sales pattern by kind of retail outlet for items such as health and beauty aids, housewares, and certain soft goods.

Manufacturers and wholesalers of food products reviewed their marketing programs in an attempt to obtain greater distribution of their lines in supermarkets. Frequently manufacturers sold directly to supers. Food wholesalers were able to reduce their costs of operation through cost-plus plans; [9] many worked closely with

[9] R. D. Tousley, "Reducing Distribution Costs in the Grocery Field," *Journal of Marketing*, XII, no. 4, April, 1948, p. 455.

supers on narrow margins or even sponsored their own supermarts.

All these salient aspects offer challenging facets for study. While these and other factors are considered in this text, attention is mainly centered on the innovation, growth, operational features, and impact of the supermarket on the pattern of food store sales which occurred simultaneously with the supermarket development.

2 | DEVELOPMENT OF THE SUPERMARKET

INTRODUCTION

In the preceding chapter, the significance of the supermarket industry, its definition, the plan of approach, and the scope of this text were considered. It is the objective of this chapter to study the development of large markets in the United States from the time of the earliest Boston public market to the modern supermarkets of today. Included are the forces that had a bearing on the start of supermarkets in the Los Angeles area and the East. For convenience in presentation, the data are examined in chronological time periods. These are as follows:

1. Large markets prior to 1930
2. The era of the "cheapy" supermarket, 1930 to 1935
3. The period of experimental growth and development, 1935 to 1946
4. The postwar period of "modern" supermarket expansion, 1946 to date

LARGE MARKETS PRIOR TO 1930

In this section the history of early large markets prior to 1930 is reviewed to ascertain if any met the accepted definition of a supermarket as outlined in this book. This includes an examination of: (1) early public and private concession-type markets, (2) Piggly Wiggly stores, (3) "market stores" of the Los Angeles area, and (4) large markets in the Southwest.

Early Public and Private Concession-Type Markets

The concept of a large market is not a recent innovation in the United States.[1] Large markets operating under public ownership date back to 1658 in Boston.[2] Some of the very early ventures were the Faneuil Hall Market of Boston, the Lexington Market of Baltimore, and the Catherine Market of New York City. The Catherine Market by 1860 had 60 enclosed stalls in addition to the areas used by the open-air vendors. By 1918 the U.S. Bureau of the Census listed 174 of these large retail markets in cities of over 30,000 population.[3]

Not all the early markets were publicly owned. Privately financed and operated markets included the Reading Terminal Market of Philadelphia, the Euclid and 46th Street Market of Cleveland, and the Pike Place Market of Seattle.

These early markets were housed in a variety of buildings, varying from sheds or booths (frequently built on public property to enable farmers to sell their products) to the more elaborate structures found in New Orleans and San Francisco. They all had common characteristics: (1) a large area, (2) many stalls, booths, or departments leased to various proprietors who operated individually, and (3) a large over-all volume for the market, although each section had a relatively small sales volume.

Were these supermarkets? A brief description of the mode of operation of one—the Crystal Palace Market of San Francisco—is presented to see how it measured against our current definition of a supermarket.

Crystal Palace Market

This establishment, founded in 1922 and controlled by the owners of the Emporium, was housed in a 68,000-sq ft building located in

[1] Paul H. Nystrom, *Economics of Retailing* (New York: The Ronald Press Co., 1936), Vol. 1, p. 335.
[2] Arthur E. Goodwin, *Markets Public and Private* (Seattle: Montgomery Printing Co., 1939), p. 22.
[3] *Ibid.*, p. 27.

the downtown district.[4] Public transportation was good; 80 per cent of all street cars in the city passed its door. In addition, a 4,350-car parking lot was immediately adjacent. The multimillion dollar sales volume of 1929 was divided among the following product classes: [5]

	% sales
Meat	18
Fruit and vegetable	16
Grocery	15
Delicatessen	13
Drugs, tobacco, etc.	12
Restaurant	10
Dairy	7
Fish and poultry	5
Bakery	3
Miscellaneous	1
	100

There were 110 departments, with concessions leased on a minimum guarantee basis and every lease containing a percentage-of-gross-sales clause. Management had control over the kind and quality of merchandise sold. Extensive advertising was done, with the market drawing 150,000 people weekly. The appeal was not one of price; rather, extensive promotions were planned, including car raffles and public drawings.

This operation, founded in the 1920's, certainly had many of the characteristics attributed to a supermarket in Chapter 1. While it was not a supermarket as defined, since it lacked self-service, it certainly was a forerunner of the modern super. The lack of self-service also characterized the other typical, large early markets of the United States.

Piggly Wiggly Stores

During 1916 in Memphis, Tennessee, Clarence Saunders started his first revolutionary self-service store in a location formerly oper-

[4] The Emporium is a San Francisco department store.
[5] Emil Dollenger, "Quality, Not Price, Built San Francisco's Grand Crystal Market," *Super Market Merchandising*, II, no. 1, January, 1937, p. 3.

ated by a regional chain.[6] He emphasized basic principles of stand-ardization and simplification found in industrial management books of today.

In the first six months of operation, this store did $114,000 gross sales at an expense of $3,400—a 3 per cent of sales expense rate—and experienced a stock turnover of 39 times a year.[7] This success was partly attributed to the innovation of self-service. The idea grew into a chain of owned and leased stores, with the latter li-censed to use the name, equipment, and method of operation.

After a series of financial maneuvers, Saunders lost control in 1923. However, the chain continued to expand, and by 1928 reached a peak of 2,700 stores in 41 states; this was prior to sale of its stores to Safeway Stores and the Kroger Company.[8]

Unfortunately, only fragmentary information is available on the complete operating results of this chain. It was reported in 1920 that the operating subsidiary, Piggly Wiggly Store Company, had 404 units with a yearly volume of almost $60,000,000.[9] The average yearly store volume was $150,000, although the peak store did a $10,000 weekly sales volume while operating as a self-service com-bination grocery and meat market.[10] The resulting net profits of this chain from 1919 to 1925 as a percentage of sales were mediocre (less than 1 per cent); however, detailed expense breakdowns were not published.[11]

A separately controlled chain, Piggly Wiggly Western States Company, reported for the fiscal year 1923 a gross margin of 11.8 per cent and an operating expense of 8.3 per cent.[12] These ex-tremely favorable results compare with today's supermarket, but they steadily declined thereafter until the chain was sold in 1927.

[6] Walter Hayward and Percival White, *Chain Stores* (New York: McGraw-Hill Book Co., Inc., 1922), p. 180.
[7] *Ibid.*
[8] *Ibid.*, p. 186.
[9] R. P. Crawford, "Piggly Wiggly, How It Has Grown," *Forbes,* October, 1921, p. 15.
[10] *Ibid.*
[11] *Moody's Industrial Manual,* 1920–1926.
[12] *Ibid.*

Based on the available information, a few of the Piggly Wiggly Stores were supermarkets according to our current definition. The limited data indicated the system, in part, operated at a smaller expense rate than the existing independent grocer or the chain economy store whose clerks serviced the trade. But in the era of the 1920's, the chains were concentrating on clerk-service economy stores and did not develop the potentialities of self-service.

"Market Stores" of the Los Angeles Area

Two kinds of "market stores" that flourished in the Los Angeles area prior to 1930 were also supermarkets according to the definition set forth in this book. These were:

1. The large, self-service food store, which was operated under centralized control and which, by current standards, would be judged as an excellent example of a supermarket

2. The open-front, drive-in market, which comprised a group of independent units in a single building

Ralph's Grocery Company. The first type of these market stores was exemplified by Ralph's Grocery Company, although there were others such as Carty Brothers and Alpha Beta Food Markets. Ralph's, still a large supermarket operator today, started in downtown Los Angeles in 1872 with one store.[13] By 1911 the company had built a flourishing operation featuring clerk-service and delivery. As the city grew, attractive branches were opened in modern, elaborate buildings. The units recognized the advantages of self-service and started conversion in 1926. By 1928 delivery was abandoned: 74 trucks were auctioned in one day. By 1929 the chain had 16 large, well-developed supermarkets.[14]

Drive-in markets. The second type of market store was the open-front, drive-in market that appeared in the Los Angeles area about 1925.[15] This type of operation comprised a group of food stores in

[13] Lucius Flint, "The Los Angeles Super," *Chain Store Age*, Grocery Executive Edition, June, 1950, p. j34.

[14] *Ibid.*

[15] Walter Van de Kamp, "An Innovation in Retail Selling," *Magazine of Business*, July, 1929, p. 28.

a one-story building located in neighborhood and outlying sections. Parking was immediately adjacent. Each of the units of the large market store was individually owned and operated; yet, shoppers looked on the market as a single entity. Certain of these units met our current definition of a supermarket. One of the most elaborate of these drive-ins was Chapman Park Drive-in Market of Los Angeles. The land and building alone represented an investment of over $400,000.[16]

Factors influencing the supermarket innovation in the Los Angeles area. It is not known definitely whether all these units met the self-service requirement. But writers in this era were of the opinion that the following reasons were responsible for this development:[17]

1. Los Angeles had no elevated, subway, or other good means of transportation to the central business district. Thus, individuals were forced to use private motor cars as the chief source of transportation. In 1928 the population of California was 4,556,000.[18] Passenger car registrations were 1,799,890; approximately 35 per cent of the inhabitants had cars.[19] This percentage of the population owning cars was substantially higher than the national average.

2. Parking in the central area was limited, and restrictions were severe. Therefore, secondary or outlying sections developed. These invariably had some facilities for parking.

3. The wide use of the automobile for shopping prevailed. People throughout the year were able to circulate more freely. The climate was favorable for outdoor living and activity.

4. The open-front, drive-in markets did not have to be erected

---

[16] "495 Autos Can Park in This New Drive-In Market," *Progressive Grocer*, XIII, no. 10, October, 1929, p. 30.

[17] These are synopses of the opinions of three authors: Walter Van de Kamp, "An Innovation in Retail Selling," *Magazine of Business*, July, 1929, p. 28; S. L. Brevit, "Drive-In Department Stores Gaining Popularity in the West," *Sales Management*, XXX, no. 3, January 17, 1931, p. 118; and H. M. Foster, "Threat of the Supermarket," *Sales Management*, XXXII, no. 9, April 20, 1933, p. 436.

[18] U.S. Bureau of Census, *Statistical Abstract of the United States, 1929*, Government Printing Office, Washington, D.C., 1930, p. 7.

[19] *Ibid.*, p. 387.

as substantially as in colder communities. The required building investment was less, and therefore business men were more likely to experiment with a new type of market.

5. Land was plentiful and reasonably priced. This growing territory spread over a large area and was not subject to central transportation limitations.

6. The people had a pioneer spirit, believed in change, and were more adaptable to innovations than the inhabitants of the East or Middle West.

It was surprising to note that none of the literature in this era prior to 1930 mentioned low price appeal in connection with these "market stores." These factors indicate that this supermarket development was viewed as a regional affair suitable for California or possibly the Southwest.[20]

Large Markets in the Southwest

One of the earliest and the largest supermarket operations in the Southwest was Henke & Pillot of Houston, Texas. This firm had its origin in 1872.[21] By 1900 its downtown store had 50,000 sq ft of space and operated 13 departments, including its own bakery and coffee-roasting plant. The store grew to a yearly volume of $5,-000,000. As Houston spread out and the automobile came of age, two modern and well-equipped outlying stores featuring large parking lots were added in 1926 and 1928. Some self-service operation was adopted in the following year, and the concern became a full-fledged supermarket.[22]

Other supermarket operators in the Southwest at this time were J. Weingarten, Incorporated, and the ABC Stores, Incorporated. Mr. Joe Weingarten, chairman of the board of J. Weingarten, Incorporated, has stated that his first large market operation which

[20] C. B. Larrabee, "Grocery Manufacturers Condemn Supermarket Price Cutters," *Printers Ink*, CLXII, no. 9, March 2, 1933, p. 41.

[21] Charles N. Bunnell, "Henke & Pillot Supermarket Grew from Houston Public Demand," *Super Market Merchandising*, II, no. 2, February, 1937, p. 3.

[22] "Big Volume in 1922," *Chain Store Age*, Grocery Executive Edition, June, 1950, p. j22.

could be considered a supermarket was started in 1918.[23] This store had both self-service grocery and dairy departments.

ERA OF THE "CHEAPY" SUPERMARKET, 1930 TO 1935

A new type of supermarket developed in 1930. It was a depression product and was very different in appearance from the attractive California and Texas markets. Yet this "cheapy," as it was referred to, still conformed to our definiton, and its development in New York and New Jersey awakened the country to this retailing innovation.

King Kullen and Big Bear Markets

Michael Cullen, an ex-chain-store executive, opened the first successful "cheapy" in August, 1930, in Jamaica, Long Island, New York.[24] By the end of 1932, the King Kullen Markets had increased to eight outlets. Big Bear, a similar "cheapy" supermarket, followed King Kullen. In December, 1932, Roy O. Dawson and Robert M. Otis, together with the American House Grocers, a local wholesaler, opened the Big Bear in Elizabeth, New Jersey. The location was an abandoned factory of the Durant Motor Car Company.[25]

The word "cheapy" was synonymous with price structure and appearance. The interior had no partitions, crude floors, bare ceilings, unpainted fixtures, glaring lights, gaudy signs, and merchandise piled everywhere. The units thrived in low-rent locations on the fringe of thickly populated sections. Later, other "cheapy" units were opened in abandoned warehouses, empty department stores, garages, and factories.

The price structures were even more fantastic when compared with the existing forms of food merchandising. Their promotional names (King Kullen, The Price Wrecker; and Big Bear, the Price Crusher) were in conformity with their price schedules. Compare

[23] M. M. Zimmerman, *The Super Market* (New York: McGraw-Hill Book Co., Inc., 1955), p. 26.

[24] "The Cheapy Thrives," *Business Week,* no. 179, February 8, 1933, p. 11.

[25] M. M. Zimmerman, *Super Market Spectacular Exponent of Mass Distribution* (New York: Super Market Publishing Co., 1937), p. 25.

the following King Kullen Market prices with those of other stores: [26]

	Elsewhere	King Kullen
All 10-cent drug items	$ 0.10	$ 0.09
Campbell's tomato soup	0.07	0.04
U.S. Rubber tires for Fords	5.50	3.78
General Electric vacuum cleaners	35.00	11.94

The greater portion of space in King Kullen Markets was allocated to the grocery, meat, bakery, and dairy departments. The remainder of the space was leased to utensil, produce, paint, hardware, and auto accessory concessionaires. A King Kullen Market required an investment of $30,000, which included $23,000 for merchandise, $2,500 for grocery equipment, and $4,500 for meat department equipment.[27]

Two of King Kullen's operating principles were (1) the other departments must all sell merchandise at reduced prices, and (2) the income from the concessions should pay the rent of the entire establishment.[28]

During this time Big Bear operated only the grocery department, which occupied 30 per cent of the 50,000-sq ft floor space.[29] It leased concessions for meat, produce, dairy, bakery, candy, tobacco, drugs, luncheonette, and paints. The concessionaires were charged 5.13 per cent on their gross sales in lieu of rent and other overhead expenses. The Big Bear made a substantial profit on the leased departments.

The markets that mushroomed following King Kullen and Big Bear were generally of the same "cheapy" type. Many of these early supers—The Whale, Giant Tiger, Big Chief, Little Bear—were strange stores, frequently referred to as monstrosities because of their method of operation, location, appearance, and type of structure occupied.[30] The King Kullen markets in modified form are still in operation.

26 "The Cheapy Thrives," *op. cit.*
27 Zimmerman, *The Super Market, op. cit.*, p. 32.
28 Zimmerman, *Super Market Spectacular Exponent of Mass Distribution, op. cit.*, p. 10.
29 *Ibid.*
30 Carl W. Dipman, "Merchandise Trend in Food Trade," *Journal of Marketing*, III, no. 3, January, 1939, p. 269.

Factors Influencing the Development
of the "Cheapy" Supermarket in the East

The innovation of the "cheapy" supermarket in the East was attributed to the fact that low income and unemployment made low price of paramount importance in the early 1930's.[31] The supermarket was a lower-cost type of operation than the existing food stores. It passed on to the consumer some of its savings, in the form of lower prices.

Income and employment statistics. The year 1932 was a depression year. Statistics in Table 2-1 indicate that the number of em-

TABLE 2-1 *

National Income and Employment in the
United States for the Years 1929 to 1936.

Year	National income (in billions)	Number of gainfully employed
1929	$83.3	35,563,000
1930	68.9	33,122,000
1931	54.3	29,715,000
1932	40.0	26,222,000
1933	42.5	26,133,000
1934	50.3	28,402,000
1935	55.9	29,725,000
1936	65.1	31,858,000

* U.S. Bureau of the Census, *Statistical Abstract of the United States,* Government Printing Office, Washington, D.C., 1940, p. 315.

ployed persons dropped 9,341,000 between 1929 and 1932, or by 27 per cent. Unemployment stood at an all-time twentieth century high of 12,300,000 persons.[32] Wages were sharply cut; many of the working population were on a part-time basis. The national income dropped from $83.3 billion in 1929 to a low of $40.0 billion in 1932.

[31] Larrabee, *op. cit.*
[32] Bureau of Labor Statistics, *Monthly Labor Review,* Vol. 35, no. 1, Government Printing Office, Washington, D.C., 1933, p. 140.

The country as a whole was "dissaving"—living on past capital accumulation. This was the economic setting for the "cheapy" supermarket.

Early price policies of supermarkets. Low price was the basic appeal of the "cheapy" supermarket as it invaded the food store field.[33] Everything about the market had an air of cheapness. Nationally advertised brands were placed on sale at ridiculously low prices. Loss leaders were common. Many of the customers drove as far as 50 miles to the Big Bear.[34]

King Kullen's pricing format [35] was to sell

> 300 items at cost
> 200 items at 5% above cost
> 300 items at 15% above cost
> 300 items at 20% above cost

The appeal of low price was nothing new.[36] Chains had used it successfully for years and generally undersold the independents.[37] But the supers "stole the thunder" from the chains and were able invariably to quote lower prices than the economy stores or independents.[38]

Charles F. Phillips cited that on June 20, 1935, he checked the prices on 34 well-known branded items in the Big Bear and in a chain store. The chain store prices for these items averaged 12.8 per cent in excess of those of Big Bear.[39] A study of advertised staple merchandise prices made by M. M. Zimmerman in 16 cities throughout the country in 1935 found that the supers undersold the chains on comparable products from 4.8 to 22.9 per cent.[40]

[33] Zimmerman, *The Supermarket Spectacular Exponent of Mass Distribution,* op. cit., p. 10.

[34] *Ibid.,* p. 11.

[35] Zimmerman, *The Super Market, op. cit.,* p. 33.

[36] Charles F. Phillips, "The Supermarket," *Harvard Business Review,* XVI, no. 2, Winter, 1938, p. 192.

[37] Federal Trade Commission, *Chain Stores, Final Report on the Chain Store Investigation,* submitted to 74th Congress, 1st session, Senate, Document 4, Government Printing Office, Washington, D.C., Dec. 14, 1934, p. 67.

[38] Phillips, *op. cit.,* p. 196.

[39] *Ibid.,* p. 198.

[40] Zimmerman, *The Supermarket Spectacular Exponent of Mass Distribution,* op. cit., p. 53.

With regard to their loss-leader policies, Phillips stated:

There is no doubt but that many supermarkets have been large users of loss leaders in the sense that many items have been sold at prices only slightly above their actual cost to the operator. This practice, of course, gives the supermarket the appearance of being a low price institution. At the same time it is evident that much of the cry against this type of operation for the use of loss leaders is not valid because many supermarkets are in a position to quote prices below those of their competitors primarily because of their low cost of operations, but also in some degree because of their buying practices.[41]

Comparative margins, expenses, and profits of independents, chains, and early supers.   Prior to the development of the supermarket industry in the 1930's, the retail grocery distribution industry had its battle lines drawn between chains and independents. The operating costs of independents in the Louisville area in the late 1920's are indicated in Table 2-2.

TABLE 2-2 *

Profit and Loss Statement for the Average Grocery Store in the Louisville Survey as a Percentage of Sales for the Year 1929.

Sales		100.00
Cost of sales		74.19
Gross margin		25.81
Expenses		
Miscellaneous	2.53	
Owners' salary	4.01	
Other salaries	6.31	
Rent	.98	
Utilities	1.23	
Delivery	2.77	
Advertising	.31	
Insurance	.15	18.29
Net profit		7.52

* U.S. Department of Commerce, *Distribution Cost Studies Number 1, Louisville Grocery Survey, Part IIIA,* Government Printing Office, Washington, D.C., 1932, pp. 15–23.

[41] Phillips, *op. cit.*

Other studies of independent store operations showed gross margins to be closer to 20 per cent and profits varying from 1.6 to 2.6 per cent of sales, depending upon the type of operation.[42]

The Great Atlantic and Pacific Tea Company for the year 1929 operated 15,150 smaller-type economy stores, with the average weekly sales of $1,317 per store. A breakdown of these operations for 1929, 1933, and 1935 is shown in Table 2-3. The gross margin

Table 2-3 *

**Condensed Profit and Loss Statement of the Retail Store
Operation of the Great A & P Tea Company as a
Percentage of Sales for the Years 1929 to 1935.**

	1929	1933	1935
Sales	100.00	100.00	100.00
Cost of sales	81.64	78.10	80.50
Gross margin	18.36	21.90	19.50
Total operating expenses	15.52	19.08	17.56
Net profit	2.84	2.82	1.94

* *United States* v. *The Great A & P Tea Company,* U.S. Circuit Court of Appeals, 7th district, Docket 9221, Records & Briefs, Vol. II, p. 162.

for chain stores as a group for 1929 was 18.99 per cent, and for independents, 23.01 per cent of sales.[43] These statistics, published later, support Professor Schmalz's contention that, generally, the chains were in a position to undersell the independent grocer at that time.

When the "cheapy" supermarket entered the field in the depression years, it operated at even a lower gross margin than the chain. The operating statement of the Big Bear super in Elizabeth, New Jersey, for 1933 is shown in Table 2-4.

Big Bear earned a substantial profit from concessions and was in a position to operate its grocery department on a 12 per cent gross.

[42] A series of studies made in the 1920's were quoted by Carl N. Schmalz, "Independent Stores vs. Chains in the Grocery Field," *Harvard Business Review,* IX, no. 4, July, 1931, p. 431.
[43] Federal Trade Commission, *Chain Stores, op. cit.*

TABLE 2-4 *

Operating Statement of the Big Bear, Elizabeth, New Jersey, for the Year 1933.

		Dollar		% of sales
Grocery department sales		$2,188,403		100.00
Cost of sales		1,925,795		87.99
Gross profit		$ 262,608		12.01
Expenses				
Rent	$15,516		.71	
Payroll	79,545		3.64	
Light and heat	7,881		.35	
Advertising	28,974		1.32	
Handling	20,157		.93	
Administration	11,248		.51	
Clerical	6,915		.32	
Insurance	3,523		.16	
Miscellaneous	7,462		.34	
Taxes	1,094		.05	
Depreciation	219	182,534	.01	8.34
Net profit from grocery operators		$ 80,074		3.67
Rental from concessions		86,434		
Net profit		$166,508		

* M. M. Zimmerman, *The Supermarket Spectacular Exponent of Mass Distribution* (New York: Super Market Publishing Company, 1937), p. 14.

Furthermore, the accounting system did not adequately show the operating profit because all rental and light for the store was charged to Big Bear grocery department even though it occupied only 30 per cent of the space.

Similarly, King Kullen stores made a gross profit of 9 per cent on grocery and fruit and vegetables and a net profit of 2½ per cent! Their net profit on meat sales was 3 per cent. These remarkable operating results and profits were the result of the innovation of the "cheapy" supermarket.

During the early 1930's other mushrooming supermarkets maintained an operating advantage over the chain economy stores and the small independents. Gross margins varied from 10 to 14 per cent of sales.[44] John Hartford, president of the A & P, reported that supermarket competitors in Detroit during this period operated on a 12.5 per cent gross and earned a 2.5 per cent net.[45] He said that the established A & P aim was to operate at a 12 per cent gross and 2 per cent net.[46]

The statistics on supermarket operation in this era indicate that it was extremely difficult for the conventional A & P economy store and the average independent combination market to compete with supers.

PERIOD OF EXPERIMENTAL GROWTH AND DEVELOPMENT, 1935 TO 1946

The markets that mushroomed following King Kullen and Big Bear were generally of the same "cheapy" variety. This type of store, however, rapidly lost its appeal when more attractive supermarkets were opened, starting in 1935.[47] By this time the principle of the supermarket operation had been proved sound. National income and employment had risen; new capital began to be attracted to the industry. "Traded up" supermarkets began to multiply in superior locations. Larger investments in equipment and buildings followed and resulted in improved external and internal appearances of the stores, which began to take on the semblance of supermarkets as we know them today.

Statistics on supermarkets kept yearly, beginning in 1936, are recorded in Table 1-2 and indicate the number of supers and their volume increase every year thereafter. Such chains as A & P, Kroger, First National Stores, and American Stores opened experimental supermarket units at this time.[48] But it was not until 1937, that the

[44] Phillips, *op. cit.*, p. 192.

[45] *United States* v. *The Great A & P Tea Company*, U.S. Circuit Court of Appeals, 7th district, Docket 9221, Records & Briefs, Vol. II, p. 194.

[46] *Ibid.*, p. 194.

[47] Carl W. Dipman, "Merchandise Trend in Food Trade," *Journal of Marketing*, III, no. 3, January, 1939, p. 269.

[48] M. M. Zimmerman, "The Supermarket and the Changing Retail Structure," *Journal of Marketing*, VI, no. 2, April, 1941, p. 403.

TABLE 2-5 °

Operating Statement of an Average Independent Combination
Market as a Percentage of Sales for the Year 1935.

Sales			100.0
Cost of sales			81.7
Gross margin			18.3
Expenses			
Utilities	.8		
Advertising	.6		
Rent	1.4		
Wages	5.4		
Owner's	4.7		
Taxes	.4		
Other	3.4		16.7
Net profit			1.6

° *Standard Ratios for Retailing* (New York: Dun & Bradstreet, Inc., 1936),
p. 8.

industry leader, the A & P, decided to make the supermarket the
next step in its development.[49] Some of the first chain supers were
opened under different names; for example, the Kroger Company
operated stores in Cincinnati under the name "Pay'n Takit." The
increase in the number of supermarkets in the late 1930's was due
largely to the switch of chains to supers (see Table 1-2). From 1936
to 1938 the number of supermarkets skyrocketed from 1,200 to 4,982.
Statistics on the number of supers for the industry leader (A & P)
are given in Table 2-6; they indicate the rapid shift to supermarket
operation. In many urban areas the most strategic locations for
supermarkets already were well developed with such outlets.[50]

The first supermarket convention in 1937 gave the industry a degree of unity. At that time the industry's trade association, Super
Market Institute, was founded. The Institute, which has lent organization to the industry and has furnished the widely scattered

[49] *United States* v. *The Great A & P Tea Company, op. cit.,* p. 192.
[50] William Applebaum, "Adjustment of Retailing to 1941 Conditions," *Journal
of Marketing,* V, no. 4, April, 1941, p. 438.

TABLE 2-6 °

**Number of A & P Supermarkets and Small Economy Stores
for the Years 1936 to 1943.**

Year	Number of supers	Number of small economy stores
1936	20	14,426
1937	282	12,776
1938	771	9,900
1939	1,119	7,902
1940	1,396	5,677
1941	1,552	4,490
1942	1,633	4,188
1943	1,646	4,105

° *United States* v. *The Great A & P Tea Company*, U.S. Circuit Court of Appeals, 7th district, Docket 9221, Records and Briefs, Vol. I, p. 323.

members a common bond, has grown from 32 pioneer members to the point where it currently embraces over 744 companies operating 11,388 outlets.[51] In addition to sponsoring the annual meetings at which current major industry problems are discussed, the Super Market Institute fosters educational activities, establishes ethical business practices, promotes research activities, and serves as a clearing house for information. More recently adopted activities include the intra-industry figure exchange and the executive training program. Credit also must be given to M. M. Zimmerman for the development and guidance of this industry, especially in the formative years. In 1936 he founded the publication, *Super Market Merchandising*, which has been a major source of information for the supermarket operators.

The years 1941 and early 1942 showed one of the largest increases in the number of supers. The number of units increased by 2,000. Many chains and independents displayed feverish activity, apparently in an attempt to beat the impending building restriction that

[51] *The Super Market Industry Speaks—1959* (Chicago: Super Market Institute), p. 15.

resulted from World War II.[52] During the ensuing war years, the industry showed little or no expansion. This was accounted for by building material shortages, lack of adequate help, food rationing, price controls, rationing which limited the use of the automobile, desire of people to know their grocers more intimately so as to obtain advantages in food purchasing, reduced significance of price as a result of swollen consumer incomes, and food shortages.[53] Nevertheless the supers survived this era, partly through the increased employment of women, the addition of nonfood lines, the maintenance of as large an inventory of national brands as possible, and self-service expansion.[54]

Prior to World War II supermarkets as a whole concentrated mainly on the sale of foods. During the war the supers began to feature more nonfood lines. The success of this policy led to the addition of more nonfood departments after the war.[55]

POSTWAR PERIOD OF MODERN SUPERMARKET EXPANSION

The industry again experienced renewed impetus in 1946. The population increase and outward push from the center of cities, plus the building of new homes in the suburbs, offered new location opportunities. Satisfactory profit margins continued to make this a mecca for expansion. Furthermore the industry was able to obtain capital. Many of the firms which less than 15 years earlier were small operations or nonexistent entered the capital markets by publicly selling securities in order to obtain funds for expansion. Many of the independent food retailers realized they could not compete with this new method of merchandising and converted their stores into supermarkets. In this they were aided by voluntary chains and alert

[52] Carl W. Dipman, "Changes in Food Distribution," *Journal of Marketing*, VI, no. 4, April, 1942, p. 48.

[53] M. M. Zimmerman, "Super Market Sales & Profit Trends 1941–43," *Journal of Marketing*, X, no. 2, October, 1944, p. 162.

[54] M. M. Zimmerman, "Tomorrow's Super Market," *Journal of Marketing*, X, no. 4, April, 1946, p. 384.

[55] M. M. Zimmerman, *Super Market—Its Growth and Future* (New York: Super Marketing Merchandising Publishing Co., 1948), p. 4.

wholesalers who helped them to streamline their methods of operation. New stores were built with greater floor space and parking facilities. Many stores were remodeled. More elaborate interiors and exteriors became the vogue, with services such as music and air conditioning added. The statistics in Table 1-2 indicate an increase of 213 per cent in the number of supers from 1945 to 1958 and a rise in sales volume of 637 per cent for the same period. By 1958 the number of supermarkets had reached 20,413 units.

Other features that aided this tremendous postwar expansion included the further shift of local, regional, and national chains from small to large store operation. In addition, the increased promotion and ballyhoo techniques of supermarket operators to increase store traffic made the suburban shopping center and the supermarket a sociological mecca for the American family. Finally, the constant pressure to reinvest earnings into profitable merchandising operations aided the expansion movement.

One of the most recent trends in the postwar era is the increased emphasis on horizontal integration through acquisition on the part of the larger concerns. Examples of this are the recent foragings of the National Tea Company and the ACF–Wrigley Stores, Incorporated. The keynote seems to be "acquire or expire." More and more the emphasis is not on "big business" but on "bigger business."

SUMMARY

The first supers were a relatively few Piggly Wiggly stores. These were followed by the California supers and drive-in markets, which appeared to be a product of primarily local forces. Then came a new supermarket, the "cheapy," which flourished in the depression years of the 1930's and which made low price its basic appeal. This was followed by the policy of "trading-up" the stores. The national food chains joined the movement after 1936 and gave it impetus. The World War II period saw changes in policies but relatively no change in number of markets. The postwar period was one of vast expansion in number of units, size of stores, services, and dollar volume. The industry has become one of bigger and bigger business.

3

EXTERNAL FACTORS
THAT INFLUENCED THE
GROWTH OF THE
SUPERMARKET INDUSTRY

INTRODUCTION

The development of the supermarket, including the factors that influenced its innovation, was discussed in the preceding chapter. It was shown that the early supers, with the exception of California and the Southwest, were largely of the "cheapy" variety. But from 1935 on, the supermarket industry continued to gain new members at a remarkable rate and began to improve the appearance, equipment and location of its stores.[1]

This chapter and the subsequent four analyze the factors that aided this remarkable growth. For expedience these are broken down into external and internal considerations. The former are examined in this chapter and include:

1. Changes in personal disposable income and personal consumption expenditures
2. Shifts in upper income shares
3. Changes in expenditures in food stores
4. Changes in the pattern of food consumption

---

[1] Charles F. Phillips, "The Supermarket," *Harvard Business Review*, XVI, no. 2, Winter, 1938, p. 192.

5. Technological developments and their adoption
6. Population growth and shift to the suburbs
7. Retail trend toward decentralization
8. Shifts in consumer buying habits (including one-stop shopping and scrambled merchandise) [2]
9. Additional external factors

Still other external influences were present in the economy such as industrial decentralization, concentration of power among food manufacturers and higher literacy; but the above listed factors appeared to be the most pertinent to the problem.

CHANGES IN PERSONAL DISPOSABLE INCOME AND PERSONAL CONSUMPTION EXPENDITURES

As previously indicated, the national income of the United States suffered a substantial drop from $83 billion in 1929 to $40 billion in 1932.[3] Employment decreased from 35,563,000 in 1929 to 26,222,000 in 1932.[4] It was at this time that the "cheapy" supermarket started its expansion—offering "food for less." But the "cheapy" depression product was short-lived and soon was replaced by the more elaborately equipped and housed super.

From 1935 to date, the total and the per capita disposable personal income and personal consumption expenditures increased substantially. These statistics are shown in Table 3-1 together with the cost of living index which also rose in this interval, although by a lesser amount than the per capita income and expenditures. The trend thus has been for each person to have more income to spend and to need relatively less of this larger income for basic living purposes. The large personal consumption expenditures indicate that

---

[2] The term *scrambled merchandise* was used by Malcolm P. McNair to indicate the merchandising of a commodity in retail stores in which the product was basically foreign. This discussion is found in an article by Malcolm P. McNair, "Trends in Large-Scale Retailing," *Harvard Business Review*, X, no. 1, Fall, 1932, p. 31.

[3] These statistics are contained in Table 2-1.

[4] *Ibid.*

TABLE 3-1

Total Disposable Personal Income, Total and Per Capita
Personal Consumption Expenditure, and the Cost of
Living Index in the United States for
the Years 1935 to 1958.

Year	Disposable personal income * (billions)	Personal consumption expenditures † (billions)	Per capita personal consumption expenditure ‡	Cost of living index §
1935	$ 58.0	$ 56.2	$ 443	58.7
1936	66.1	62.5	486	59.3
1937	71.1	67.1	520	61.4
1938	65.5	64.5	496	60.3
1939	70.2	67.5	508	59.4
1940	75.7	72.1	545	59.9
1941	92.0	82.3	616	62.9
1942	116.7	91.2	673	69.7
1943	132.4	102.2	745	74.0
1944	147.0	116.6	841	75.2
1945	151.1	123.1	879	76.9
1946	158.9	146.9	960	83.4
1947	169.5	165.6	1,150	95.5
1948	188.4	177.9	1,200	102.8
1949	186.4	180.6	1,210	101.8
1950	204.3	194.0	1,280	102.8
1951	225.0	208.3	1,358	111.0
1952	237.4	218.3	1,401	113.5
1953	250.2	230.5	1,456	114.4
1954	254.4	236.5	1,467	114.8
1955	274.4	254.0	1,546	114.5
1956	290.4	269.4	1,602	116.2
1957	305.1	284.4	1,661	120.2
1958	311.6	290.6	1,669	123.5

* Statistics for 1935 to 1950, U.S. Bureau of the Census, *1951 Supplement,
Survey of Current Business,* Government Printing Office, Washington, D.C.,
1952, p. 8. Statistics for 1951 to 1956, U.S. Bureau of the Census, *Statistical
Abstract of the U.S.,* Government Printing Office, Washington, D.C., 1959, p.
305.

† *Ibid.*

‡ This is the Bureau of Labor Statistics Cost of Living Index in which statistics for the years 1947–49 equal 100. U.S. Bureau of the Census, *Statistical
Abstract of the U.S.,* 1959, *op. cit.,* p. 338.

§ Calculated by dividing Personal Consumption Expenditure by total population data contained in the *Statistical Abstract of the U.S., op. cit.,* p. 5.

people did spend liberally in this era; and as shown later in this chapter, food stores did capture a greater portion of the consumer dollar through the sale of "luxury" food items and newly added nonfood lines.

SHIFTS IN UPPER INCOME SHARES

A parallel to the above is the study by Simon Kuznets on the upper income shares of the national income.[5] During the interwar decades (1919–1938) before income taxes, the top 5 per cent of the population had 30 per cent of the income; during 1947–1948, they had only 18 per cent of the income.

Up to 1938 the income percentage of the top 5 per cent varied only by 4.7 percentage points in either direction from the 1919–1938 average of 30 per cent; [6] but from 1938 on, the upper-share income declined steadily. This decline was unparalleled in the financial records for its magnitude and persistence.

The most recent statistics on the distribution of personal income indicate that the basic trend in upper-share income has continued. Between 1946 and 1955, the top 20 per cent of the income units dropped from 46.1 per cent to 44.6 per cent of total personal income.[7] The biggest gains were registered by the middle income groups.

There were various causes for this shift. The most important were (1) the reduction of unemployment, (2) the growth of unions, (3) the tax structures, and (4) the marked increase in total income that flowed to the lower income groups, particularly the farmers and wage earners.[8] This increase in income that precipitated to the lower income groups was more likely to be spent on food as well as other purchases.

[5] Simon Kuznets, *Shares of Upper Income Groups in Income and Savings* (New York: National Bureau of Economic Research, Inc., 1953).

[6] *Ibid.*, p. XXXV.

[7] U.S. Department of Commerce, *Survey of Current Business,* Government Printing Office, Washington, D.C., July, 1958, p. 13.

[8] Kuznets, *op. cit.*

CHANGES IN THE PATTERN OF FOOD CONSUMPTION

Shifts in the dietary habits of the American people significantly altered the pattern of food store sales from 1929 to 1954. The trend in consumption was away from less expensive bulk foods such as potatoes and grain products and toward the more costly leafy green vegetables, fresh fruits, and meat and dairy products as noted in Table 3-2. On a per capita basis the consumption of potatoes in 1954 was only 106 lb as compared with 169 lb in 1929. The consumption of dairy products in the same period rose from 379 lb to 417 lb per person; and meat, poultry, and seafood increased on a per capita basis from 134 to 169 lb. These changes in food consumption habits benefited in general the food store industry and in particular the supermarket. The latter increased its volume in the above lines and realized larger margins.[9]

TABLE 3-2 *

Yearly Consumption of Food Products per Capita,
Retail-Weight Equivalent (in pounds), by Major
Food Groups for the Years 1929, 1948, and 1954.

Product	1929	1948	1954
Dairy products	379	412	417
Eggs	40	47	52
Meat, fish, and poultry	134	151	169
Potatoes and sweet potatoes	169	116	106
Leafy green and yellow vegetables	102	111	112
Citrus fruit and tomatoes	79	116	108
Flour and cereal products	234	169	156
Ice cream	11	18	17

* Bureau of Agricultural Economics, U.S. Department of Agriculture, *Consumption of Food in the U.S.*, Agriculture Handbook No. 62, Government Printing Office, Washington, D.C., October, 1955, p. 43.

[9] Herman L. Myers and Forrest Scott, *The Rise of the Super Market*, U.S. Department of Agriculture, Bureau of Agricultural Economics, MTS–103, Government Printing Office, Washington, D.C., December, 1951, p. 10.

CHANGES IN EXPENDITURES IN FOOD STORES

Statistics in Table 3-3 indicate that food store sales, both on a total and a per capita basis, rose substantially from 1935 to 1958. This gain has been attributed not only to a rise in prices but also to an increase in total and per capita quantities of products sold in food stores.[10]

Furthermore, the food store group not only gained absolutely in dollar sales but captured a greater portion of the consumer's dollar. The statistics in Table 3-4 show that 15 cents out of every dollar of personal consumption expenditure went to the food store in 1935. The trend from 1935 to 1958 has been upward, and in 1958, 17.31 cents out of every consumer dollar spent went to the food store group.

TECHNOLOGICAL DEVELOPMENTS AND THEIR ADOPTION

Technological developments such as the automobile and the refrigerator, and their wide use in daily living, enabled a change to take place in the food store sales pattern. These developments influenced changes in buying habits, which in turn benefited certain types of food stores (particularly the supermart) to the detriment of other kinds of food store outlets. Of the many developments that occurred, three are selected for study as logically being the most important:

1. The automobile
2. Refrigeration
3. New food manufacturing and processing techniques

[10] The Retail Food Price Index of the Bureau of Labor Statistics (recorded in Table 3-3) increased from 49.7 in 1935 to 120.3 in 1958. However, this rise was relatively less than the total food store sales and the per capita food store sales.

TABLE 3-3

Total Food Store Sales, Per Capita Food Store Sales,
and Retail Food Price Index for the Years 1935 to 1958.

Year	Food store sales (in billions) *	Per capita food store sales †	Retail food price index ‡
1935	$ 8.4	$ 66	49.7
1936	9.0	72	50.1
1937	9.7	75	52.1
1938	9.5	73	48.4
1939	10.2	78	47.1
1940	10.9	83	47.8
1941	12.6	95	52.2
1942	15.8	117	61.3
1943	17.5	128	68.3
1944	19.0	138	67.4
1945	19.8	141	68.9
1946	24.2	171	79.0
1947	28.4	197	95.9
1948	31.0	210	104.1
1949	31.0	208	100.0
1950	32.8	215	101.2
1951	37.6	244	112.6
1952	39.8	254	114.6
1953	40.8	255	112.8
1954	41.6	257	112.6
1955	42.0	264	110.9
1956	44.2	274	111.7
1957	47.8	280	115.4
1958	50.3	289	120.3

* These statistics do not contain sales of the country general store. U.S. Bureau of the Census, *Statistical Abstract of the U.S.*, Government Printing Office, Washington, D.C., 1959, p. 833.

† Calculated by dividing food store sales by the total population statistics contained in the *Statistical Abstract of the U.S.*, 1959, p. 5.

‡ *Ibid.*, p. 328.

TABLE 3-4 *

Percentage of Personal Income Expenditure Spent in Food Stores.

Year	%
1935	15.00
1940	15.18
1945	16.15
1950	16.75
1955	17.17
1956	17.29
1957	16.83
1958	17.31

* Calculated by dividing total food store sales (data contained in Table 3-3) by total personal consumption expenditures (statistics found in Table 3-1).

Automobile

Statistics on car registrations are shown in Table 3-5. From 1915 to 1920, motor vehicle registration increased 308 per cent. From 1920 to 1930 an additional 190 per cent gain was experienced. By 1930 cars in operation totaled 26.5 million. These substantial increases on a national basis occurred when the supermarket, except in the Los Angeles area, was a rarity. In California there was early acceptance and wide use of the automobile for shopping.

The "cheapy" supermarket of the early 1930's had "low prices" as the basic appeal, and the significance of the automobile was to furnish transportation to the supers and to haul away the food bargains, since the units in general were located in fringe areas poorly serviced by public transportation.

From 1930 to 1950 car registrations increased from 26,532,000 to 48,567,000. By 1958 registrations rose to 68,299,000 cars. These statistics are contained in Table 3-5. This substantial gain occurred concomitantly in the era of vast supermarket growth. Not only did car registration increase, but cars were distributed widely among the population. They were used more in daily living, driven more by women, and used actually for shopping. It was in this manner that the automobile and its use can be said to have played an integral part in the supermarket development.

Refrigeration

A second technological development that influenced the pattern of food store sales was the principle of refrigeration. In Table 3-6

TABLE 3-5 *

Motor Vehicle Registrations (in thousands) in the
United States for the Years 1915 to 1958.

1915	2,491
1920	9,239
1925	19,941
1930	26,532
1935	32,035
1940	30,638
1945	44,140
1950	48,567
1955	62,020
1956	64,437
1957	67,131
1958	68,299

* U.S. Bureau of Census, *Statistical Abstract of the U.S.*, Government Printing Office, Washington, D.C., 1959, p. 559.

are statistics on manufacturers' unit sales of refrigerators. The adoption for home use started in the late 1920's and continued through the 1930's, although unit sales varied in some years because of economic conditions.

The major influence of the refrigerator on buying habits was to reduce the frequency of shopping trips. The refrigerators enabled the storage of foods, particularly meat, for longer periods of time than the old conventional ice box.[11] Following World War II, a variation of the refrigeration principle—the deep freeze or home freezer—enabled storage of foods for even longer periods. The sales of home freezers, which totaled 8,983,800 units through 1956, along

[11] A. A. Brown, "Competition in Refrigeration Demands the Retelling of the Food Protection Story," *Edison Electric Institute*, April, 1937, p. 123.

TABLE 3-6

Manufacturers' Sales by Number of Units of Refrigerators and
Home Freezers for the Years 1926 to 1956.

Year	Refrigerators	Home Freezers
1926 *	205,000	
1927	375,000	
1928	535,000	
1929	778,000	
1930	791,000	
1931	906,000	
1932	798,000	
1933	1,016,000	
1934 †	1,283,000	
1935	1,568,000	
1936	1,996,000	
1937	2,310,000	
1938	1,254,000	
1939	1,900,000	
1940	2,700,000	
1941	3,500,000	(None recorded
1942 ¶	520,000	before 1946)
1945	263,860	
1946	2,100,000	210,300
1947 ‡	3,400,000	607,000
1948	4,766,000	690,000
1949	4,450,000	485,000
1950	6,020,000	884,000
1951	3,731,000	1,032,500
1952	3,196,000	1,118,200
1953 §	3,287,000	1,049,800
1954	3,135,000	943,000
1955	3,820,000	1,045,000
1956	3,382,000	919,000

* Sales from 1926 to 1934 are found in *Electrical Merchandising*, Vol. 55, no. 1, January, 1936, p. 3.
† Sales from 1934 to 1945 are found in *Electrical Merchandising*, Vol. 76, no. 1, January, 1946, p. 37.
‡ Sales from 1947 to 1952 are found in *Electrical Merchandising*, Vol. 85, no. 1, January, 1953, p. 75.
§ Sales from 1953 to 1956 are found in *Electrical Merchandising*, Vol. 90, no. 1, January, 1957, p. 102.
¶ None were manufactured during the years 1943 and 1944.

with the growing popularity of refrigerators with frozen food compartments also influenced the pattern of frozen food sales.

In addition to reducing the frequency of shopping trips, refrigeration brought about still another and more revolutionary change in the food pattern. It made possible the development of a myriad of new frozen food products which gained popularity. The supermarkets took greater advantage of this new food trend than the small food store by providing the space and the large capital for the refrigerated units required to store and display these new foods.[12]

New Food Manufacturing and Processing Techniques

Manufacturers developed products that made it more convenient to prepare and serve foods. For example:

1. Baby foods, which got their start in 1925, built up to a $251,-000,000 retail volume in 1958.[13]

2. The preservation of foods by quick freezing was pioneered by Clarence Birdseye in 1925.[14] The first line was introduced in the food stores by General Foods in 1930. Frozen foods, which not only included the conventional fruit juices and vegetables but also complete dinners, attained an estimated retail volume of $2.331 billion in 1958.[15] Dehydrated food processing currently looks promising.

3. New, instant-type desserts, ready cake mixes, and beverages (to name but a few) were developed. These new products generally were more expensive than the older types of products which they replaced.[16] The distribution of gourmet specialties by General Foods is a recent innovation.

4. Packaging changes have resulted that not only facilitate self-service selling but also require additional display space. One example is the growing use of multiple packaging that requires room

[12] Edwin T. Gibson, "Frozen Foods in the Super Market," *Super Market Merchandising*, XV, no. 6, June, 1950, p. 72.
[13] *What the Public Spends for Grocery Store Products* (New York: Food Topics Publishing Co., 1959), p. 3.
[14] *Frozen Food Industry* (Philadelphia: Curtis Publishing Co., 1952), p. 4.
[15] *What the Public Spends for Grocery Store Products, op. cit.*
[16] "Stocks Have Trebled," *Progressive Grocer*, XXXI, no. 10, October, 1952, p. 41.

for display in order to differentiate the product from the 5,710 other items in supermarkets.[17] Another example is the innovation of larger packages for soap and cleansers, which require additional space for proper merchandising.

The many new items and innovations required the food store to carry larger inventories, to provide more display space, and to have sizable investments in refrigerated cases. These new products, easily sold by self-service techniques, in the main benefited the supermarket as compared to the small grocer who lacked the needed facilities.[18]

POPULATION GROWTH AND SHIFT TO THE SUBURBS

The population of the United States increased during the years 1930 to 1950 from 123,070,000 to 151,240,000.[19] By January, 1958, the number of inhabitants soared to 171,970,000.[20] This rise of 23.4 per cent was associated with a rising food store volume. However, locational shifts in the population appeared to affect more significantly the shifting of the pattern of food store sales than did the increase in the number of inhabitants.

Data on 140 central cities in the United States, which in 1940 had 50,000 or more population, are given in Table 3-7. From 1930 to 1940 the percentage increase of population in the central cities was 6.1 per cent, while the areas adjacent rose 16.9 per cent, as calculated from statistics contained in Table 3-7.

In the period of 1940 to 1950 the number of central cities increased to 168, as noted from the figures in Table 3-8. The central city population grew 13.9 per cent, but the areas adjacent rose 35.5 per cent. National population from 1940 to 1950 increased from 131,936,000 to 151,240,000, or only 14 per cent. The estimated

[17] Frank J. Charvat, "Growth Trend in Multiple Packaging," *Advertising Agency,* Vol. 51, no. 17, August 15, 1958, p. 16.

[18] "Stocks Have Trebled," *Progressive Grocer, op. cit.*

[19] U.S. Bureau of the Census, *Number of Inhabitants, U.S. Summary 1950 Census of Population,* Government Printing Office, Washington, D.C., 1952, pp. 1–51.

[20] U.S. Bureau of the Census, *Current Population Reports,* Government Printing Office, Washington, D.C., 1958, p. 1.

TABLE 3-7 *

Shift in Population in 140 Central Cities of the
United States with 50,000 Population and Over,
for the Years 1930 and 1940.

	1930 Population	1940 Population	% increase 1940 over 1930
Central cities	40,343,442	42,796,170	6.1
Outside central city area †	17,259,423	20,109,603	16.9

* U.S. Bureau of the Census, *Sixteenth Census of the U.S., 1940 Population,* Vol. 1, Government Printing Office, Washington, D.C., 1942, p. 61.

† The area "outside the central city" is, by census definition, immediately adjacent to the city.

changes in population to 1958 indicate a continuation of this trend, with the inhabitants literally racing to the suburbs to live.

An additional factor of this national shift to suburban living was the composition of the population.[21] The median family income in 1950 for the suburban area was $5,100 against $3,600 for the city proper. About 75 per cent of the suburban families owned their homes, as compared with 41 per cent for the city. Approximately 27 per cent of the residents in the suburbs were under 14 years of age, whereas in the city itself, this age group claimed only 21.4 per cent.

These changes in urban and suburban population were attributed in part to World War II, to the desire for home ownership, to the requisite for larger space around homes, to more families, and to the increase in personal disposable income. The automobile was a tool in this development, since it helped to provide transportation. These outlying areas, not so densely populated per square mile as the cities, required shopping facilities. New secondary shopping centers mushroomed; some assumed major significance. The extent to which supermarkets and other forms of retailing took advantage of these new suburban markets is examined in the next section.

[21] "The Lush New Suburban Market," *Fortune,* XLVIII, no. 5, November, 1953, p. 131.

TABLE 3-8 *

**Shift in Population in 168 Central Cities of the
United States with 50,000 Population
and Over, for the Years 1940 and 1950.**

	1940 Population	1950 Population	% increase 1950 over 1940
Central city	43,391,718	49,412,792	13.9
Outside central city area	25,887,957	35,087,888	35.5

* U.S. Bureau of the Census, *Number of Inhabitants, U.S. Summary, 1950 Census of Population,* Government Printing Office, Washington, D.C., pp. 1–69.

RETAIL TREND TOWARD DECENTRALIZATION

The development of outlying shopping sections was an adjunct to the suburban movement of the population. The supermarket was part of this movement. While it can be contended that the locating of supermarkets is a management prerogative and should be included in the next chapter under operating practices, the whole retail movement to the suburbs was pronounced. This forced retail management generally to open outlets in the suburbs.[22] The need for retail outlets was made greater when manufacturing plants were given special tax advantage to encourage new factories in outlying areas.[23]

In Table 3-9 are statistics on retail sales volume by size of city. Generally, the period from 1939 to 1954 showed a trend toward a greater percentage of sales in smaller communities. However, the movement by large retailers to the suburbs has further gained momentum.[24] Companies participating in shopping centers read like a "Who's Who of Merchandising." Many of these outlying shop-

[22] "The Changing American Market," *Fortune,* XLVIII, no. 2, August, 1953, p. 232.
[23] V. B. Smith, "Industry Disperses Plants," *Engineer-News,* March 27, 1952, p. 241.
[24] "The Changing American Market," *op. cit.*

TABLE 3-9 *

Retail Trade by City Size for the Years 1954, 1948, and 1939.

Size	Sales (in billions)			Percentage distribution		
	1954	1948	1939	1954	1948	1939
500,000 and over	$ 35.8	$ 30.3	$10.2	21.1	23.2	24.3
250,000 to 499,999	13.4	9.9	3.9	7.8	7.6	9.4
100,000 to 249,999	15.9	12.5	3.8	9.4	9.6	8.9
50,000 to 99,999	14.5	11.0	3.5	8.5	8.4	8.3
10,000 to 49,999	34.6	26.3	8.0	20.4	20.1	19.1
5,000 to 9,999	12.8	9.7	3.0	7.5	7.4	7.2
2,500 to 4,999	9.9	7.0	2.3	5.8	5.4	5.6
Under 2,500	33.1	24.0	7.3	19.5	18.3	17.2
Total	$170.0	$130.7	$42.0	100.0	100.0	100.0

* Data for 1939 and 1948 from U.S. Bureau of Census, *Census of Business, 1948, Retail Trade, Part 11*, Vol. II, Government Printing Office, Washington, D.C., 1952, p. 14. Data for 1954 from U.S. Bureau of Census, *Census of Business, 1954*, Bulletin R-2-2, Government Printing Office, Washington, D.C., 1957, pp. 2–309.

ping centers located in unincorporated areas in order to obtain low-cost land and to avoid annoying local ordinances. This phenomenal shift is reflected in the data contained in Table 3-9. Total retail sales made in areas of under 2,500 rose from 17.2 per cent of all retail sales in 1939 to 19.5 per cent of all retail volume by 1954.

Three types of centers have developed.[25] The smallest—5 to 10 acres with a maximum of ten stores and referred to as the neighborhood type—has one dominant store in the group acting as the magnet to attract shoppers. This core store frequently has been a large supermarket. The investment ranges from several hundred thousand dollars to several million dollars. The second type—the intermediate community center of 10 to 25 acres with a junior department store as the focal point—needs a minimum of 5,000 families for its support. This type of center is reflected by Lincoln Village in the Chicago suburbs, which required an investment of about $3,000,000. The third type is a regional center with a minimum of 35 acres and serv-

[25] "Shopping Centers," *Barrons*, XXXVI, no. 32, August 6, 1956, p. 3.

ing 100,000 persons. Examples of the latter are the $100,000,000 extravaganza of Lakewood Center in Los Angeles, which has a 12,000-car parking lot, or the new $25,000,000 Roosevelt Field center in New York, which contains 110 stores and expects to transact an $80,-000,000 yearly volume.

In 1957, 35 regional centers, 200 intermediate community centers, and 600 of the neighborhood type of center were opened.[26] Shopping centers continue to flourish, but they appear to be losing some of their momentum. A 1958–59 directory of the large suburban shopping centers lists 1,914 centers with 14,750 tenant stores.[27]

The decentralization movement was a factor in supermarket development.[28] The "cheapy" supers were first located in low-rent districts adjacent to densely populated areas of New Jersey and New York. It was considered that a population of 75,000 to 100,000 was required to support a million-dollar yearly volume market and that the saturation point of the number of these units would be reached quickly.[29]

With the shift to better equipped and housed supers, stores were opened in a variety of other sections and communities throughout the country. Many of the new locations were selected to house larger stores and to provide necessary parking. The changing pattern is shown by the statistics in Table 3-10. In 1940, 28.4 per cent of the supers were in cities with a population of 500,000 and over, and 50 per cent in cities with an excess of 100,000 inhabitants. Although the number of supermarkets increased numerically in these large cities during the next 14 years, there was an over-all trend toward small-town locations; and the large cities lost relatively in the number of supers by almost 13 per cent. All classes of communities under 100,000 population gained relatively in this 14-year period. More than 38 per cent of all supermarkets in 1954 were in towns of less

[26] *Business Week,* no. 1499, May 24, 1958, p. 50.

[27] *Directory of Shopping Centers in the United States and Canada 1958–59* (Chicago: National Research Bureau, Inc., 1959).

[28] "Store Locations," *Chain Store Age,* Grocery Executive Edition, January, 1950, p. 143.

[29] Carl Dipman, "Merchandising Trends in the Food Trade with Special Reference to Supermarkets," *Journal of Marketing,* III, no. 3, January, 1939, p. 272.

TABLE 3-10 *

Number of Supermarkets in the United States by Size of the Community
for the Years 1940, 1950, and 1954, and the Percentage That
Each Community Is to the Total.

| | 1940 | | 1950 | | 1954 | |
Population	Number	%	Number	%	Number	%
500,000 and over	2,119	28.4	2,854	20.1	3,073	17.8
100,000 to 499,999	1,599	21.4	2,929	20.7	3,441	19.9
25,000 to 99,999	1,647	22.0	3,276	23.5	3,938	22.8
10,000 to 24,999	967	12.9	2,218	15.8	3,025	17.5
5,000 to 9,999	545	7.3	1,289	9.1	1,592	9.2
2,500 to 4,999	352	4.7	784	5.3	1,038	6.0
Under 2,500	244	3.3	814	5.5	1,191	6.8
Total	7,473	100.0	14,164	100.0	17,298	100.0

* *Super Markets in the United States* (Philadelphia: Curtis Publishing Co.,
1954), p. 7.

than 25,000 inhabitants. These statistics indicate that supermarkets
followed the trend of the population to the outlying areas. The
supermarkets were here at an advantage in that they could erect
facilities suitable to the shopping needs. Moreover, in these outlying
locations, there tended to be less competition from small food stores
than in the older sections where rental facilities for small food stores
were greater.

SHIFT IN CONSUMER BUYING HABITS, INCLUDING ONE-STOP SHOPPING AND SCRAMBLED MERCHANDISING

Certain consumer buying habits underwent a considerable change
after the 1920's. These shifts were associated with the supermarket
development inasmuch as the supers adopted practices in line with
the change in shopping wants.[30] Supermarkets were thus in a more

[30] The changes in shopping habits occurred concomitantly with the development of the supermarket. No attempt is made to determine which preceded the
other. The entire movement was part of a trend toward "simplified selling."

favorable position than other types of food stores to benefit from these changes.

Thirty-seven different studies were reviewed to determine changes in shopping habits that differed from those of the pre-supermarket era.[31] An example is the *McCall's Magazine* "Consumer Diary Study," the results of which are found in Table 3-11. The findings of the various research projects are summarized as follows:

1. There has been a decided increase in one-stop shopping preference. Women shoppers first go to stores they believe will give them the best opportunity of making all their purchases. This desire has led to the diversified lines of merchandise handled by supers.

2. Visits to the food store have become less frequent. The average seems to be about three times per week. There is a decided increase in the number of people who shop once a week.

3. There has been a substantial increase in the use of the automobile for shopping.

4. The average expenditure per customer in the stores has increased substantially, more than the rise in price level.

5. Shopping seems concentrated on certain days of the week, with Friday and Saturday the key days.

6. People tend to travel farther to shop than they did prior to the supermarket development.

7. While shopping is still done predominantly by women alone, the increase in number of men shoppers has been substantial. The general findings indicate men alone, or accompanied by women, purchase about 40 per cent of the food.

8. Impulse buying has become a significant factor in food shopping. Display techniques and ability of the buyer to wander through the store have resulted in the purchase of a significant number of items that the customer had not intended to buy upon entering the store.

[31] A comprehensive file of consumer-shopping studies is contained at the library of the Super Market Institute. These studies were made by advertising agencies, private research firms, universities, and the research departments of corporations, newspapers, and periodicals.

9. Preference for self-service is indicated by answers to surveys and also by the heavy patronage of self-service food stores.

10. There is a desire for more convenient and attractive shopping.

TABLE 3-11 °

Findings from McCall's Magazine Consumer Diary
Study of Food Purchases Made by 1,090
Families for One Week in the Year 1956.

A. FOOD PURCHASES MADE BY THE PANEL:

Products purchased	Number of families that purchased these products	Total number of purchases of each product made	Dollar value of purchases
Meat, poultry, fish	1,051	4,515	$ 6,066
Produce	1,030	4,211	1,951
Dairy	1,067	7,278	4,530
Frozen foods	653	1,603	974
Baked goods	1,069	4,984	1,723
Grocery items	1,090	23,491	11,378

B. FOOD PURCHASING HABITS:

1. Approximately 86.6 per cent of the food shoppers always use an automobile, and an additional 1.8 per cent use an automobile for food shopping only part of the time.

2. Approximately 90.7 per cent of the families do some shopping at supermarkets, and 75.8 per cent shop exclusively at supermarkets.

3. Major reasons for shopping at supermarkets expressed as a percentage of total responses:

Large selection	49.0%
Economy	37.8%
Self-service selection	28.7%
One-stop shopping	22.2%
Easy-to-find items	20.5%
Freshness	13.9%

4. Two major dislikes are (a) impersonal relationship due to large size of store, and (b) difficulty of finding items because of the size of the store.

° Home Testing Institute, Inc., *McCall's Food and Grocery Products Diary Study* (New York: McCall Corp., 1956).

11. Advertising helps women in their search for merchandise. They examine the newspapers prior to making shopping expeditions.

These changes in buying habits in general have favored the supermarket industry as compared to other types of food stores.[32] Perhaps the most significant of these changes in shopping in relation to the growth of supermarkets has been the preference for one-stop shopping.[33] This in turn has been one of the reasons that has intensified competition among different types of retailers in selling the same product—scrambled merchandising.[34] Supermarkets have always been one of the proponents of scrambled merchandising. Aided by large customer traffic, supers have added many lines of merchandise that were foreign to food stores in the 1920's and have turned them into substantial sources of profit.[35]

ADDITIONAL EXTERNAL FACTORS THAT INFLUENCED THE SUPERMARKET DEVELOPMENT

An examination of the literature in this field has disclosed a variety of additional external factors that had varying degrees of influence on the supermarket growth. Some of the most important of these are summarized below.

1. There was a trend following the early 1930's for a greater percentage of married women to work outside the home. Generally they were able to spend this income, or at least part of it, as they wished. The display techniques of supermarkets and the addition of nonfood lines have attempted to capture this income.[36]

2. Manufacturers of food products increased the brand and package advertising of their merchandise in an effort to presell the customers.[37]

---

[32] The operating practices of supermarkets that enabled them to benefit more from these buying habit changes than other types of food stores are presented in Chapters 4 through 7.

[33] *Here's How We Shop for Our Big Grocery Order* (New York: Batten, Barton, Durstine & Osborne, 1959).

[34] Richard Alt, "Competition among Types of Retailers in Selling the Same Commodity," *Journal of Marketing*, XIV, no. 3, January, 1948, p. 444.

[35] Milton Alexander, "Where We Stand in Non-Foods Merchandise," *Progressive Grocer*, XXXI, no. 10, October, 1952, p. 197.

[36] "Supermarket Revolution in Retailing," *Business Week*, no. 1189, June 28, 1952, p. 38.

[37] John R. Gilman, "Why Package Products Face Super Competition in Supermarkets," *Advertising Agency*, Vol. 45, no. 6, June, 1952, p. 64.

3. There was a growing trend for manufacturers to identify their products in the mind of the consumer as to constant quality and value. This ready recognition and acceptance of brand names aided the self-service movement, one of the keystones of the super-market.[38]

4. Following World War II there was a trend toward larger family units than in the 1930's. With more members of the family to take care of, women found it difficult to shop frequently. When they did go to the store, they bought in greater quantity and tended to patronize supermarkets because of price appeal and convenience offered.[39]

5. The scarcity of cheap household help today, compared to the availability in the 1930's, influenced women to seek easier-to-prepare foods. This in turn necessitated that the merchant carry a greater variety of these foods. The larger facilities and resources of the supers enabled them generally to benefit more than the small food store.[40]

6. The growing baby crop, which began during World War II and which has continued unabated since then, has placed an ever-larger percentage of the population under 21 years of age. These growing bodies have made it necessary for families, in order to sustain this age group, to place an increasing portion of their expenditures into food and related items sold in supers.

MARKET OF THE 1960's

Continuation of a favorable market for the "sizzling sixties" is portrayed by the recent forecast of the magazine *Life*.[41] The 55 million families of 1960 are expected to increase to 66 million by 1970. One out of every four 18-year-old girls would be married by the

[38] E. B. Weiss, "Food Supers Will Find Going Tougher," *Printers Ink*, Vol. 239, no. 13, June 27, 1952, p. 71.

[39] Charlotte Montgomery, "The Woman and the Modern Market," *Progressive Grocer*, XXXI, no. 10, October, 1952, p. 170.

[40] *Ibid.*

[41] The magazine *Life* employed many market research experts to plan a research project forecasting the market of the 1960's. The findings were published in a booklet entitled *The Market of the Sixties* (New York: Time, Inc., 1960).

end of 1960, the survey predicted. Prior to World War II, 53 per cent of the women between 20 and 24 were married; in 1960, 65 per cent of the women in this age group would be married, and the continued outlook is for a leveling off at that percentage. Furthermore, women of today are bearing larger families, with the 1970 population estimated at 210 million persons. A new baby boom is anticipated to start around 1965 when the girl babies born in the early postwar years reach marriageable age. The 1970 birth rate is expected to be over 5 million compared with slightly more than 4 million currently in 1960.

Families with teen-agers, which comprise the major market of the 1960's, will continue to spend out of proportion to their number, especially for food and soft drinks. The number of inhabitants over 65 will increase by 19 million; and for the first time, this class will have sizable incomes to spend. Wives between the ages of 35 and 64 are expected to have continued increase in income as a result of their employment outside their homes. From 1940 to 1960, the number of working women between the ages of 35 and 64 more than doubled.

During the 1950's, the population of suburban areas of metropolitan markets grew seven times as fast as the rest of the United States. Suburbs are expected to continue to expand. Overlapping areas from one metropolitan center to another will create vast new interrelated markets. Continued decentralized industry and service organizations will strengthen the tendency toward convenience shopping, with greater dependence on cars. The consumer will be of a higher intellectual level.

In 1947, family units in the $4,000 to $7,500 income bracket represented about 23 per cent of all units but had 43 per cent of all disposable income. This group destroyed the traditional gap between a mass market for necessities and the small class market for luxuries. By 1960, 22 million family units comprised this middle income group, a gain of 30 per cent over 1947. The families earning more than $7,500 yearly have doubled since 1947 to over 12 million. The number of family units under $4,000 annual income has declined both relatively and absolutely since World War II and comprises today only two-fifths of the families, whereas in 1947 they represented about 70 per cent of the family units. By 1970, 45 per cent of all families will have annual incomes over $7,500; approximately 39 per cent will be middle income units from $4,000 to $7,500 income, and only 16 per cent will have incomes under $4,000. This substantial group of high income families will have broad, discretionary purchasing power, from caviar and champagne to world travel.

The market of special interest to the supermarket industry, that for food, drink, and tobacco, is currently estimated at $91 billion. This is expected to rise to $117 billion in 1970, a gain of 29 per cent. Household and recreation goods, which totaled $35 billion in 1960, are expected to rise to $53 billion by 1970, a gain of 51 per cent. Another item of possible interest to the supermarket industry is clothing. This totaled $35 billion in 1960 and will increase 18 per cent by 1970 to $43 billion. The supermarket industry, faced with these optimistic forecasts, can plan accordingly.

SUMMARY

The economic setting in which the supermarket developed was pictured statistically in this chapter. These data, including shifts in upper income shares, the rise in personal disposable income, and increased expenditures in food stores, were presented to support the qualitative discussions. The technological and psychological environment in which the supermarket grew was depicted. The acceptance of the automobile as a shopping aid and the shift in consumer buying habits were but two aspects covered. No numerical claim was made as to the extent of the association between the supermarket development and each of these external factors, individually or as a group. The contention presented has been that the growth of the supermarket industry since the "cheapy" development occurred concomitantly with various external factors which furnished a favorable atmosphere. Simply, the economic, technological, and psychological setting for the development of the supermarket was extremely favorable. And the period of the "sizzling sixties" promises more of the same.

4 | SELLING OPERATIONS

INTRODUCTION

The preceding chapter covered the favorable economic, technological, and psychological setting in which the supermarket industry grew. Statistics in Table 4-1 indicate that the total retail sales rose from $48.3 billion in 1929 to $170 billion in 1954. Almost 15 per cent of this $121.7 billion increase was accounted for by the supermarket. By 1954 supermarket sales of $18.2 billion represented almost 11 per cent of all retail store sales of $170 billion. The supermarket volume grew far more than that of the other food store members. Yet, all were in the same economic setting during this period. Therefore the supermarkets must have adopted or developed operating practices that induced consumers to come to them in preference to competitors.

The purpose of this and the subsequent three chapters is to examine what the supermarket industry did to promote such progress. What practices within the control of the operators themselves were pursued? Whereas diversity among the members is great, certain general or common characteristics of operation set the supermarket apart from other types of retailers.

These characteristics are discerned through study of operating and financial statistics of individual concerns as well as industry surveys. The operating data are examined in this and the subsequent two chapters in the framework of the main sections of an operating statement; i.e., sales, cost of sale and gross margin, cost or expense, and profit divisions. Selling practices are reviewed first; cost of sales and margins will be examined in Chapter 5; expense and profit analysis will be contained in Chapter 6. The financial prin-

53

TABLE 4-1 *

Sales of Certain Classes of Retail Stores
and Total Retail Sales
in the United States for the Years
1929, 1939, 1948, and 1954 (in billions of dollars).

Type of outlet	1929	1939	1948	1954
All retail store sales	$48.3	$42.0	$130.5	$170.0
Nonsuper grocery stores	7.3	6.2	16.9	16.2
Supermarkets †	—	1.5	7.8	18.2
Specialty food stores	3.4 §	2.4 ‡	6.2 ‡	5.4
All retail sales except food store group ¶	37.6	31.9	99.6	130.2

* Data for 1929, 1939, and 1948 are found in U.S. Bureau of the Census, *Retail Trade—General Statistics, Part 1,* Vol. 1, Government Printing Office, Washington, D.C., 1952, p. 1.04. Data for 1954 are found in U.S. Bureau of the Census, *1954 Census of Business,* Bulletin R-2-2, Government Printing Office, Washington, D.C., 1957, p. 2–2.

† These statistics are found in Table 1-2.

‡ U.S. Bureau of the Census, *Statistical Supplement, 1951 Survey of Current Business,* Government Printing Office, Washington, D.C., 1952, p. 25.

§ U.S. Bureau of the Census, *Food Retailing—Retail Distribution,* M–93, Government Printing Office, Washington, D.C., 1934, p. 9.

¶ Calculated by subtracting total food store sales from total retail sales for the respective years.

ciples of supermarketing will be studied in Chapter 7 in the framework of the major asset and liability classifications of a balance sheet.

At the outset, to exemplify approximate supermarket operations, the published results of two different operations are presented in Tables 4-2 and 4-3. The findings of the Harvard Business School Study of Food Chains, expressed as a percentage of sales, are contained in Table 4-2. The operating results of Wilt's, an independent supermarket located in Elkhart, Indiana, are presented in Table 4-3. These statements are submitted to exemplify approximate supermarket operations for both chains and independents. They are not presented to show chain versus independent operation; nor are the data to be considered as typical for the entire industry. The operating statements indicate merely approximate margin, expense, and profit relationships for a supermarket. Operating policies adopted by management can result in variations from these statistics.

TABLE 4-2 *

Operating Statistics of Selected Food Chains Expressed as a Percentage of Sales for the Years 1955 to 1958.

	1958	*1957*	*1956*	*1955*
Sales	100.00	100.00	100.00	100.00
Cost of sales	79.50	79.63	80.61	81.89
Gross profit	20.50	20.37	19.39	18.11
Expenses				
Payroll	10.07	10.01	9.74	9.68
Real estate	1.77	1.64	1.54	1.45
Equipment costs	1.38	1.42	1.39	1.36
Utilities	0.67	0.62	0.61	0.60
Supplies	1.14	1.18	1.11	1.08
Services purchased	0.25	0.26	0.26	0.27
Advertising (includes stamps) .	1.88	1.87	1.44	0.82
Traveling	0.10	0.09	0.08	0.08
Insurance (except real estate) .	0.14	0.13	0.15	0.16
Taxes (except real estate or income)	0.53	0.54	0.49	0.48
Miscellaneous	0.61	0.61	0.63	0.56
Interest paid	0.24	0.25	0.27	0.24
Total expense	18.78	18.62	17.71	16.78
Net operating profit	1.72	1.75	1.68	1.33
Other income (primarily cash discounts earned and interest) . .	1.17	1.21	1.22	1.17
Less income tax	1.48	1.50	1.48	1.28
Net profit	1.41	1.46	1.42	1.22

* Wilbur B. England, *Operating Results of Food Chains in 1958* (Cambridge: Harvard Business School, Bulletin No. 156, 1959), p. 2.

VOLUME—A SUPERMARKET NECESSITY

The stress on volume in a supermarket is inherent in the basic nature of operation of this type of retail institution. The early super,

TABLE 4-3 *

Operating Statistics of Wilt's Supermarket, Elkhart, Indiana, Expressed as a Percentage of Sales for the Year 1956.

Sales	100.0
Cost of sales	80.7
Gross profit	19.3
Expenses	
Premiums	1.1
Advertising	0.6
Regular payroll	9.2
Executive payroll	0.5
Supplies	1.0
Utilities	0.3
Insurance	0.4
Rent	0.3
Taxes	0.9
Depreciation	0.7
Interest	0.2
Other expense	1.5
Total expense	16.7
Net operating profit	2.6
Cash discounts	0.3
Net profit before income tax	2.9

* "Change or Die, Says Wilt's," *Super Market Merchandising*, XXIII, no. 8, August, 1958, p. 47.

appealing on a price basis, needed volume to compensate for a narrow gross margin and net profit. The market of today, operating on a larger but still relatively small gross margin compared with other types of retailers, also needs volume operation to compensate for tight gross margins. In addition, the modern market has added materially to its expense of doing business and its investment. Competitive conditions prevent most markets from operating continuously at a level which will yield the greatest dollar net return. Unused capacity appears to exist in most markets. Therefore stress must be placed on added possibilities for volume to bring the market more in line with its capacity and optimum profit potential. These relationships are examined in detail in Chapter 7.

SALES PRACTICES OF SUPERMARKETS

The basic technique of supermarket operation has been to transact a large dollar volume.[1] This has been accomplished by devices such as:

1. Price appeal
2. Display techniques
3. Self-service
4. Attractive and convenient shopping facilities
5. Advertising and promotion
6. Large inventories but well regulated with regard to turnover
7. Addition of diversified lines of merchandise including nonfood items

Each of these devices for building volume is examined in detail in the remainder of this chapter.

Price Appeal

With regard to price, from the inception of the "cheapy" supermarket to the modern supers of today, the general practice has been to sell for less.[2] Through its low-cost methods, the supermarket, more than any other food store, has passed on to the customer over the past 25 years greater values plus additional services.[3] The "cheapy" super rode to fame by its "price wrecking" policies and large volume. Supers still stress low prices as a means of attracting customers and building volume. Witness the full-page newspaper ads of special values offered by supers. Price studies dating back to the "cheapy" supers indicate the constant endeavor of modern supers to sell for less, and this is further substantiated by the small gross

---

[1] M. M. Zimmerman, "Ten Years of Supermarket Growth," *Super Market Merchandising*, XI, no. 12, December, 1946, p. 45.

[2] Victor Lebow, "What Department Store Managers Should Know About Supermarkets," *Journal of Retailing*, XXIX, no. 1, Spring, 1953, p. 17.

[3] William Applebaum, "Is Supermarket Efficiency Slipping?" *Chain Store Age*, Grocery Store Executive Edition, February, 1952, p. 169.

margin of the supermarkets in comparison with that of other forms
of retailing.[4] Even though supers generally have modernized their
stores and made them attractive, studies have revealed customers
still have the "opinion" that supermarkets quote low prices.[5] Akin to
price appeal is the concept of quality. In the main, whether it be
nationally advertised, branded merchandise, or chain store brands,
supermarkets have been associated with the concept of giving satisfactory quality in relation to price.[6] One of the keystones of supermarket operation, self-service, is in part predicated on the customer's
recognition of price bargains on known lines.

Pricing Policies

The pricing policies of individual supermarkets can vary widely
as a result of local factors. In the main, however, supers basically
follow a policy of normal markup pricing, tempered by competitive
conditions and price leadership. As a simple example consider that
a can of tomato soup costs a super 10 cents and the normal markup
is 9. 2 per cent, based on selling price; then

$$\text{Selling price} = \frac{\text{cost} \times 100\%}{100\% - \text{markup \% at retail}} = \frac{10\cancel{c} \times 100\%}{(100\% - 9.2\%)}$$
$$= 11 \text{ cents}$$

or, the soup would sell at 11 cents per can.

Most comparable concerns in that immediate trading area, unless a particular store is differentiated by offering different services,
will price the soup competitively. However, if a store faces little
competition, markup on the tomato soup could range as high as 23
per cent, with the soup selling at 11.5 cents per can, or 2 cans for
23 cents. Chain stores in a given city, except for advertised specials

---

[4] Gross margins are discussed in detail in Chapter 5.
[5] In a study conducted by the magazine *Super Market Merchandising* in 1948,
the number two reason advanced for trading in supermarkets was "Low Price."
The findings of the *1958 Survey of Super Market Shoppers, Their Buying Habits
and Attitudes,* published by Burgoyne Grocery and Drug Index, Inc., and the
results of a study by Newel Comish, "What Influences Customer Choice of Food
Store?" *Journal of Retailing,* Summer, 1958, indicate price is still a significant
factor in the patronage of supers.
[6] Lebow, *op. cit.*

which are announced throughout the area, have marked similar merchandise at different prices at different locations.

A smaller independent supermarket, not associated with a wholesale or retail-sponsored voluntary chain, may even be forced to operate on a smaller markup in a highly competitive area or differentiate the store because of its lack of buying power. To attract customers to the market some stores have differentiated by offering unusually high quality meat or by remaining open longer hours.

A manufacturer of soup, desiring more display space and a resulting greater share of the market, may offer comparable buyers a deal involving cooperative advertising or price concessions. The tomato soup possibly can be advertised and sold at 10 cents a can. Deals such as this on a wide variety of merchandise occur daily and constantly upset the market equilibrium. Witness the week-end, advertised specials offered in the Thursday night ads in which supers still use the price appeal as an attraction to customers.

The particular store or stores accepting the special soup deal in a certain trading area will have a temporary price advantage. Stores not participating in the arrangement may either cut the price of tomato soup to 10 cents or push some other price special in their weekly promotions, continuing to sell tomato soup at 11 cents per can to the shoppers attracted by other bargains or patron-buying motives. At the end of the special promotion (several days to a week) the price of tomato soup will revert back to the original equilibrium price of 11 cents per can. No one company can continue to enjoy indefinitely the advantages of a special promotion or purchase because the normal markups established for the various classes of commodities in the industry are a function of cost of selling and profit on the one hand and giving the consumer what he or she desires on the other. Supers are forced by their customers to handle some products that yield low profits per linear foot of display space. The establishment of normal markups or margins is discussed in Chapter 5.

Produce marketing is complicated further by varying degrees of product deterioration, fluctuations in supply, and great number of products handled. Managers apply suggested markups on the individual products to make an over-all initial markup for the department of 30 to 35 per cent and a maintained markup of about 25 per cent after allowances for markdowns. Spoilage losses average from 1 to 3 per cent of sales.

Meat pricing is complicated by the wide fluctuations that occur in wholesale prices for meat. Furthermore, production costs are incurred in the super to prepare the meat in proper cuts and packages for the consumer. While an over-all yearly markup percentage generally is set as a standard, a super must operate daily in the approximate spread between selling prices set by competition plus what consumers will pay and the cost of the meat set by factors over which the super has no control. The supermarket must know the fixed and variable costs of handling all kinds of meat, as well as which types of meat cuts pay off. Skill in pricing joint products (for example, short ribs and roasts from the same rib) is essential to maintain the general gross margin and still attract customers on a price basis.

Display Techniques

A second means of developing large volume is to display mass stocks of inventory.[7] At an early date in its history the super found that mass displays of merchandise psychologically tended to make people buy. Mock-ups, mirrors, and lighting have been used to give the illusion of bigness. Modern display fixtures, refrigerators, and freezers have been developed. Manufacturers constantly have studied package design to make the product more appealing. Studies have been made on the value of display space to increase sales.[8] Multiple packaging has been developed to create "billboard illusions" in stores, as well as make display space more usable directly on floors of supermarkets. The placing of related merchandise, such as wash cloths adjacent to toilet soap, has boosted sales. Other re-

[7] William S. Ireland, "Mass Sells More," *Chain Store Age*, Grocery Executive Edition, August, 1950, p. 68.

[8] "Merchandise Location," *Chain Store Age*, Grocery Executive Edition, December, 1958, p. 52.

lated items include cellophane wrapped footballs with vitamin pills and table cloths with baby food.[9] Studies on impulse buying have indicated that approximately 25 per cent of the purchase in supers are unplanned. Other surveys have shown that 77 per cent of women who shop with children purchase items at the suggestion of children who see the item on display. Shoppers, surrounded by an assortment of related merchandise such as health and beauty aids in a supermarket, respond to the display of the merchandise and do not take into account the type of store in which they are shopping.[10] The supermarket has been an unusually lucrative source of unplanned purchases. Increased volume is thus obtained.

Self-Service

Akin to mass displays is the policy of self-service. Supermarket operators generally are of the opinion that letting people roam with push carts has paid off in increased sales.[11] Shoppers can feel, pinch, smell, and handle the merchandise; they can compare brands and read labels. To feel is reassuring. No clerk anxiously stands by to finish the sale or hurry the customer. Shoppers can budget as they go along. The *McCall's* study of 1,090 families disclosed 28.7 per cent of the respondents preferred to shop in supermarkets because they could make their own selection.[12]

While the supers originally had only self-service in groceries, they have adapted this technique to meat, dairy, produce, and bakery departments, with outstanding results. The facts are that when a supermarket operator puts in a self-service meat department, his sales usually increase because customers [13]

1. Hate to wait.
2. Want to search among a broad variety of kinds of meat.

[9] "New Angles on Related-Item Display," *Supor Market Merchandising,* XXII, no. 4, May, 1957, p. 99.

[10] John R. Gilman, "Why Package Products Face Super Competition in Supermarkets," *Advertising Agency,* 45, no. 6, June, 1952, p. 64.

[11] *Ibid.*

[12] Home Testing Institute, Inc., *McCall's Food and Grocery Products Purchase Diary Study* (New York: McCall Corp., 1956).

[13] Don Parsons, "The Supermarket Formula," *Food Business,* Vol. 6, no. 5, May, 1958, p. 17.

3. Like to make their own choice.

4. Like to see what they are getting.

5. Like to take their own time to select purchases.

The self-service technique originated in supers was adopted by other forms of retailing on a growing scale since about 1950. Walgreen, Woolworth, and Kresge are examples in the drug and variety store field. Self-service, called "quick service," had swept the variety industry to the point in 1958 where 42 per cent of total variety stores had adopted quick service.[14] Department stores have re-examined the problem of determining the amount of assistance to be given to a customer and have developed new store layouts and display techniques with the aim of not only increasing sales but of also reducing selling costs.[15] This simplified selling, as it is referred to in department store terminology, is exemplified by the Fedway Stores division of Federated Department Stores, Incorporated.

Attractive and Convenient Shopping Facilities

Another device to increase volume has been to make the store attractive, convenient, and pleasant for shopping.[16] The "cheapy" super maintained an air of cheapness which contributed to the feeling of obtaining bargains. Since the advent of the supers, the general policy has been to make the stores more appealing through more attractive interiors, better lighting, music, air conditioning, rest rooms, and parking lots. This trend of "trading up" the stores has been questioned as an unnecessary expenditure, since it has tended to increase expenses and raise gross margins.[17] These expenditures possibly could result in the super losing its basic competitive advantage of price appeal. On the other hand, it has been contended that these expenses for comfortable shopping are a rela-

[14] "Self-service in Variety, 1958," *Variety Store Merchandiser,* Vol. 54, no. 4, May, 1958, p. 67.

[15] C. W. Barker, I. D. Anderson, and J. D. Butterworth, *Principles of Retailing* (New York: McGraw-Hill Book Co., Inc., 1956), p. 136.

[16] "Appearance Counts at Penn Fruit," *Super Market Merchandising,* XIII, no. 9, October, 1949, p. 74.

[17] "Schwegmann Brothers, Inc.," *Business Week,* no. 1136, June 9, 1951, p. 120.

tively small percentage of sales; the resultant increase in volume has improved the earnings effectively.[18]

An example of a recently opened modern super with decor is Eavey's Super Market in Fort Wayne, Indiana. It has 50,250 sq ft of selling space, a "kiddie korral," post office, flower shop, liquor department, utility payment booth, and a carillon for time and weather.[19] Despite the cost of these attractions, advertised prices are in line with chain competition and the concern appears to be successful.

The term "convenience of the supermarket to the customer" is concerned with the ease by which the consumer gets to the supermarket. This varies by particular kind of store location—central business district, neighborhood location, planned outlying shopping center, or highway market. Management has come to realize that nearness in itself is not a basic prerequisite per se, inasmuch as from 80 to 90 per cent of the customers use a car for grocery shopping.[20] General factors to be considered in selecting a supermarket site to make the location convenient include:

1. Street walking traffic
2. Street driving traffic
3. Congestion of streets to get to the market
4. Intersection of other streets
5. Availability of parking
6. Ease of access or egress of the parking lot
7. Public transportation
8. Zoning in the neighborhood

Furthermore, management must examine other location factors in the selection of a market site, including:

1. Land size
2. Suitability of store rental property
3. Number of competing stores

[18] Applebaum, *op. cit.*
[19] "Eavey's Young Giant," *Super Market Merchandising,* XXII, no. 1, January, 1957, p. 85.
[20] Home Testing Institute, Inc., *McCall's Food and Grocery Products Purchase Diary Study, op. cit.*

4. Standards of competition
5. Population trends
6. Income trends
7. Diversity of income sources
8. Type of customers
9. Population density
10. Taxes
11. Neighborhood changes
12. Size of trading area

The *McCall's* Food Study disclosed that the average family spends $25.27 per week or $1,314.04 per year on grocery store products. If $110 of yearly sales per square foot of space is used as a standard, a market of 10,000 sq ft of total covered space would need 837 families in order to transact a yearly volume of $1,100,000. This average figure can vary in specific instances, but it is presented to illustrate the importance of having sufficient potential in the area from which patronage is drawn.

Rules of thumb are difficult to establish in locating a supermarket. In a built-up neighborhood of one- and two-family units, a supermarket should control at least 20 per cent of all food business in its primary trading area of a 1-mile radius of the store, at least 10 per cent within the 1- and 2-mile radius, and an additional 1 to 2 per cent within the 2- to 5-mile radius of the store. Mr. Ray Harb, general sales manager for Red and White, Incorporated, reported that a metropolitan location can pull customers who buy all requirements from a distance that takes a maximum of 20 minutes to drive.[21] In rural areas the allowance for driving should be 30 to 40 minutes. Other results of a study made by *Food Topics* on the maximum trading area of a supermarket are shown in Table 4-4. In a city with inhabitants of 500,000 or more, a super can draw from a radius of 7.1 miles from the store. In a small town of less than 10,000 persons, the trading-area radius ranges up to 22.4 miles. Again it is cautioned that locational problems of each store are unique and subject to individual variation.

[21] "Store Locations," *Food Topics*, January 23, 1956, p. 1.

Trends in supermarket location indicate that management has followed the movement of the population to outlying residential or suburban areas in an endeavor to make the facility convenient for shopping. In fact, even highway locations have been pioneered in recent years to satisfy this demand.

TABLE 4-4 *

Maximum Trading Area Radius for a $500,000
Yearly Volume (and over) Supermarket by
Size of Community.

City size	Trading area radius (miles)
500,000 and over	7.1
100,000–499,000	8.8
25,000–99,000	10.4
10,000–24,000	12.1
Under 10,000	22.4

* "Store Locations," *Food Topics,* January 23, 1956, p. 1.

Advertising and Promotion

Promotion and advertising have been attempted to increase sales. Attractions for inducing people to shop at supers have ranged from automobile and money raffles to guest appearances by movie stars.[22] While stores differ as to the extent of promotion, an endeavor has been made to make the super a family place to shop, a source of evening entertainment, a place to go. Snack bars, magazine sections for children, soda fountains, kiddyland rides, and special attractions galore have abounded in certain supers. Yet, the food-chain operating statements for 1958, shown in Table 4-2, indicated advertising and promotion expense (including trading stamps) to be 1.88 per

[22] Pragmatic operators will find of extreme value a series of articles entitled *1,000-and-one Super Promotion Ideas,* which started in the March, 1951, issue of *Super Market Merchandising* and continued intermittently until September, 1952. These ideas, together with practical illustrations, cover the topics of grand openings, storewide promotions, institutional campaigns, anniversaries, and specific product promotions. Also of value is an article "51 Public Relations Ideas," *Super Market Merchandising,* XXIV, no. 5, May, 1959, p. 113.

cent of sales. Surveys conducted by the magazine *Super Market Merchandising* indicated that advertising expenditures (excluding stamps) in 1955 and 1956 were 0.84 and 0.93 per cent of sales, respectively.[23]

Promotion can take two directions. One is the special, short-run type; the other is the long-run, regular promotion, usually of a premium nature. The former is exemplified by the following:

1. Grand openings: free gifts or night club shows
2. Storewide promotions: airplane ride with the purchase of $25 or more, mystery shopper sale, or finder's keepers sale
3. Institutional: polio campaign or set-up of art galleries
4. Anniversary: serve breakfast or give birthday cakes to all babies born the week of the sale
5. Holiday: free trimmings if you purchase a turkey at Thanksgiving
6. Product lines: half-cent sale or shopping bag specials full of canned goods

The regular or constant type of promotion typically involves a premium. There are four types.

1. Giveaways: Have a lottery every week or give a certain dish of a china set with a stated dollar purchase. Stagger the kind of dish given away so that it will take several months to get a whole set.
2. Discount-on-purchase plan: Offer certain merchandise at a discount if customers purchase a certain dollar amount. The merchandise sold at a discount can range from special premiums to regular merchandise carried.
3. Cash register receipt: Save receipts, and after they total a certain prescribed amount, offer the customer a premium such as a dollar salad bowl.
4. Stamp or coupon plan: Give coupons or certificates to be applied to the purchase of merchandise carried by the store. Or use the conventional type of stamp plan whereby stamps are given generally at the rate of one stamp for each 10-cent purchase. The stamps

[23] "How's Business," *Super Market Merchandising*, XXII, no. 8, August, 1957, p. 113.

are saved in a booklet and redeemed for a great variety of merchandise premiums.

Of all the regular type of promotion plans, trading stamps have become the most vital promotional tool for supermarket operators. A study made by *Progressive Grocer* indicates that the typical super which issues stamps spends 2.03 to 2.06 per cent of the sales dollar for this device.[24] The general use of trading stamps has grown unevenly and cyclically since the 1890's, with a department store generally as the core. While some supers introduced trading stamps earlier, their general acceptance dates from about 1950. For a supermarket to use this promotional tool successfully, certain prerequisites must be met. There are six discernible features.[25]

1. The user should be part of a group of different stores reasonably close to each other geographically. All should handle the same stamp, with the super or a department store as the center of influence.

2. Stamps are promotional; customers must be encouraged to save them and associate the stamps with that particular store.

3. Stamps must obtain and hold additional volume; while the volume increase varies, at least a 10 per cent increase in sales is needed to break even on the stamp cost.

4. The super must be able to handle added volume without materially increasing the overhead.

5. Stamps are not a panacea for supers whose quality and type of service are inferior to that offered by competitors.

6. Stamps do not permit much, if any, independence in pricing.

The use of trading stamps reached its zenith in 1956 when 39 per cent of the supermarkets reported using this premium.[26] In 1957 the upward trend finally halted when only 38 per cent reported using stamps; in 1958 only 35 per cent reported stamp plans in opera-

[24] *Facts in Grocery Distribution* (New York: Progressive Grocer, 1958), p. F-19.

[25] Albert Haring and Wallace O. Yoder, *Trading Stamp Practice and Pricing Policy* (Bloomington: Indiana University, 1958), p. 284.

[26] *Facts in Grocery Distribution* (New York: Progressive Grocer, 1959), p. F-13.

tion. However, there is no indication that stamps will fade into the
position of relative insignificance as their past history purports, inasmuch as the major factors that led to stamp ascendency will continue to influence the market.[27] Indications are that certain industry giants may adopt stamps as a promotional tool, with market
tests being conducted on a limited experimental basis.

Large Inventory

Merchandising is defined as the adaptation of a product to fit the
requirements of the buyer, coupled with the effective presentation
of such goods.[28] Supermarkets merchandise through their buyers
and buying committees who screen the veritable horde of items and
deals presented. Merchandising is completed by the various display
and sales techniques that result in the movement of goods to the
ultimate consumers.

Supermarkets have carried larger and more diversified inventories
in an effort to increase sales. Examine the increase of the number
of items carried: [29]

Year	Items
1928	867
1946	3,000
1950	3,750
1955	4,723
1957	5,144
1958	5,600

This increase resulted in part from the shopper's desire to select
from many lines. In addition, manufacturers produced and promoted
new items in accord with the strong desire of the housewife to want
convenience in food preparation.[30] Ingenuity and skill of food processors created new and better products, such as frozen juices and

[27] Eugene Beem, "Who Profits from Trading Stamps," *Harvard Business Review*, Vol. 35, no. 6, November–December, 1957, p. 121.
[28] T. N. Beckman, H. H. Maynard, and W. R. Davidson, *Principles of Marketing* (New York: The Ronald Press Co., 1952), p. 5.
[29] *Facts in Grocery Distribution, op. cit.*, p. F–3.
[30] "The Fabulous Market for Food," *Fortune*, XLVIII, no. 4, October, 1953,
p. 135.

cake mixes. Most supers are cramped for space; it is a constant fight to get merchandise on display. Manufacturers' salesmen do not sell merchandise to supermarket buyers; instead they sell dollar profits to the supers for granting them location and display space in the store. In the case of many new items or brands, advertising done to presell the customer is not sufficient inducement to buy. Various promotions, premiums, coupons, and deals are required to get the item carried.

Basically, an item is judged for stocking in supermarkets on turnover, gross margin, and expense of handling and selling.[31] Inherent in these major features are space for display, storage, competing lines handled, advertising allowances, promotional support, items given a store, and merchandise-returns policy. These criteria, which influence profits, vary for different kinds of merchandise. The supermarket has attempted to attain a large volume (and its resultant advantages) through a high rate of turnover.[32] Rates for selected supermarket chains for 1956 are shown in Table 4-5.[33] These range from a low of 7.8 for A. J. Bayless Markets, Inc., to a high of 14.94 for Daitch Crystal Dairies, Incorporated. A turnover of about 12 times per year, or once a month, appears to be average. The Harvard Study of Selected Food Chains indicated a stock turnover of 12.3 for 1958.[34]

The wide variation in turnover rates is in part attributed to the lines of merchandise stressed by the respective companies. The trend toward larger stores in the postwar period has offered additional shelf space for display and has made the super a bonanza for visiting salesmen. The increase in number and kind of food items carried, coupled with nonfood lines, has tended to lower turnover rates in the postwar period for many concerns. As an example, be-

[31] Malcolm P. McNair, "Thinking Ahead in Retailing," *Super Market Merchandising*, XV, no. 8, August, 1950, p. 106.
[32] Milton Alexander, "Where We Stand on Non-food Merchandising," *Progressive Grocer*, XXXI, no. 10, October, 1952, p. 200.
[33] The supermarket chains listed in Table 4-5 were those whose detailed operating statistics were published in *Moody's Industrial Manual*.
[34] Wilbur B. England, *Operating Results of Food Chains in 1958* (Cambridge: Harvard Business School, Bulletin 156, 1959), p. 33.

tween 1950 and 1956 the turnover for Colonial Stores, Incorporated, dropped from 15.0 to 10.3; for Lucky Stores, Incorporated, from 10.8 to 7.9; and for Market Basket, Incorporated, from 11.7 to 10.2. This is a merchandising trend that management must watch. How-

TABLE 4-5 *

**Annual Inventory Turnover of Selected Supermarket Chains
for the Year 1956.**

Company	Turnover
American Stores Co.	11.7
A. J. Bayless Markets, Inc.	7.8
Century Food Markets Co.	11.3
Colonial Stores, Inc.	10.3
Daitch Crystal Dairies, Inc.	14.9
Fisher Bros., Co.	11.2
Food Fair Stores, Inc.	14.8
Food Mart, Inc.	9.5
Grand Union, Inc.	11.2
Jewel Tea Co., Inc.	10.8
Kroger Co.	11.5
Lucky Stores, Inc.	7.9
Market Basket	10.2
Purity Stores	13.0
Safeway Stores, Inc.	10.9
Shaffer Stores Co.	10.2
Shopping Bag Food Stores	10.2
Sunrise Supermarkets Corp.	13.7
Thriftmart, Inc.	7.9
Weingarten, J., Inc.	9.8

* These statistics are calculated from data contained in *Moody's Industrial Manual.* Cost of sales is divided by average inventory at cost.

ever, profits have not appeared to suffer inasmuch as gross margins generally have improved for concerns that lower turnover to carry more lines. As a generalization from the 1956 data, stores with the lower inventory turnover rates tend to have the higher gross margins.[35]

Supermarkets have enjoyed a high inventory turnover as compared with that of other retailers, as shown by the statistics in Table

[35] Gross margins are discussed in Chapter 5.

4-6. The average turnover of about 12 times per year is approximately triple that for department, drug, and variety stores, which average about four times per year. Simply, the velocity of goods in and out of a super is three times that for a department, drug, or variety store; or, a supermarket buys, stocks, sells, makes a profit, and repeats the cycle about three times while a drug, department, or variety store is doing it once with the same dollar inventory. This is a vital consideration in the handling of nonfood lines.

Addition of Nonfood Products

Akin to the problem of controlling a large inventory is that of adding nonfood products to the line. The supermarket has incorporated in its operation the rapidly moving meat, dairy, and produce

TABLE 4-6

Annual Inventory Turnover of Various Lines of Retailing for the Year 1954.

Department stores	3.7 *
Drug stores	3.9 †
Hardware stores with sales over $200,000	2.3 ‡
Jewelry stores with sales over $500,000	1.1 §
Variety stores	4.2 ¶

* Controllers Congress, *1954 Merchandise and Operating Results* (New York: National Retail Dry Goods Association, 1955), p. 1.
† *Lilly Digest* (Indianapolis: Eli Lilly and Company, 1955), p. 21.
‡ "1954 Retail Hardware Survey," *Hardware Retailer*, June, 1955, p. 14.
§ *1954 Operating Statistics* (New York: American National Retail Jewelers Association, 1955), p. 4.
¶ "Harvard Report on Variety Chains," *Chain Store Age*, Variety Store Managers Edition, XXXI, no. 8, August, 1955, p. 62.

items; but it also has concentrated on fast-turnover nonfoods which have experienced higher markup and profits. For the year 1958, food stores sold $1.82 billion in nonfood items exclusive of tobacco products. Of this group, health and beauty aids, with sales of $1.10 billion, were the largest group.[36] This substantial $1.10 billion total

[36] *Facts in Grocery Distribution, op. cit.*

represented 60 per cent of the entire national volume of health and
beauty aids. Other classes of nonfoods included greeting cards, magazines and books, toys, records, stationery, clothing, dry goods, and
film. In addition, tobacco products of $1.8 billion were sold in
grocery stores during the year 1957.[37] A study made by *Chain Store
Age* disclosed that the 1959 supermarket transacted 4.3 per cent of
total sales in tobacco products, 2.3 per cent in health and beauty
aids, 1.1 per cent in housewares, and 0.5 per cent in magazines and
books.[38]

The super is basically a food store; many of these nonfood lines
create a problem of buying, stocking, rotating, and selling that differs from the food departments. While the bulk of nonfoods are
handled through the supermarket buying division, the tasks of merchandising nonfoods have been simplified partly by the use of rack
jobbers for at least part of the needs, as shown by the data in Table
4-7. The rack or short-order jobber performs the function of stock-

TABLE 4-7 *

**Source of Nonfood Products in Supermarkets
Expressed as a Percentage of Stores
Using the Source.**

Source	Drugs	Housewares	Toys	Soft Goods
Manufacturer	67.2	58.3	65.5	79.2
Rack jobber	24.1	66.8	28.4	46.6
Food wholesaler	7.6	3.6	2.0	4.8
Other wholesaler	12.1	36.4	11.4	4.7
Concessionaire	0.0	0.1	0.6	0.4

* "Non-Foods Jump to Major Rank," *Super Market Merchandising*, XIX, no.
1, January, 1954, p. 36.

ing and rotating merchandise and keeping the shelves clean. The
general practice has been for the store to receive 25 per cent as its

[37] *Supermarket News*, April 14, 1958, p. 52.
[38] "What Do Food Chains Sell?" *Chain Store Age, Grocer's Manual Issue*,
July, 1959, p. 109.

share of all merchandise sold.[39] Stock left in the store by the rack jobber normally remains the property of the jobber until sold. Merchandise is sold in the regular manner, and the consumer does not know that consigned products are being purchased.

In a study covering the influence of nonfood merchandise on food products, the following data were disclosed: [40]

1. Supers reduced the amount of space for food products by less than 10 per cent in order to stock nonfoods.

2. New stores were built larger so as to handle both lines.

3. The food lines that suffered most were the slow turning, less profitable ones.

4. The nonfood lines carried had to turn over rapidly, to take up little room, and to be adapted to self-service sale and not require technical selling.

Furthermore, studies revealed that visits to food stores were about four times more than those to every drug store and eight times more than to every hardware store.[41] Mathematically there was greater chance for displayed merchandise to be purchased in a super. The trend toward the sale of nonfoods in supers has been pronounced in the postwar period.

One of the more recent nonfood trends has been the marriage of the discount house and the supermarket in the form of giant merchandising colossi.[42] Safeway Stores, Incorporated, has opened a discount center within one of its food markets in Bakersfield, California, in which appliances, sporting goods, and related items are featured. Schwegmann Brothers has opened a store in New Orleans with 189,000 sq ft of space on the first floor and 55,000 sq ft of selling space on the mezzanine to merchandise an infinite variety of stock. Two Guys from Harrison and the National Grocery Company

[39] Interview with Chris Tarrant, Secretary, Grocerland Co-operative, Inc., Chicago, Illinois, on June 20, 1957.

[40] "Supers Bid Welcome to Soft Goods," *Super Market Merchandising*, XVIII, no. 7, July, 1953, p. 27.

[41] Gilman, *op. cit.*

[42] "The Super Super Market," *Super Market Merchandising*, XXII, no. 7, August, 1957, p. 56.

have opened a 110,000-sq ft operation estimated to do $20,000,000 in food, durable goods, auto accessories, and promotional items. Merchandise is received directly from the manufacturer in drop shipments. Retailing innovations of this type may cause an upheaval in the world of retailing.

SUMMARY

Supermarkets have adopted practices that have led toward increased sales per store. These practices have included low price policies, mass displays, large stocks (but carefully selected as to turnover), self-service, promotions, addition of certain nonfood departments, and improved appearance and services. Excellent merchandising practices to obtain increased sales per square foot of floor space and linear display space have been pursued. Management has taken advantage of the desire of the consumer for one-stop shopping by selection of merchandise and expanding store building programs. Simply, the policy is to attract the consumer and attractively display a variety of fast-turning merchandise that can be purchased as a result of planned purchases as well as impulse buying.

These selling policies are a must if a store is to realize its full potential during its lifetime, the length of which is governed by unpredictable factors. Detrimental population shifts may take place in a store's trading area, competition may move in, or the facilities of the store may become outmoded. A given store has certain facilities with which to make a profit, and in the main, these resources do not always appear to be used at maximum capacity. Thus management must strive to make the most out of the facilities over a predetermined period of time. In a store's trading area, management must strive to obtain its maximum share of the available market commensurate with the store facilities. The marginal customer attracted or the extra dollar of sales to the established customer has a significant impact on profits of a store. Not only does the added sales dollar reflect in the normal profit percentage, but it also contributes to an increased profit percentage. This interesting phenomenon will be presented in Chapter 7 after margin, expense, and profit relationships have been examined.

5 | BUYING OPERATIONS AND MARGINS

INTRODUCTION

The preceding chapter pointed out the necessity for a large volume per super and examined the selling techniques designed by supermarkets to generate this needed large volume. It is the purpose of this chapter to continue the study of supermarketing principles, still in the framework of an operating statement. Attention in this section is focused on (1) cost of goods sold and (2) principles involved in the establishment of gross margins. The former includes a review of buying practices and techniques developed by this industry.

COST OF GOODS SOLD

There is a maxim in retailing that anything well bought can be sold at a profit. Department stores recognized this principle early, as did food chains. Buying is an area of specialization in itself, and the demise of the small food store can be attributed to a large extent to improper or inept purchasing.

Balance of Buying Power Favors Supers

Supermarkets in 1958 had sales of $28.7 billion.[1] Inasmuch as cost of goods sold in a supermarket averages about 79.50 per cent of the sales dollar, merchandise purchases approximated $22.8 billion in 1958, assuming no major change in inventory position by the members.[2] Supers, in the aggregate, wield a powerful buying force.

79.50

[1] See Table 1-2.
[2] See Table 4-2.

Furthermore, the strong trends toward larger stores and more stores under a common ownership through horizontal integration have given the individual members of this industry more potent bargaining power. Even an individually owned store with typical yearly sales of $1,000,000 is a highly respected customer, since purchases for that operation approximate $800,000. As a result, transactions today between the buyer (the super) and the seller (the manufacturer) are more of a cooperative venture in which the manufacturer needs the assistance and cooperation of the supermarket.

Routine Buying Policies

Many of the purchases of a supermarket are of a routine nature from established sources of supply. It would be difficult to envisage a super without Ritz crackers or Campbell's tomato soup. Responsibility for buying, the actual placing of the order, varies according to the size and organizational structure of the company. Specialized buyers are used by the large chains for routine buying, with store managers requisitioning from the warehouses. In some smaller organizations the entire buying responsibility for routine purchases is handled by one individual. Some firms become members of wholesale or retail voluntary chains in order to procure staple items at low cost. Department managers, specializing in certain areas such as produce and meat, have assisted in routine procurement for the one-or-few unit operations. Ordering and shelf stocking of certain items frequently are handled by manufacturers' salesmen under the authorization of the owner, manager, or person responsible for buying.

Yet, even in the purchase of regular items, care must be taken to make certain that the best possible prices and deals are obtained. The purchase of routine merchandise must be an integral part of the selling program. The buyer must be aware of special promotions, displays, local and national advertising, economical handling of merchandise, warehousing, promptness of delivery, and turnover. Some of the larger firms, such as Jewel Tea Company, have acquired electronic computers to handle the logistics problem of most economical handling and warehousing of merchandise. In turn, manufacturers must not be complacent about their established brands in a super. Commodity analysis constantly takes place, either subjectively by a busy owner or manager or objectively by accountants and statisticians who compute dollar profit per linear foot of display space. No item on the shelves of a super is in a haven. It must sell or be eliminated.

New Products—Life Blood of a Super

Merchandise that is well established in a supermart under a system of cooperation between the manufacturer and the supermarket is "bread and butter" volume. These items reflect customers' needs and wants and move off the shelves. However, a dynamic supermarket that is striving for added volume and a greater profit percentage must evaluate successfully new products on a continuous basis. New items that sell are the volume builders that a super needs to add increased profits to the store. A supermarket retains its basic competitive position in a trading area by [3]

1. Offering an expanding variety of merchandise.
2. Developing a good reputation for offering new items.
3. Functioning as the purchasing agent for the community.
4. Differentiating its store from competition.
5. Associating with the news value inherent in new products.

The problem of adding new merchandise to the line becomes more acute because of the difficulty in defining exactly what a new product is. A new item can be [4]

1. A product that hasn't existed previously or a product so changed as to make most existing items obsolete.
2. A product that has been changed in varying degree in construction, design, color, size, or package.
3. A product on the market not previously handled by the particular super.

[3] E. B. Weiss, *Winning Chain Store Distribution for New Products* (New York: Doyle, Dane, Bernbach, Inc., 1956).
[4] *Ibid.*

4. An old item made by a new manufacturer.

Supermarket attitude toward new items will vary, depending upon how new products fall into these divisions as well as upon the prestige and record of the supplier.

Buying Committee

As a result of buying complexities of stocking the myriad of new items and the importance of integrating purchasing, sales, advertising, and promotion into a unified merchandising program, supermarkets have developed buying or merchandise committees. Approximately 88 per cent of the supermarkets have these committees, which replaced food retailing by a federation of individual apron-stringed grocers with a select group of skilled merchandisers having the power to match giant manufacturers.[5] The stated purpose of these committees is to [6]

1. Remove buying decisions from an emotional atmosphere.

2. Prevent a buyer's personal likes and dislikes from entering into a decision.

3. Help store and field personnel to understand buying operations at headquarters better through rotating participation of some members.

4. Capitalize on collective knowledge.

5. Provide for the orderly continuity of buying operations.

Buying committees range from 3 to as many as 17 members. They are made up of a buyer and other top advertising, promotion, merchandising, and sales executives. Frequently store managers are included to make their operation more democratic. Each member on the committee has one vote, and it takes a simple majority to add a new item to the line. Faced with the problem of buying many lines of merchandise, some firms have organized two buying committees.

Activities of these committees are as varied as their composition. Some assemble once every week, and depending upon the number

[5] From an address by William C. Nugent to the Grocery Manufacturers of America, Inc., on November 12, 1957, at New York City.
[6] *Ibid.*

of products to be considered, the meetings run from 1 to 6 hours. A buying committee's decision is binding in that a buyer cannot overrule or ignore it. The group decision, however, is not irrevocable. For example, if a product is rejected, another presentation generally can be given in a period of from 60 to 90 days after the rejection. Some committees will review an item as many as three times. After a merchandise group selects a product, store managers must introduce the item. But if it doesn't sell, a manager need not reorder. In turn, store managers in some supermarket chains can request buying committees to adopt a product. It must be remembered that the buying committee decisions involve the entire store system and not just one store.

The results of merchandise committee decisions have been examined in several studies. One large food chain reports that its buying office has presented for consideration as many as 150 to 200 new items per week.[7] If all were accepted, 10,000 new items per year would be added to this chain, which normally carries 4,000 items. A study of the activities of 12 buying committees of some of the largest supermarket chains showed that out of 496 products examined, 220 were voted favorably, 61 were deferred, and 215 were rejected.[8] In another study, the buying practices of eight chains were examined for the period of March, 1954, to June, 1955.[9] Thousands of items were presented to the buyers. They in turn screened new items and submitted only 1,433 products to the respective merchandise committees. These committees disposed of the new items as follows: [10]

Rejected	987
Held for reconsideration	16
Accepted for testing	10
Recommended for special promotion only	13

[7] Weiss, *Winning Chain Store Distribution for New Products, op. cit.*
[8] Nugent, *op. cit.*
[9] William Applebaum and Richard Moulton, *An Exploration into Reasons Why Supermarkets Add and Discontinue Items* (New York: McCall Corp., 1956).
[10] *Ibid.*

Accepted part of the line   29
Accepted   378
Items reviewed 1,433

In all, 69 per cent of the items presented to the committees of these eight chains were rejected and only 26 per cent were accepted unconditionally.

As a corollary to this same study of the eight chains, the major reasons for discontinuing 3,725 items from the line during this same 16-month period were: [11]

	Per cent
Slow movement	42
Did not fulfill expectations	22
Replaced by superior product	15
Due to manufacturers' action	11
Other	10

Merchandise that doesn't sell is eliminated.

In cases where a decision to add an item is questioned, some companies resort to consumer panels of up to 16 housewives whose opinions are respected. Other companies have a designated test-store group where product tests are regularly conducted in order to assist the merchandise group.

This trend of employing the buying committee has shifted the duties of a buyer from one of making decisions to one of communications. Buyers make decisions on the original screening. After this, they generally present the product to the merchandise committee for a group decision. In the committee the buyer carries but one vote. In turn, this has made selling on the part of the manufacturer more impersonal, since the salesmen seldom appear personally before the committee. The salesman merely sells the buyer and fills out comprehensive data sheets so that the buyer in turn can do a creditable job of presenting the proposal. Table 5-1 contains a suggested form of the Super Market Institute to be filled out by the salesman for use in the buying function. This type of impersonal selling in turn requires manufacturers to

[11] *Ibid.*

1. Open up channels of communication with all executives having a voice in new-item determination.

2. Develop new methods of presenting data to the buying committee.

3. Understand problems confronting chains and their difficulties in adopting new products.

Supermarkets in turn must review and improve the functioning of the committee as to operating techniques and organization in order to make it more effective.

TABLE 5-1 *

Grocery Promotion and New Item Fact Sheet.

1. ITEM _____   PROMOTION NUMBER _____

2. Date presented _____   Buyer _____

3. Starting date _____   Accepted (date) _____

4. Closing date _____   Rejected (date) _____

5. Type of promotion _____

_____

FOR BUYER'S USE		
This Item		*Reg. Mdse.*
$_____	cost/case	$_____
$_____	cost/unit	$_____
$_____	suggested retail	$_____
$___ : ___%	profit/unit	$___ : ___%
$___ : ___%	profit/case	$___ : ___%

6. Pack and size _____

7. Invoice price per case _____

8. Freight, if any _____

9. Terms (cash discount) _____

10. Promotional allowance _____

11. Total cost per case _____

12. Performance requirements for promotional allowance _____

13. Promotional allowance paid by: Check___ Off invoice___ Free mdse.___.

14. Display allowance: Yes_____ No_____.

15. Advertising allowance: Yes___ No___. If "yes," is it in addition to promotion and display allowance?___ Tear sheet to be furnished?   Yes___ No___

16. Are allowances over and above regular contract?   Yes___ No___

17. Floor stock protection on regular merchandise?   Yes___ No___

18. Will regular merchandise be picked up while deal is in effect? Yes___ No___

19. Display material available? Yes___ No___ Delivered to: Store___ Warehouse___.

20. Will deal be advertised by manufacturer? Yes___ No___. If "yes," to what extent? _____
    National media _____
    Local media _____

* Super Market Institute.

21. Will case be marked "Deal?" Yes___ No___ How many sides?_____
22. Is sale guaranteed? Yes___ No___ If "yes," what basis?_____
23. Is price guaranteed against decline? Yes___ No___ If "yes," what limits, if any? _____
24. Manufacturer's name _____
25. Manufacturer's address _____
26. Local representative _____
27. Local representative's address _____
    Additional information: _____
    _____
    _____

NEW ITEMS
(Complete in addition to first sheet)

1. Who handles this product in this market?
   Name_____ SRP †_____
   Name_____ SRP _____
   Name_____ SRP _____
2. What advertising and promotion is being done in this market by manufacturer? _____
   _____
3. What advantage is there in stocking this item? _____
   _____
4. If approved, when will item be available for delivery? _____
5. Shipping point _____
6. Transit time _____
7. Best routing _____
8. What quantities must be purchased to obtain lowest cost? _____
9. LCL price_____ Pool car price_____ Car price_____
   Minimum_____ Minimum_____ Minimum_____
10. Are drop shipments available? Yes____ No____.
    Additional Information _____
    _____
    _____

† Suggested retail price.

Factors Involved in Selecting Individual Products

While buying committees vary as to composition and method of operation, they generally are in accord as to the factors involved in the selection of merchandise. Following are criteria used to judge a product: [12]

[12] Address by William C. Nugent presented at the United States Wholesale Grocers' Convention, April 21, 1957, St. Louis, Missouri.

1. Will product return a fair dollar profit in terms of potential volume and shelf space?
2. Does the consumer want the product?
3. What is its sales potential?
4. Is there a need for the product?
5. How will the product be advertised and promoted?
6. Are there advertising, promotional, or display allowances available?
7. Is there a retailer incentive (deal goods)?
8. Is a product of good quality?
9. Is packaging proper?
10. Is the manufacturer reliable?
11. Does competition have the item?
12. Was the product market-tested?
13. Is the product timely—in season?
14. Is the introduction timely?
15. Will it bring new customers to the store?
16. How many items are in a carton?
17. Does stock of item conflict with company policy?
18. What is the merchandise returns policy of the manufacturer?
19. What is the quantity that must be bought?
20. What discounts are offered?

A manufacturer will do well to weigh these factors in merchandising his line to fit in with these requirements. There is an ever-increasing problem of obtaining distribution of new products in the supermarkets.

Make or Buy

Akin to the problem of product selection is the alternative of a supermarket: whether to manufacture or to purchase. Different stores have different policies in this regard, and it is difficult to generalize.

The industry leader, the Great Atlantic and Pacific Tea Company, has long been an advocate of manufacturing as well as marketing. Other large chains have entered manufacturing operations on a more limited scale, primarily in bakery and coffee lines. The factors that determine whether a product should be manufactured or purchased include:

1. Investment in manufacturing facilities
2. Alternative use of funds
3. Frequency of depressed conditions in the line so that advantageous purchases can be made
4. Total dollar volume of the specific item
5. Total dollar volume of any one item within a line
6. Strength of brand preference for competing products
7. Strength of the emotional buying motive for the item as a result of strong brand preference (e.g., baby food)
8. Need for a yardstick to insure proper costs for the product

Policy on Packer versus Private Brands

Closely related to the problem of "make or buy" is that of brand selection. Supermarkets got their start in the self-service sale of nationally known brands. In today's market, however, there are both packer and private brands crowding the shelves. Packers' brands include nationally known products—Del Monte and Dole—as well as little known or unadvertised brands of small and medium-sized packers. Private labels exist at both retail and wholesale levels and include chain brands. The private labelers acquire their merchandise from manufacturers of various sizes. Some of the private brands also are packed by the chain factories and sold as chain brands. Thus chain brands can be both private brands and packers' brands.

For example, in the canned goods field, nationally advertised products generally command a higher price than private labels or unknown packers' brands. Competition between them is primarily on a price basis. Major packers who know possible total demand and supply conditions, inventory carry-over, costs, and profit possibilities attempt to establish prices on their branded products, quality considered. In turn, they are underpriced by unknown brands that arrive on the market at various times and in varying quantities. A retailer may never again carry a particular private brand. In bumper crop years, the price spread between the two tends to increase as smaller packers literally dump their pack on the market and force the major packers to take a new price position.

Add to this the growing importance of chain-branded goods that are brought into the store under the broad family brand of the retailer and which embrace a variety of food products, from bread to cheese. Little advertising or promotional expense is incurred other than that related to the store special sales. As a result of astute buying, display policies, and tie-in of the product with the general reputation of the store, the chain labels have been taking an increasingly larger share of the market.

Factors involved in the decision to use chain brands are for the most part similar to those involved in the decision whether to manufacture or to purchase. One additional feature is that funds need not be expended for plant and equipment because chains have been able to obtain items under their brand from small manufacturers as well as large national sellers of branded products.

Use of Buying Associations

Food chains and large, independent supermarkets have integrated their operations by performing more and more of the wholesale marketing functions and even some of the manufacturing activities. For example, approximately 80 per cent of the supermarkets obtain their grocery products through their own central warehouses, from 9 to 10 per cent obtain their merchandise through retailer-owned cooperatives, 3 per cent through voluntary chain wholesalers, and 7 per cent through no central warehouse or affiliation.[13] As a result of their own wholesale operations, the integrated retailers generally have been able to place merchandise in their stores at a cost less than that of small independent merchants who buy from service wholesalers. This has placed the large operators at a competitive advantage in this high-volume, narrow-profit industry in which a 10 cent price advantage on a case of tomato catsup is significant. To adjust for this competitive disadvantage in buying,

[13] *Super Market Industry Speaks* (Chicago: Super Market Institute, 1956).

many of the independent merchants have cooperated with each other for the purpose of purchasing primarily staple merchandise. In 1957 there were 88,000 food stores that were members of voluntary and cooperative buying organizations.[14] Although most of these units were not supermarkets according to the definition established in this text, inasmuch as their volume was under $500,000 annually, a fair amount of their sales of $20.46 billion was transacted by supermarket members. Independent Grocers Alliance of America, commonly referred to as IGA, is the largest of the voluntary chains. The 5,300 member stores in 1957 transacted approximately $2.9 billion sales.[15] While only 234 of their United States outlets and 20 Canadian stores were classified as supermarkets, these units are reported to have done at least 5 per cent of the retail volume of this voluntary organization. Therefore this procurement channel must be considered in a text on supermarkets even though the voluntaries were developed to aid the smaller merchant.

There are basically two types of buying associations in the food industry. One is the wholesale-sponsored voluntary chain, such as the Red and White Corporation or IGA. Red and White is owned by its wholesale members throughout the country. Its headquarters in Chicago conducts many varied activities. It makes arrangements with manufacturers to pack merchandise for its wholesalers, handles all quantity and net buying arrangements which are available to the wholesalers on a national basis, and arranges for quantity discounts on a national basis where available. Red and White also arranges for private labeling, furnishes advertising service, and works with the member stores at the retail level to improve their operation. The independent retail stores in turn agree to purchase a certain portion of their requirements through the respective local wholesale member. There is no requirement that an individual retailer purchase all requirements through this wholesaler. In the similarly operated IGA

[14] *Facts in Grocery Distribution* (New York: Progressive Grocer, 1958), p. F–5.

[15] Interview with Mr. Don R. Grimes, assistant to the president, IGA, July, 1957.

voluntary chain, the retailer members pay 2 per cent above cost of the merchandise to their IGA local wholesaler, who gets "cash on the barrel head." Cash discounts vary from 1 to 2 per cent, and the local retailer also pays drayage.

The other principal method of purchasing through an affiliation is that of the retail-sponsored voluntary chain in which a group of retailers form a cooperative to purchase some or all of their joint requirements. The association is financed by its retail members, whereas financing is done by the wholesaler in the method described previously. Some cooperatives require members to have on deposit funds equal to each week's purchases. In return, merchandise is delivered to the respective members at cost plus a slight percentage for operation of the association plus drayage. In some cases the cooperative even owns and operates its own warehouse facilities. Cooperative profits paid to the members are based on the ratio of the percentage of each member's purchases through the cooperative to the total sales of the cooperative. This type of operation is used primarily to procure staple merchandise.

Consigned Merchandise

The final method of acquiring merchandise is that of consignment selling. The vast majority of the merchandise sold by supers is purchased outright. It turns over rapidly, and thus inventory investment is kept at a minimum. Yet, some manufacturers and wholesalers leave merchandise with supermarts who become the agents for the purpose of selling the goods. Title remains with the manufacturer, and the super receives its compensation in the form of a percentage of the selling price at which the goods actually are sold. A supermarket will use this arrangement in cases in which it does not desire to tie up capital in merchandise that may prove to be unsalable. This situation arises primarily with unknown new grocery products of questionable merit or nonfood items with which the super has limited experience. It is in conjunction with the latter case, nonfood merchandise placed in supers by rack jobbers, that consignment selling is significant. Nonfood sales in a 1958 super averaged 5 per cent of total sales.[16]

Basically, a rack jobber sets up display equipment in a supermarket, arranges the merchandise, services the account by exchanging defective goods and rebuilding stocks, and suggests how the store manager can tie in with national advertising. The super receives, as its compensation for rental of space and for the selling of the product, from 25 to 35 per cent of the sales price of each item. The margin depends upon the type of goods handled by the particular rack merchandiser. Some jobbers carry a complete line; others specialize in certain merchandise categories. It is possible for a large super to be serviced by as many as ten specialized rack jobbers in such areas as hardware, housewares, health and beauty aids, tobacco, soft goods, toys, stationery, auto supplies, pet food, and electrical items.

Wide diversity exists among members of the supermarket industry in the use of rack jobbers. Even divisions within the same company may vary as to policy. For example, the stores of the Great Atlantic and Pacific Tea Company in Baltimore employ an old drug wholesale house to handle their health and beauty aids on a rack-jobbing basis.[17] The same company in Jacksonville, Florida, buys all stationery items and health and beauty aids direct from manufacturers.[18] As supers become more familiar with the merchandising of nonfood items, they take over certain lines of this activity. The items taken over from rack merchandisers generally are small in size and moderately priced; they contain a minimum of style obsolescence, sell in volume, are consumed quickly, display easily, and offer a fair profit margin. The extent of consignment selling by rack jobbers is shown by the data in Table 4-7. Consignment sellers are the second most important source of nonfood merchandise in supers.

[16] *The Super Market Industry Speaks* (Chicago: Super Market Institute, 1959).

[17] "How Rack Jobbers Open Doors for Sale of Non-foods in Supers," *Sales Management,* Vol. 82, no. 7, April 3, 1959, p. 44.

[18] *Ibid.*

GROSS MARGINS

In the preceding section, buying practices and techniques developed by this industry were reviewed. The importance of scientific purchasing was stressed as a vital requisite to the fundamental method of operation of this volume merchandiser. The vast array of merchandise carried must be sold at relatively low prices in order to represent good value to the customer. This in turn requires skillful buying.

Like all retailers, a supermarket purchases merchandise at one price and in turn sells it at a higher price. In turn, out of its sales dollar it must obtain the cost of the merchandise and leave a balance (gross margin) to cover expenses and net profit. In order for a balance to exist in the form of gross margin, the supermart must, of necessity, furnish services for which its customers are willing to pay. While a super does nothing to the fundamental form or shape of the goods, it does give them added value in the form of time, place, and ownership utility. For example, it enables butter produced in the summer in Wisconsin to be purchased and consumed by a family in New York in the winter. This measure of value added by the supermarket to the products it sells is its gross margin.

Margins differ within product lines and among individual supermarkets and various types of retailers. Markups also vary over time. It is the purpose to examine these facets in the remainder of this chapter.

Trends in Margins

The early supermarkets were able to operate on gross margins varying from 10 to 14 per cent of sales.[19] This was a considerable reduction from the generally accepted 19 to 20 per cent for the chain economy store and the independent grocers in the early 1930's.[20]

---

[19] Charles F. Phillips, "The Supermarket," *Harvard Business Review*, XVI, no. 2, Winter, 1938, p. 192.

[20] *United States v. The Great A. and P. Tea Company*, U.S. Circuit Court of Appeals, 7th district, Docket 9221, Records and Briefs, Vol. II, p. 162.

The Great Atlantic and Pacific Tea Company strove for a 12 per cent gross profit once it had adopted supermarket operation.[21]

(Industry studies on gross margin first were made in the period following World War II. The magazine, *Super Market Merchandising,* conducted an industry-wide survey in the years 1947 to 1956 and reported that the average gross margins were: [22]

Year	% sales
1947	18.2
1948	17.7
1949	17.6
1950	17.7
1951	17.4
1952	17.9
1953	18.4
1954	18.8
1955	19.0
1956	19.6

The food chain supermarkets indicated gross margins that ranged from 18.11 to 20.50 per cent of sales, as shown by the data in Table 4-2.)

Statistics in Table 5-2 comprise the gross margins for selected supermarket chains. The 1956 range was 16.27 for Shaffer Stores Company and 22.98 for A. J. Bayless Markets, Incorporated. The general trend of gross margins for the selected chains has been upward in line with that for the industry. For example, between 1950 and 1956 the gross margin for Colonial Stores, Incorporated, rose from 17.7 to 18.7 as a percentage of sales; for Food Fair Stores, Incorporated, from 17.1 to 18.7; and for Market Basket, Incorporated, from 18.8 to 19.6. The much publicized Schwegmann Brothers, Incorporated, New Orleans, constantly strove for a gross margin of only 10 per cent, but in recent years legal difficulties in connection with fair trade laws have forced it upward.[23]

[21] *Ibid.*

[22] These statistics from 1947 through 1951 are from the yearly surveys published in the May editions, 1948 through 1952, respectively, of *Super Market Merchandising*. Statistics for 1952 through 1956 are from the yearly surveys published in August 1953 through 1957 editions of *Super Market Merchandising*.

[23] "Schwegmann Bros., Inc.," *Business Week,* no. 1136, June 9, 1951, p. 120.

Forces Behind Increases in Margins

Four movements have been present since the 1930's, particularly since World War II, which have tended to force gross margins upward.

TABLE 5-2 *

Gross Margin, Expense, and Net Profit (Before Taxes) as a Percentage of Sales for Selected Supermarket Chains for the Year 1956.

Company	Gross margin	Expense	Net profit
American Stores Co.	17.72	15.15	2.57
A. J. Bayless Markets, Inc.	22.98	17.75	5.23
Century Food Markets Co.	20.54	18.59	1.95
Colonial Stores, Inc.	18.68	15.94	2.74
Daitch Crystal Dairies, Inc.	19.91	18.36	1.55
Fisher Bros., Co.	17.01	14.23	2.78
Food Fair Stores, Inc.	18.68	15.24	3.44
Food Mart, Inc.	19.33	15.88	3.45
Grand Union Co.	19.68	16.99	2.69
Jewel Tea Co., Inc.	19.32	15.48	3.84
Kroger Co.	17.83	15.52	2.31
Lucky Stores, Inc.	20.92	17.36	3.56
Market Basket	19.63	16.34	3.29
Purity Stores, Ltd.	18.46	16.09	2.37
Safeway Stores, Inc.	17.75	15.07	2.68
Shaffer Stores Co.	16.27	15.01	1.26
Shopping Bag Food Stores	22.22	19.34	2.88
Sunrise Supermarkets Corp.	18.60	16.20	2.40
Thriftimart, Inc.	16.54	13.77	2.77
Weingarten, J., Inc.	19.84	17.13	2.71

* Calculated from statistics contained in *Supermarket News Food Industries Financial Manual* (New York: Fairchild Publications, Inc., 1957).

1. The first is a tendency during and since the postwar era to expand into nonfood lines which earn a higher markup than grocery products. For example, health and beauty aids are handled at about 28 to 31 per cent gross margin as shown by the statistics in Table

5-3. Toys and certain of the soft goods are handled at about 30
per cent markup. Arrangements with rack jobbers return to the
super about 25 to 35 per cent of the selling price. Moreover, many
of the nonfood lines are fair traded.[24]

2. Second is a tendency for families to purchase better and more
convenient kinds of food products. Per capita consumption of meat
and fresh produce has increased. While margins vary depending
upon store policies, meat returns a gross margin of about 17 to 22
per cent and produce from about 25 to 31 per cent, as shown by the
data in Table 5-3. Frozen foods, including prepared dinners, currently account for about 5 per cent of supermarket sales and re-

TABLE 5-3

Gross Margins in Supermarkets by Major Product Lines.

Product	Food Town study [*]	Super Valu study [†]
Meat	16.9%	21.3%
Produce	25.4	30.8
Frozen foods	22.2	20.3
Bakery	18.0	17.8
Paper products	23.9	23.4
Health and beauty aids	27.7	31.3
Food specialties	24.9	23.9
Beer and wine	26.3	
Toys	. . .	29.5

[*] "The Foodtown Study," *Progressive Grocer*, XXXIV, no. 1, January, 1955,
p. 43.
[†] *Facts in Grocery Distribution* (New York: Progressive Grocer, 1958), p.
F-18.

turn from 20 to 22 per cent gross margin. Stores incur added expense
for stocking and displaying the assortment of frozen foods. Per
capita use of paper products has mounted, and these products gross
from 23 to 24 per cent margin.

3. Third is the fact that supermarkets in recent years have adopted

[24] Milton Alexander, "Where We Stand on Non-food Merchandising," *Progressive Grocer*, XXXI, no. 10, October, 1952, p. 200.

merchandising policies in line with consumer desires and habits that necessitate more diversified inventories. Merchandise turnover, which is a vital factor in determining retail price, has decreased. General price policy in supers has been for the fastest movers, usually products essential to the health and well being of the family, to carry the lowest margins. As sales movement declines, percentage of margin usually increases. This realistic pricing philosophy builds volume, strengthens consumer confidence in the store, and at the same time produces a satisfactory competitive over-all store margin.[25]

4. Fourth is a tendency to increase customer services and comfort—"trade up" the supers. This trend has resulted in larger expenses and, in turn, higher margins.[26]

Comparison of Margins with Other Retailers

Although these four pressures have tended to force gross margins upward, supermarkets still operate at a lower over-all markup than the chain economy stores and the small independent grocers of the 1920's. In comparison with other types of retailers, few maintain such low markups as the supermarket, as shown by the statistics in Table 5-4. Department and variety stores have both maintained margins of over 35 per cent or about double that for the supermarket. The nature of the products sold, competitive conditions, and policies of manufacturers, wholesalers, and retailers are a few of the factors that have a bearing on the margins. But the fact that the super could operate on such a narrow margin influenced other retailers. Those who handled the same nonfood products easily sold in supers attempted to improve their competitive position.

The average 1957 margin for a small, combination grocery and meat market was 18.25 per cent of sales.[27] This was lower than the

---

[25] "The Food Town Study," *Progressive Grocer*, XXXIV, no. 1, January, 1955, p. 43.

[26] Actually margins could have been left the same and profits reduced. This has not been the case, as will be seen in the next section on expenses.

[27] *Facts in Grocery Distribution* (New York: Progressive Grocer, 1958), p. F–17.

margin for its counterpart in the 1920's. Supermarket margins, as shown by the data in Table 4-2, ranged from 18.11 to 20.50 for chain units. Because of differences in products handled by various supers, no attempt can be made to compare their margins with those for

TABLE 5-4

Gross Margin for Various Kinds of
Retail Establishments for the Year 1954.

Type of store	Gross margin as % of sales
Department store	36.5 [a]
Drug store	33.2 [b]
Furniture store (large)	39.0 [c]
Hardware store	29.5 [d]
Meat market	21.4 [e]
Supermarket	18.8 [f]
Variety store	37.7 [g]

[a] Controllers Congress, *1954 Merchandise and Operating Results* (New York: National Retail Dry Goods Association, 1955), p. 1.

[b] Lilly Digest (Indianapolis: Eli Lilly & Co., 1955), p. 21.

[c] *1954 Furniture Operating Experiences* (Chicago: National Retail Furniture Association, 1955), p. 5.

[d] "1954 Retail Hardware Survey," *Hardware Retailer,* June, 1955, p. 77.

[e] *Meat Markets—Operating Results in 1954* (New York: Dun & Bradstreet, Inc., 1954), p. 2.

[f] *Facts in Grocery Distribution* (New York: Progressive Grocer, 1957), p. F–15.

[g] "Harvard Report on Variety Chains," *Chain Store Age,* Variety Store Managers Issue, XXXI, no. 8, August, 1955, p. 65.

the small combination market. The comparison should be by product classes. For staple food items, supers continue to be the price leaders.

This trend of rising gross margins has resulted from policies of supers endeavoring to furnish goods and services desired by the consumer. However, the supermarket managements must not fail to realize that they have an Achilles heel in rising gross margins necessitated by increased expenses. Since 1957 the full-line but limited-brand "vest pocket" super has gained popularity in the Southeast,

Southwest, and in some areas of the Pacific Coast.[28] These stores, with from 2,000 to 4,000 sq ft of space, sell every type but not every size or brand of product at low prices. This and other innovations in retailing must be watched by supermarket management.

Margins by Product Lines

While the over-all gross margin of a supermarket averages about 18 to 20 per cent of the sales dollar, individual departments and products within these departments have gross profit percentages and dollar gross margins that vary widely from the store average. Furthermore, sales by product lines and the resulting dollar margins are not equally important. For example, the 1957 Harvard Study of Food Chains disclosed the following product-line sales of the medium-sized food chains:

Item	*% total sales*
Groceries	66.2
Produce	9.9
Meat	23.9

In turn, these same food chains had product-line, gross-margin percentages as follows:

Groceries	17.4
Produce	26.9
Meat	20.8

The percentages of total-dollar gross margin earned by product classes for these same stores were:

Groceries	61.3
Produce	13.5
Meat	25.0

Therefore all three product classes did not contribute equally to the store margin of 18.9 per cent. For example, if these percentages were applied to a store doing $1,000,000 volume, the dollar gross margin for the entire store would be $189,379. However, produce sales

[28] *Facts in Grocery Distribution, op. cit.,* p. F–4.

would total only $99,000 but would return $24,479 gross margin. Thus, while produce sales were only 9.9 per cent of the total volume, they returned 13.5 per cent of the store's dollar gross profit.

A further breakdown of margins of grocery items suggested by *Progressive Grocer* in its widely distributed margin card include the following:

Margin %	Item
9 or less	Butter, coffee, sugar
10–15	Eggs, cereals, soup, soap
16–19	Dog food, flour mixes, syrup
20–22	Catsup, frozen food, canned fruits
23–25	Jelly, olives, paper towels
26–28	Pie filling, waxes, brooms, pectin
29 and over	Drug sundries, napkins, facial tissue

These margin percentages illustrate the wide variation in gross profit among different products. Gross profit percentage is a function of the competitive situation in the respective market areas, volume and resulting turnover of each item, handling and display costs, and the nature of the product. A super generally must price its products competitively, and thus it is limited in its control over specific product margins. In addition, if a product such as coffee has a high turnover and sells in volume, the margin percentage may be small, but the total-dollar gross margin may be large. A premium margin normally is placed on products that are bulky and difficult to display, such as brooms and paper goods.

Improvement in Supermarket Margins

Gross margin is the difference between the selling price and the cost of the goods sold. Management is under constant pressure to improve store margins in order to increase the profit possibilities. It can do this by holding selling prices constant and reducing cost of sales, raising selling prices generally and holding cost of sales constant, raising selling prices generally and lowering cost of sales, or concentrating effort on selling products which normally have the largest gross margin percentages.

Any activity on the part of management that can reduce the cost of the merchandise which the super sells can increase the gross margin. That is why scientific purchasing has played such a vital role in the development of this industry. Astute purchasing is the heart of a super's merchandising strategy. Management also must strive to keep cost of sales down through close control of inventory in order to prevent losses or shrinkages from accruing. Losses that appear in inventory increase the cost of goods sold during that period and thus reduce the dollar margin. Losses occur as a result of:

1. Failure to get the merchandise that was purchased. This involves proper inspection.

2. Excessive discounts offered to employees on merchandise bought for their own consumption.

3. Pilferage on the part of customers, personnel, or suppliers. This can vary from 0.35 per cent to 0.50 per cent of the sales dollar and thus increase the cost of sales by a like amount.[29]

4. Spoilage or shrinkage of merchandise, particularly in produce and meat departments.

The competitive situation in the respective trading area of a super has a bearing on prices charged. An individual store normally may find it difficult to raise prices above competition unless the store is differentiated in some manner. But the merchandising skill of the store executives can augment margins. Special promotions or sales can be used more effectively to draw customers who buy related merchandise not on sale and which carries larger margin percentages. A store executive may be able to merchandise specific products to advantage through knowledge of local factors and flexible operations. A product in short supply in the market may be raised in price and return a higher margin. Merchandising skills must be developed and employed to plan operations more completely, take advantage of special events, promote seasonal merchandise sales and display merchandise more effectively.

[29] These figures were obtained from a letter from Mr. G. L. Mattei, District Manager, William J. Burns International Detective Agency, to the Super Market Institute on January 22, 1958.

Managerial ability is important to make certain that selling prices are not understated. This can occur if checkers undercharge for merchandise or do not record the sale of every item. Improperly marked merchandise can lower margins. It is vital to get the money due the super. The proper combination of merchandising and managerial skills on the part of the store executives, coupled with skillful buying, can improve the gross margin in a super.

SUMMARY

Merchandise "well bought" can be sold at a profit. This is a cardinal rule in the supermarket industry which purchases over $20 billion in merchandise each year. The term "well bought" means the purchase of merchandise that meets the needs and wants of the customer and which can be sold at a price that reflects good value.

Trends within the industry toward larger stores and more stores under a common ownership, coupled with the development of group purchasing (the buying committee), have given the industry advantageous bargaining power with suppliers. Furthermore, the wide use of the buying committee has resulted in a more unified merchandising program—greater coordination of buying, selling, advertising and promotion. The role of the buyer has changed. Although he performs executive tasks, he must also be a communication expert, taking the manufacturer's message to the committee. This impersonal buying has forced food manufacturers to revamp their selling programs.

In turn, the margins in the supermarket industry have tended upward. This has been brought about by four fundamental forces present in the industry. There has been a tendency during and since the postwar era to expand into nonfood lines that earn a higher markup than grocery products. Second is the tendency for families to purchase better and more convenient kinds of food products that carry a wider margin. Third, supermarkets have adopted merchandising policies in line with consumer desires and habits that necessitate more diversified inventories to be handled. This has lowered turnover and resulted in higher margins. Finally, there has been a tendency to increase customer services and comfort. This trend has resulted in greater expenses and, in turn, higher margins. Yet, the supermarket continues to afford the consumer values in its respective area substantially better than those offered by other forms of retailing.

6 | EXPENSES AND PROFITS

INTRODUCTION

The preceding chapter examined (1) the buying practices of supermarkets and (2) the principles involved in the establishment of gross margins. The purpose of this section is to continue the study of the principles of supermarketing within the framework of an operating statement. Attention in this chapter is focused on operating expense and net profit relationships.

OPERATING EXPENSES

The third step in the plan to identify characteristics of supermarket operation that set it apart from other forms of retailing is to study expense relationships.

At the outset, reference is made to the data in Tables 4-2 and 4-3, which list detailed expenses as a percentage of sales for supermarket food chains and for an independent supermart. Other expense ratios can be found in Table 6-1 which presents operating data from the annual surveys conducted by the Super Market Institute among its members for the years 1954 through 1958. Akin to other retailers, the major expense items of supermarkets are for store payroll, administrative salaries, occupancy or real estate, advertising, and store supplies.

Trends in Supermarket Total Operating Expense

Yearly surveys conducted by the staff of *Super Market Merchandising* for 1947 through 1956 indicate that operating expenses as a percentage of sales were: [1]

---

[1] The statistics for the years 1947 to 1950 are from the yearly surveys published in the May editions, 1948 through 1951, respectively, of *Super Market*

Year	% sales
1947	14.8
1948	14.9
1949	13.9
1950	14.3
1951	15.4
1952	15.7
1953	16.1
1954	15.8
1955	16.1
1956	16.9

These data are comparable with the total expense statistics of the Super Market Institute figure exchange data shown in Table 6-1. This organization reported in its 1958 study that total operating ex-

TABLE 6-1 °

Operating Statistics of Selected Super Market Institute Members as a Percentage of Sales for the Years 1954 to 1958.

	1958 †	1957	1956	1955	1954
Sales	100.00	100.00	100.00	100.00	100.00
Cost of sales	81.88	81.89	.82.06	82.24	82.63
Gross profit	18.12	18.11	17.94	17.76	17.37
Expense	10°|o				
Store labor		6.87	7.10	7.08	7.16
Advertising	—	0.87	1.00	0.89	0.90
Store supply	—	0.88	0.88	0.80	0.80
Store rent and real estate . . .	—	1.12	1.07	1.07	1.01
Heat, light, power . .	—	0.50	0.50	0.48	0.47
All other expenses . .	—	5.80	5.41	5.05	4.38
Total expenses . .	16.19	16.04	15.96	15.37	14.72
Net profit ‡ . .	2.20	2.26	2.13	2.56	2.46

° *Facts in Grocery Distribution* (New York: Progressive Grocer, 1959), p. F–21.

† *The Super Market Industry Speaks* (Chicago: Super Market Institute, 1959), p. 17.

‡ These statements do not include other income and expense items. Therefore net profit cannot be added to total expense to obtain gross margin.

Merchandising. Data for 1951 through 1956 are found in the August editions, 1952 through 1957, respectively, of the same magazine.

penses ranged from 14.54 to 17.49 per cent of sales for the middle
range of respondents and 16.19 per cent for the typical supermarket.[2]

The expense rates as a percentage of sales for certain supermarket
chains for 1956 are shown in Table 5-2. These rates ranged from a
low of 13.77 for Thriftimart, Incorporated, to a high of 19.34 for
Shopping Bag Food Stores. The diversity of characteristics of stores
within the industry, including the method of operation and lines
stressed, had a direct bearing on these ratios.

The expense rate for supers in the postwar period was considerably larger than that for supermarkets in the late 1930's. And the
expense trend each year has continued upward. The rise is attributed
to improved customer shopping conveniences and services and to a
higher percentage of sales expended for salaries and wages. It was
not unusual for the expense rate of supers in the 1930's to average
10 to 11 per cent of sales.[3] In 1941 the entire supermarket operation
of the A & P worked on a 10.51 expense ratio.[4] However, the expense
rate for supers in recent years has still been lower than that for the
grocery stores and combination markets, including the A & P economy stores of the early 1930's.

Comparison of Total Expense with Other Retailers

The general trend of total expense in a supermarket has shown
consistent increase over the years. Yet, the supermart is still a low
cost marketer when compared to other types of retailers. The total
expense rate of the supermarket industry compared with that of the
variety and department stores is substantially lower; in fact, it is
about 50 per cent less, as illustrated by statistics in Table 6-2. Expenses vary according to the type of business, lines handled, and
operational policies, to name but a few factors. But the low supermarket rate becomes even more significant when nonfood items that
are stocked by similar stores, including supers, are considered.

[2] The middle-range figures are the values at the one-quarter and three-quarter
points from the array of data listed, from the smallest to the largest. Extremes in
the top and bottom quarters are thus omitted.

[3] *United States* v. *The Great Atlantic and Pacific Tea Company*, U.S. Circuit
Court of Appeals, 7th District, Docket 9221, Records and Briefs, Vol. II, p. 194.

[4] See Table 8-7.

TABLE 6-2

**Operating Expenses as a Percentage of Sales for Various
Types of Retail Stores for the Year 1954.**

Type of store	Expense % of sales
Department store	33.50 [a]
Drug store	27.80 [b]
Furniture store (large)	37.44 [c]
Hardware store	27.55 [d]
Meat market	20.00 [e]
Supermarket	15.80 [f]
Variety store	32.90 [g]

[a] Controllers Congress, *1954 Merchandise and Operating Results* (New York: National Retail Dry Goods Association, 1955), p. 1.

[b] *Lilly Digest* (Indianapolis: Eli Lilly & Co., 1955), p. 21.

[c] *1954 Furniture Operating Experiences* (Chicago: National Retail Furniture Association, 1955), p. 5.

[d] "1954 Retail Hardware Survey," *Hardware Retailer*, June, 1955, p. 77.

[e] *Meat Markets—Operating Results in 1954* (New York: Dun & Bradstreet, Inc., 1954), p. 2.

[f] *Facts in Food Distribution* (New York: Progressive Grocer, 1955), p. F–17.

[g] "Harvard Report on Variety Chains," *Chain Store Age*, Variety Store Managers Issue, XXXI, no. 8, August, 1955, p. 52.

Comparison of Major Expense Items by Retailers

Data in Table 6-3 present major expense breakdowns for certain types of retail stores, including supermarkets. The four most significant expense items confronting retailers, as shown by the statistics in Table 6-3 are (1) employees' salaries, (2) owners' or administrative salaries, (3) occupancy, and (4) advertising, publicity, and promotion. In almost every instance the supermarket was able, more than any other type of retailer shown, to operate at a considerably lower expense rate as a percentage of sales.)

Owner or administrative expense in supermarkets was 1.92 per cent of sales in 1954 compared with 7.7 per cent in drugstores, 5.8 per cent in variety stores, and 7.8 per cent in department stores for the year 1954. Simply, supermarkets are geared for large-volume operation, and they require a small percentage of the sales dollar for supervision. Operations are routinized, sales are largely on a self-service cash basis, and a high degree of division of labor is obtained. Efficiencies through central management in chain supermarts have been attained. Management at the store level in chains generally is paid a fixed salary plus a small percentage of sales above a set goal. Local management emphasis is on volume.

Similarly, self-service, division of labor, and large-volume operation have kept employees' salaries as a percentage of sales smaller than those paid by most types of retailers, except the small stores where the owner does most of the work personally. In the larger

TABLE 6-3

Major Operating Expenses as a Percentage of Sales for Certain Types of Retail Outlets.

Expense	Super-market [a]	Drug store [b]	Depart-ment store [c]	Variety store [d]	Hard-ware store [e]	Meat market [f] (complete or partial self-service)
Administration	0.78 to 1.26	7.70	18.40 [g]	17.50 [g]	17.75 [g]	6.40
Employees' salaries	5.24 to 5.89	10.60	—	—	—	6.40
Occupancy	0.82 to 1.01	2.40	6.10	5.90	2.45	2.70
Advertising, promotion, publicity	2.93 to 3.07 [h]	—	4.30	0.40	1.40	0.70

[a] *Facts in Grocery Distribution* (New York: Progressive Grocer, 1958), p. F–18.

[b] *Lilly Digest* (Indianapolis: Eli Lilly & Co., 1954), p. 62.

[c] Controllers Congress, *Merchandising and Operating Results* (New York: National Retail Dry Goods Association, 1955), p. 2.

[d] "Harvard Report on Variety Stores," *Chain Store Age*, Variety Store Managers Edition, August, 1955, p. 62.

[e] "1954 Retail Hardware Survey," *Hardware Retailer*, June, 1955, p. 77.

[f] *Meat Markets—Operating Results in 1954* (New York: Dun & Bradstreet, Inc., 1954).

[g] Administration and employees' salaries are included under one classification.

[h] This includes trading stamps of approximately 2 per cent of sales. Advertising expense alone for the 1954 typical super was reported at 0.87 to 1.02 per cent of sales. Only 36 per cent of the supers offer trading stamps.

super operations, personnel departments have been established to hire, train, set job descriptions, and determine promotion, transfer, and layoff policies. Most operations especially train the check-out girls through whom contact with the public is maintained. Not only are trained check-out girls more efficient from the use of equipment and error standpoints, but the consumer receives faster service. Variety and drugstores had employees' salaries expressed as a percentage of sales of 11 and 10.6 per cent, respectively, for 1954; supermarkets have averaged between 5 and 6 per cent. With only 55 per cent of department store employees active in selling, their compensation alone in 1954 was 7 per cent of sales.[5]

The low percentage expenditure for salaries and wages has been aided further by simplifying and eliminating work. Manufacturers perform some of the retail functions. Supermarkets are one of the few retailers that require manufacturers to do this. Baby food manufacturers and biscuit bakers, to name but two, have taken on such functions as ordering, stocking shelves, keeping merchandise clean, and arranging displays. Unions oppose this practice.

The policy of self-service obviously requires the customer to take over some of the functions of the clerk. Not only has this practice been successful in grocery operation (by definition, the grocery division of a supermarket must be self-service), but the principle has spread to other departments within the supermarket. In 1950 a study by the research staff of the Super Market Institute reported 8 per cent of its members operated completely self-service stores.[6] By 1958, 57 per cent of all supermarkets were on a completely self-service basis in all major departments.[7] The meat department is now fully self-service in 88 per cent of the supermarkets, with most of the remainder semi-self-service. Only 2 per cent of the meat departments are still operated on a complete service basis. The produce department is the principal division not operated on a full self-service basis.

[5] Controllers Congress, *1954 Merchandise and Operating Results* (New York: National Retail Dry Goods Association, 1955), p. 21.
[6] *The Super Market Industry Speaks* (Chicago: Super Market Institute, 1951), p. 17.
[7] *Ibid.*, 1959, Part II, p. 9.

Occupancy or real estate cost is the third significant expense item faced by retailers. This cost as a percentage of sales also favors the supermarket type of operation. Data in Table 6-3 indicate that the typical supermarket expended 0.82 to 1.02 cents out of every sales dollar for occupancy as compared with a minimum of 2.4 cents for all other types of stores. This does not mean necessarily that supermarkets obtain cheaper dollar rental. In some cases the super has been given a rental advantage where the mart is the key store in a shopping center. However, the low percentage of the sales dollar expended for rent primarily is the result of their policy to exploit customer traffic to the fullest so that increased volume can reduce rental expense as a percentage of sales.

Advertising, publicity, and promotion for a typical supermarket shown by the data in Table 6-3 ranged from 2.93 to 3.07 per cent of the sales dollar. Of this, advertising itself ranged from 0.87 to 1.04 per cent. Studies since 1950 made by the Super Market Institute indicate that slightly under 1 per cent of every sales dollar is spent for advertising. Expenditures by media are shown by the figures in Table 6-4. The over-all expenditure of less than 1 per cent of the

TABLE 6-4 *

Advertising Expenditures by Media for the Supermarket
Industry as a Percentage of Total Dollar
Ad Expenditures for the Year 1956.

Medium	% of total expenditure
Newspaper	67.0
General promotion (door prizes, civic drives, etc.)	7.5
Circulars	6.9
Television	6.6
Radio	4.9
Display posters	3.4
Direct mail	3.1
Magazines	0.6
Total	100.0

* "Where Advertising Dollars Went in 1956," *Super Market Merchandising*, XXII, no. 11, November, 1957, p. 68.

sales dollar is primarily for newspaper ads, which commanded 67 per cent of the ad funds. Supermarts compare favorably with department stores, which spend about 2.6 per cent of the sales dollar for newspaper costs alone.[8]

However, this figure of slightly less than 1 per cent of the sales dollar does not give a true picture of supermarket advertising volume because of the cooperative advertising deals offered supers, particularly the large chains. Food manufacturers have agreed to sponsor ads and have paid the cooperating store for its portion, frequently at the national newspaper rate. The local store can arrange for the ad and pay the media at the local rate. Thus supers have not only passed on to the manufacturer part of the advertising expense but in addition have found a source of added income as a result of the difference between the national and local media rates. On the average, the local rate is 50 per cent less than the national rate on weekday newspaper ads.[9] Supermarkets feel they are entitled to this allowance inasmuch as they perform some of the advertising function. Manufacturers' cooperative advertising and advertising allowances come under the Robinson-Patman Act, which holds in substance that whatever allowances a manufacturer offers to one dealer must be proportionally available to all other comparable dealers of that product in the same competitive market and must be a bona fide allowance for advertising and not merely an additional trade discount. Cooperative advertising with all its implications has created vast problems among food manufacturers, supermarkets, and publishers.

Trading stamps have become the largest promotion item in the supermarket industry. While not all the stores issue stamps, this expenditure in a typical super averages slightly above 2 per cent of the sales dollar. Other forms of promotion, publicity, and advertising are practiced by nonstamp stores; some have contended they sell for less than stamp stores.

[8] Controllers Congress, *1954 Merchandise and Operating Results, op. cit.*, p. 2.
[9] Otto Kleppner, *Advertising Procedure* (Englewood Cliffs, N. J.: Prentice-Hall, Inc., 1950), p. 297.

Governmental agencies, universities, and business have endeavored to study this nebulous concept of trading stamp impact on margins, prices, and restraint of trade. Factors for successful use of stamps have been discussed before.[10] No clear-cut results are available. Some supers have found the needed volume to use this tool successfully and have spread fixed and semifixed costs over larger sales. In addition, some stamp users also shifted from other kinds of advertising or promotional effort. This cyclical promotion tool appears to have passed its zenith at this time, however, with a drop in its use reported for the second consecutive year. About 35 per cent of the supers used stamps in 1958 according to *Progressive Grocer*. The failure of supers to attain needed volume increase apparently was a major factor in the end of this boom. Stamp-giving supers have made no volume headway at the expense of the non-stamp supermarkets in the past three years, as shown by the data in Table 6-5. The movement could be revived if one or several of the large chains adopted their use.

TABLE 6-5 *

How Stamps Affect Supermarket Sales.

Years	Average % sales gain in stores giving stamps	Average % sales gain in stores not giving stamps
1954 vs. 1953	18	12
1955 vs. 1954	25	12
1956 vs. 1955	13	14
1957 vs. 1956	14	14
1958 vs. 1957	10	12

* *Facts in Grocery Distribution* (New York: Progressive Grocer, 1959), p. F–11.

Functional Expense Analysis

Diversity exists in the operating statistics of member stores of the supermarket industry owing to size of stores, size of concerns, merchandise handled, location, method of operation, and merchandising

[10] The use of trading stamps was discussed in Chapter 4.

policies. Still, operating data from surveys and studies made by the four major statistical sources in this industry—Super Market Institue Figure Exchange, *Super Market Merchandising, Progressive Grocer,* and the Harvard Study of Food Chains—are generally in accord with each other. In the postwar period, total operating expenses have been on the increase in the supermarket industry.

It is imperative to know in what areas and for what reasons expenses are increasing. This can be ascertained by two basic types of distribution cost analyses. One is the familiar examination of operating statements, in which expenses are listed and then analyzed by the nature of cost items or the object of expenditure. Reference is made to the operating statistics of selected food chains shown in Table 4-2. Expenses expressed as a percentage of sales are itemized by the nature of the cost such as payroll, real estate, and supplies. Changes in specific items over the years can be detected. (For example, data in Table 4-2 indicate that payroll, real estate costs, fixture and equipment costs, and advertising expenses in recent years have been taking a larger share of the sales dollar.)

These increases in expenses could be attributed to added functions or activities assumed by the supermarket chains. Therefore a second type of distribution cost study was undertaken in the Harvard Report, namely, an analysis of functional operations performed. In the department store field, the Controllers' Congress of the National Retail Dry Goods Association has set up five major functional divisions of expense: administration, occupancy, publicity, buying, and selling and delivery. The classification set forth in the Harvard Study of Food Chains includes the store or selling function, warehousing or storage function, transportation, and administration and general expense. These functions are of importance for food chains faced with store, warehouse, and transportation problems. An individual super may not find this breakdown of value.

Changes in these functions over the years can be detected by a study of the data in Table 6-6. A breakdown of these classifications by the specific expense items for the year 1958 is shown by the statistics in Table 6-7. Food chains have kept their storage, transportation, and general and administrative costs in line from 1950 to 1958. In fact, efficiencies in the transportation function are shown by the statistics, with transportation costs dropping slightly almost yearly from 1.07 cents out of the sales dollar in 1950 to 0.91 cents in 1958. Lower transportation costs are accounted for by fewer and larger stores better located geographically. Warehousing costs have been aided by better handling, modern equipment, new buildings, and supervision. The larger sales over which to spread overhead have benefited the ratios of general and administration expenses.

It is in conjunction with the stores, the selling function, that expenses have mounted. Store expense rose from 10.85 per cent of the sales dollar in 1950 to 13.58 per cent in 1958, as shown by the data in Table 6-6.

In turn, the specific store expenses that principally have accounted for this increase were store payroll, real estate costs or occupancy, equipment costs, advertising, and supplies. Payrolls have increased faster than sales. This results from higher hourly wages, primarily for the same type of work, in line with the industrial wage-rate pattern. It does not appear as though the industry has added a different quality of labor performing new and specialized services which require a boost in wages per hour; for example, in areas such as pre-packing meat. Real estate costs as a percentage of sales have risen as a result of higher store construction costs, mounting interest rates, increased real estate taxes, more elaborate stores, larger parking lots, and higher land costs. Even when a super does not own its own buildings, it faces increased rental charges for new locations inasmuch as the owner passes on increased costs. Similarly, new equipment not only tends to make older fixtures obsolete but costs more than the item replaced so that depreciation charges are higher. The sharp increase of advertising expenses is attributed primarily to certain respondents of the survey adopting trading stamps in this period. Other factors that have led to increased advertising costs are higher space rates, increased use of radio and TV time, and larger

TABLE 6-6 *

Functional Expense Analysis of Selected Food Chains as a Percentage of Sales for the Years 1950 to 1958.

	1958	1957	1956	1955	1954	1953	1952	1951	1950
Gross margin	19.51	19.38	19.08	18.43	18.87	18.76	17.97	17.50	18.51
Expenses									
Store	13.58	13.22	12.85	12.30	11.83	11.51	11.01	10.80	10.85
Warehouse	1.12	1.11	1.15	1.15	1.17	1.19	1.14	1.17	1.17
Transportation	0.91	0.92	0.95	0.99	1.01	1.02	1.03	1.03	1.07
General and overhead	1.85	1.90	2.01	1.96	2.07	2.15	1.99	2.00	2.02
Total	17.46	17.15	16.96	16.40	16.08	15.87	15.17	15.00	15.11
Net operating profit	2.05	2.23	2.12	2.03	2.79	2.89	2.80	2.50	3.40

* Wilbur B. England, *Operating Results of Food Chains in 1958* (Cambridge, Mass.: Harvard Business School, Bulletin No. 156, 1959), p. 8.

TABLE 6-7 *

Itemized Expenses Classified by Functions for Selected Food Chains as a Percentage of Sales for the Year 1958.

Item	Store	Warehouse	Trans-portation	Adminis-trative and general	
Payroll	6.86	0.54	0.21	1.41	9.02
Real estate cost	1.27	0.16	0.01	0.06	
Equipment expense	1.10	0.09	0.16	0.11	ADD
Utilities	0.54	0.04	—	0.01	FOR
Supplies	0.91	0.01	0.05	0.09	
Advertising	2.39	—	—	—	TOTALS
Travel	0.01	—	—	0.09	
Insurance	0.16	0.02	—	0.03	
Taxes	0.37	0.07	0.02	0.05	
Services purchased	—	—	0.16	—	
Miscellaneous	0.32	0.04	0.01	0.26	
Total	13.93	0.97	0.62	2.11	

* Wilbur B. England, *Operating Results of Food Chains in 1958* (Cambridge, Mass.: Harvard Business School, Bulletin No. 156, 1959), p. 20.

promotional costs involved in the introduction of new stores. Furthermore, nonstamp users have intensified their promotional activities to retain their respective market shares.)

Increased costs of supplies have resulted from higher paper costs, changes in store packaging policies, and wider use of office supplies such as punch cards. As a result, supermarket food chains have been forced to increase gross margins; but this increase has not been sufficient to offset higher costs, with the result that net operating profit before taxes has tended to decrease for these chains.

Although these results are for food chains, similar results can be assumed for smaller concerns and independent supermarkets which face the same slowly rising costs of doing business. Yearly surveys conducted by the Super Market Institute indicate that the majority of members report encountering continually higher costs over the past decade.

A third type of distribution cost study, namely the manner in which the distribution effort is applied, is considered in the next section under expense control. This involves expense studies of product lines, customers, or other segments of the business and is exemplified by a study to determine net operating profit for the dairy department.

Expense Control

The supermarket industry has been faced almost since its inception with gradually rising costs of operation. Concomitant with the rise in costs has been added services furnished and activities assumed by this industry. However, in a narrow profit-margin field such as this, the trend could prove to be especially dangerous if increased costs resulted from services not desired or if no improvement in services were offered. In time the supermarket conceivably could lose its competitive position or see its profits erode if consumers believed the value added to the goods by the supers was not worth the prices charged. Marketing is dynamic in nature; nothing is so certain as change. Therefore control of operating expenses is vital.

The wide diversity among industry members makes it difficult to generalize as to policies adopted to gain effective control. However, the following practices have been instituted to some degree by members of the industry in an effort to keep expenses under control.

Expense budgeting. A budget is a plan of expected future operations. A complete budget should include anticipated sales, margins, expenses, and profits. It should serve as a guide or a control mechanism for management. A budget is not only a tool for large organizations but also a useful device for the small concern. The activity of preparing a budget is at least as important as the budget document that results because the activity itself forces formalized planning. This may be even more significant for the smaller concern, which is often less likely than a large organization to formalize its plans. An example of the budget program of one chain is shown below. This program also can be adopted with some modification by the smaller concern.

In the short run, at the most a year, an expense budget can serve as a valuable tool to supermarket management. It can point out discrepancies between actual and anticipated results, illustrate the need for adequate records, and show the information that must be

Outline of Budgeting Procedure *

Step 1: Data to be furnished to the divisions.

DATA	SOURCE
a. Last year's experience for period to be covered	Accounting department
b. Over-all tonnage goals for existing stores	General manager
c. Store expansion and renovation plans including target dates	General manager
d. Commodity price forecast	Market research department

Step 2: Preparation of divisional budgets.

   a. Each division head shall submit to the chief budget officer budget figures broken down by department and by account classifications as listed on a standard budget form. An appropriate text explaining the bases for the budget projection is to accompany the form when submitted. The budget figures, for the present, shall be on a quarterly basis. Sales, gross profit, salaries, and wages shall be further broken down by four-week periods.

   b. The chief budget officer shall review the divisional budgets, consolidate them into an over-all company budget, and submit it with adequate explanatory text to the general manager.

Step 3: Approval of budget by general manager.

   a. The general manager will review the budget and text and will indicate such modification of plans as he deems advisable.

   b. The approved budget shall be presented to the division heads at a special meeting chairmanned by the general manager.

Step 4: Evaluation of results versus plans.

   a. Each division head shall prepare and submit to the chief budget officer a review and evaluation of the division's results versus plans on a four-week and quarterly basis.

   b. The chief budget officer shall prepare a consolidated review and submit it to the general manager, who after studying it, will indicate

* Lloyd B. Tarlin, "How a Super Market Chain Started Budgeting," *Super Market Merchandising*, XXI, no. 7, July, 1955, p. 65.

what adjustments and action are to be taken to achieve the desired
goals. The general manager will choose the time and means for con-
veying his views to the division heads.

readily available to make merchandising decisions. It can make store
managers on the firing line cost-conscious. It can aid in the movement toward decentralization of management by illustrating the
need for profits as well as volume. While the supermarket is geared
to volume operation, top management does not appear to have en-
trusted sufficient responsibility to store managers.

   Establishment of standards.   More and more the management of
a super needs guide posts by which to judge marketing efficiency.
Some of the standards already developed include:

Sales per square foot of selling space
Tons of merchandise handled in warehouse operation per man-
   hour
Sales per employee
Transactions handled per check-out stand per hour
Labor turnover
Analysis of sales per day of week and per hour of the day
Average sale per customer
Expense per linear foot of display space
Itemized expenses expressed as a percentage of sales
Cost of handling various product lines
Sales velocity by item
Profit per item

For example, various company and industry standards are published
in trade magazines and by the trade association Super Market Institute. A survey of the industry in 1957 revealed that the average
sale per customer was $4.85 and average weekly sales per square
foot of selling area were $3.00.[11] A study of warehouse costs dis-
closed that from 1947 to 1956, tons of merchandise handled per

11 "Super Market Institute Mid-Year Gives Hard Facts on Markets," *Super
Market Merchandising*, XXII, no. 1, January, 1957, p. 101.

man-hour rose from 1.06 to 1.87 tons.[12] In the 1958 study of operations conducted by the Super Market Institute, it was disclosed that sales per full-time employee equivalent averaged $41,200, or 4 per cent higher than 1957.[13] This figure is based on all employees in a company as well as the assumption that two part-time employees are equivalent to one full-time worker. Sales per man-hour were $22.97, compared with $21.66 a year earlier (Typical sales per square foot of selling area were $3.71 a week compared with $3.77 in 1957.)

Akin to the setting of standards is the problem of effective use of labor, the major expense item. Concerns have made job analyses, set up job descriptions, and developed division of labor to a high degree. Efforts have been made to reduce employee turnover.

Fixed cost-volume relationship. From its inception the supermarket has been geared to volume operation. Store managers have been rewarded by salary incentives for developing volume, with the usual arrangement being a fixed salary plus a percentage of sales above a predetermined amount. Large volume has been its basic tenet so that the multitude of fixed costs which are present can be spread over a more substantial dollar sales. The fixed costs are not reduced dollarwise, but when expressed as a percentage of a larger sales volume, they appear as a lower ratio and of lesser importance. The whole concept of profitable use of trading stamps as a promotional tool was suited for supers because it was predicated on increased volume so that fixed costs such as rent, insurance, fuel, depreciation, telephone, and other utilities could be spread over a larger volume. Simply, a super faced with a contractual rental obligation of $10,000 per year while transacting a $1,000,000 volume can reduce its rental as a percentage of sales from 1 per cent to ½ per cent if sales can be doubled. However, as vital as this principle is, emphasis also should be placed on more responsibility at the store level for expense control. This necessitates higher caliber, better educated, and more skilfully trained managers.

[12] "How to Fight Costs and Win," *Super Market Merchandising*, XXIII, no. 4, April, 1958, p. 64.
[13] *Super Market Industry Speaks, op. cit.*, 1959, p. 17.

Cost reduction. In supermarkets, reduction of expenses has been centered in six major areas. These include labor, warehouse and transportation, general operations, store department operations, back room, and construction maintenance. These divisions are more suitable for expense analysis of both large and small supermarket concerns than are the functional divisions set forth by the Harvard Study of Food Chains. Store operators who desire a comprehensive check list of 119 ways to reduce costs are referred to Appendix A.

Labor is the major expense item in a retail store. All executives in the firm must be in favor of a sound personnel program in order to obtain the greatest productivity from the employees. Every supervisory person must be sold on the idea of labor performance. Care must be taken in the selection of workers. Employees should be trained for their respective tasks. If management expects to obtain the superior profits of effective merchandising, then store managers and key personnel must be trained to be merchandisers. Whatever is expected of the workers should be transmitted in the form of work schedules, which should include a man-hour program and the payroll percentage of sales of each department. This is the result of job analysis. The desired goals of productivity should be set forth. Every effort should be expended to maintain interest and show the progress being made. The employees should be made part of a team effort. Rewards should be commensurate with performance.

The original premises of self-service in supermarket operation substantially reduced labor expense. It brought the customer "into the act" by taking over some of the functions of the clerk. Since then, self-service has spread to most departments of the super. Another factor that reduced labor expense was the requirement that manufacturers perform some of the retail functions such as ordering, stocking shelves, keeping merchandise clean, and arranging displays. Finally, supers have passed on to the customer some of the carry-out and delivery activities. For example, in many areas customers can cart their purchases home free or pay extra to have them delivered by an external delivery concern. In either instance, no entry appears in the expense records of the supermarket. The decision rests with the customer as to whether it is to be a cost to the consumer. In a department store, however, delivery appears in the store records as a cost.

Warehouse and transportation costs have been subject to intensive study to determine optimum size and layout of warehouses, order-handling systems, routing, and scheduling. The number and type of tractors and trailers, if any, must be scrutinized to obtain maximum use. Another facet open for review is the use of mechanical loaders to stock merchandise on shelves.

General operations embrace systems and devices to make the administration of the store more efficient. These range from a study of bag sizes for packing customer purchases in order to eliminate the odd sizes, to a review of insurance in force by a consulting firm.

Store department operations include systems, devices, and routines to make the operation of an individual department more efficient. In the produce department, for example, racks for display can be filled substantially quicker by the use of two hands rather than one. Or, in the meat department, specific sizes of cellophane or other wraps should be established and only those sizes should be kept on hand.

Back-room expenses include the behind-the-scenes costs. These can best be kept in hand by centering responsibility in one person and keeping that individual or a replacement for him there at all times. This assures greater productivity as well as reducing inventory shortages.

Construction and maintenance costs include expenses involved in modernization, repair, and maintenance of facilities. These range from protection of shopping carts, by assuring their proper use, to the channeling of all orders for equipment servicing through central purchasing at headquarters.

Distribution costs studies should be conducted in these six major areas of expense control to make certain maximum efficiency of operations is being obtained.

PROFIT

In the preceding section, the operating expenses of a supermarket were examined. It was shown that management in this industry faces a severe challenge from constantly rising costs that are tending to erode profits. The latter—profit—is the residue left from total sales after the goods sold and the operating expenses are taken into account. The term *profit* or *net profit* refers to earnings before income taxes. Profits before taxes are used in order to discern the operating status without having to consider the changing income-tax structure.

Trends in Net Profit

There are three major reasons for going into business, namely, altruistic purposes, desire for power, and profit. Of these, the major motive is profit. The results of yearly surveys conducted by the staff of *Super Market Merchandising* for 1947 through 1956 indicated that the average profit of the reporting supermarkets as a percentage of sales was: [14]

Year	% sales
1947	3.7
1948	3.7
1949	2.8
1950	3.4
1951	2.0
1952	2.2
1953	2.2
1954	3.0
1955	2.9
1956	2.7

Net profits expressed as a percentage of sales for the selected supermarket chains in 1956 are shown in Table 5-2 to range from a low of 1.3 per cent for Shaffer Stores Company, a Pennsylvania chain, to a high of 5.2 per cent for A. J. Bayless Markets, Incorporated, an Arizona chain.[15] For the years in the postwar period, the rate of return for the companies has ranged generally from 2 to 5 per cent

[14] These statistics are from the yearly surveys published in May editions, 1948 through 1951, respectively, of *Super Market Merchandising*. Statistics for 1952 through 1956 are from the yearly studies published in August editions, 1953 through 1957, respectively, of *Super Market Merchandising*.

[15] Diversity of ownership and operating policy within the industry plus non-standardized accounting practices have resulted in wide variation in the reported net profits of individual companies. The principal variation has been in the methods of reporting returns to the owners; that is, whether it be reported as salaries or profit.

of sales; statistics from these selected companies generally indicate a fluctuating but slightly decreasing earnings trend measured as a percentage of sales. However, dollar profits of the individual concerns have increased along with the sharp rise in sales in the postwar period.

The operating results of the Harvard Study of Food Chains and the yearly surveys of the Super Market Institute shown in Tables 4-2 and 6-1, respectively, indicate that in the 1950's there has been a rising expense trend, and while gross margins have tended upward, they have not kept pace with expenses; hence net profits have suffered.

Comparison of Profit with Other Types of Retailers

Profits of supermarkets have been shown to vary between 2 and 3 per cent of sales. Statistics in Table 6-8 indicate that drug, variety,

TABLE 6-8

Net Profit as a Percentage of Sales for Various Types of Retail Stores for the Year 1954.

Type of store	Net profit as a % of sales
Department store	4.20 [a]
Drug store	5.40 [b]
Furniture store (large)	1.58 [c]
Hardware store	1.90 [d]
Meat market	1.40 [e]
Supermarket	3.00 [f]
Variety store	5.32 [g]

[a] Controllers Congress, *1954 Merchandise and Operating Results* (New York: National Retail Dry Goods Association, 1955), p. 1.

[b] *Lilly Digest* (Indianapolis: Eli Lilly & Co., 1955), p. 21.

[c] *1954 Furniture Operating Experiences* (Chicago: National Retail Furniture Association, 1955), p. 5.

[d] "1954 Retail Hardware Survey," *Hardware Retailer*, June, 1955, p. 77.

[e] *Meat Markets—Operating Results in 1954* (New York: Dun & Bradstreet, Inc., 1954), p. 2.

[f] *Facts in Grocery Distribution* (New York: Progressive Grocer, 1955), p. F-17.

[g] "Harvard Report on Variety Chains," *Chain Store Age*, Variety Store Managers Issue, XXXI, no. 8, August, 1955, p. 65.

and department stores return a much larger profit percentage than the supermarket. Both variety stores and drugstores earned over 5 cents in the form of profit out of every sales dollar. Yet, this modest 2 to 3 per cent return for a super is significant when viewed against the large dollar volume of a supermarket.

Other measures of profitability, such as profits as a percentage of net worth and earnings on total assets, are considered in the following chapter.

SUMMARY

From its inception, the supermarket profit was predicated on volume operation. Low price policies, display techniques, advertising, and promotion were cornerstones for substantial sales. Expenses of supers to attain this volume have risen steadily since the 1930's, despite efforts to keep them in hand. These included the devising of policies such as self-service and simplified stock handling to reduce expenses as a percentage of a given sales volume, the developing of a large volume against which the more fixed expenses such as rent and utilities could be allocated, and the instituting of cost-reduction programs. However, store management has centered its attention on volume and has left unrealized a source of possible earnings through closer control of expenses at the local level. The net profit that has filtered down has appeared modest when expressed as a percentage of sales. While there has been a slight lowering of profit margins, the modest percentage return is significant when viewed against the large dollar volume per store.

7 | FINANCIAL FACTORS

INTRODUCTION

In the previous three chapters, internal operating procedures and policies developed by supermarket management were examined in the framework of an operating statement. Selling techniques, buying practices, establishment of margins, promotional strategy, and expense analysis and control were the major operating principles examined. It is the objective of this chapter to continue the study of internal supermarket characteristics that have led to the success of the industry, except that in this section, financial aspects are scrutinized in the framework of a balance sheet. The approach used in this chapter to study the financial characteristics was necessitated by the general failure of the supermarket industry to publish representative balance sheet statistics.

GENERAL ASSET STRUCTURE OF A SUPERMARKET

The finances required to open a modern supermarket have undergone considerable change from the days of Roy O. Dawson and Robert Otis, who started the Big Bear with $10,000.[1] Consider the case of Food Fair Stores, Incorporated, an expanding and progressive supermarket chain of 362 units as of January 31, 1959. According to Meyer Marcus, vice president, a modern suburban unit, occupying from 12,000 to 15,000 sq ft of space and grossing $1,000,000 to $1,500,000 yearly, required: $65,000, inventory; $65,000, equipment; and about $200,000, land and building.[2]

---

[1] M. M. Zimmerman, *Super Market Spectacular Exponent of Mass Distribution* (New York: Super Market Publishing Co., 1937), p. 8.
[2] "Food Fair Supermarkets," *Fortune,* Vol. XLI, no. 6, June, 1950, p. 99.

Harley V. McNamara, president of the National Tea Company, a supermarket chain of 932 units as of December 31, 1958, reported the costs of a new supermarket as follows: inventory, $58,000; fixtures and installations, $42,000; and real estate, $100,000.[3] Some of the recently opened "super duper" stores required: inventory, $100,-000 to $250,000; equipment and installation, $100,000 to $250,000; and monthly rental from $2,000 to $5,000.

A new 26,000 to 27,000-sq ft store in Houston, Texas, required: [4]

Land	$100,000
Building	350,000
Equipment	150,000
Inventory	150,000
	$750,000

Similarly, a new store in Oklahoma City, Oklahoma, on 72,800 sq ft of land, with a building of 18,000 sq ft of space, required: [5]

Land	$ 47,750
Building	140,000
Paving	20,000
Equipment	90,000
Inventory	95,000
Cash fund	30,000
	$422,750

John A. Logan, president of the National Association of Food Chains, reported the following asset items of an average supermarket in a statement to the Consumers Study Subcommittee of the Committee on Agriculture, House of Representatives, on May 7, 1957: [6]

---

[3] Taken from an address, "Modern Trends in Food Retailing," given before the Chicago Federated Advertising Club on October 12, 1952.

[4] M. M. Zimmerman, *The Super Market* (New York: McGraw-Hill Book Co., Inc., 1955), p. 171.

[5] *Ibid.*

[6] John A. Logan, *Progress in Food Distribution* (Washington: National Association of Food Chains, 1957), p. 20.

Building	$192,000
Parking lot	10,000
Leasehold improvements . .	34,300
Land	25,000
Sales equipment	87,100
Behind-the-scenes equipment .	65,500
Inventory	82,000

This total outlay for a modern super is a far cry from the $3,000 capital required to open an A & P unit in the 1920's or the $10,000 Big Bear in 1933.

DEVELOPMENT OF A REPRESENTATIVE SUPERMARKET BALANCE SHEET

The major assets required to open a supermarket, regardless of who owns or finances the building, have been shown to be cash, inventory, prepaid expenses, equipment, land, and building. Intangible assets in the form of good will and leasehold improvements also appear. Inasmuch as no statistics based on industry surveys as to asset and liability items have been published, a balance sheet of a representative supermarket was developed and presented in Table 7-1 along with a representative operating statement. These financial statistics were based on ratio analyses from various industry sources, particularly data submitted by certain supermarket chains which operated 6,379 stores out of total industry units of 17,024 in 1956. Other data were gleaned from statements and comments of bankers and executives in the industry, obtained through personal interview, and from speeches and trade magazines. This is the first known endeavor to depict a representative store. The estimates developed will of course vary from statistics of individual concerns because of operating policies, location, and size.

Assume that the representative super in Table 7-1 occupies a 10,-000-sq ft, single-story brick building in a suburban location. Adjacent is a lighted and paved parking lot of 40,000 sq ft—four times the store area. Using $110 yearly sales per square foot of building space as a conservative estimate, the store transacts a $1,100,000

TABLE 7-1 *

Balance Sheet and Yearly Operating Statement of a Representative Supermarket.

BALANCE SHEET

Asssets		Liabilities	
Cash	$ 30,000	Accounts payable . . .	$ 40,000
Inventory	75,000	Accruals and notes payable	20,000
Total current assets .	105,000	Total current liabilities .	60,000
Equipment	75,000	Long-term debt	104,000
Deferred charges . . .	3,000	Net worth	164,000
Building	100,000		
Parking lot	15,000		
Land	30,000		
Total assets	$328,000	Total liabilities	$328,000

YEARLY OPERATING STATEMENT

Sales	$1,100,000	100%
Cost of sales	891,000	81
Gross margin	209,000	19
Operating expenses, fixed	66,000	6
Operating expenses, variable	110,000	10
Net profit before taxes	$ 33,000	3%

* Based on ratio analyses from various industry sources.

yearly volume.) Assuming a gross margin of 19 per cent and a stable monthly inventory, yearly cost of sales will be

$$\$1,100,000 \times (100\% - 19\%) = \$891,000$$

With a turnover of 12 times per year, the average inventory in the store is

$$\$891,000 \div 12 = \$74,250$$

or, for approximate purposes, inventory is estimated at $75,000. Equipment in a store approximately equals the inventory of $75,000. Another rule of thumb employed is $3.00 of equipment for each $1.00 in weekly sales.

The ratio of inventory to total current liabilities equals from 1:1 to about 1½:1. Using a ratio of 1¼:1, current liabilities will equal

$$\$75,000 \div 1.25 = \$60,000$$

In turn, accounts payable equals about two-thirds of current liabilities, or \$40,000, with the balance accruals plus current payments on indebtedness. Cash should average from one-half to equal the current liabilities, thus assuring adequate working funds. If the one-half ratio is used, cash needed will be \$30,000. The current ratio in this typical balance sheet is 1¾:1, a figure in line with ratios that vary from 1¼:1 up to 2:1.

The 10,000-sq ft building, using an estimate of \$10 per square foot, will cost \$100,000. Land cost varies by location, but it has been estimated to be about 20 to 30 per cent of the building for suburban locations. If the 30 per cent figure is used, land cost will be \$30,000. The grading, paving, and lighting of a 40,000-sq ft parking lot will cost approximately \$15,000. Prepaid expenses are nominal and would be no more than \$3,000.

Indebtedness can vary widely among the individual markets. Total debt to net worth tends to be heavy, especially for concerns financing real estate. Under the assumption that this firm owns its building, a figure of \$1.00 of debt to \$1.00 of equity capital is used. Thus net worth will be one-half of total assets of \$328,000, or \$164,000. Total debt will be \$164,000, of which \$60,000 is already accounted for by current liabilities. The balance of indebtedness will be

$$\$164,000 - \$60,000 = \$104,000$$

This \$104,000 is long-term debt secured by equipment and building and is represented by both chattel and real estate mortgages.

To develop the picture further, an operating statement predicated on ratios established in Chapters 4 through 6 is presented in Table 7-1.

CURRENT ASSETS

The principal current items are cash and inventory. This highly simplified, current asset condition results from sales on a cash basis.

In addition, the amount of working capital needed for a supermarket tends to be less than that for most other forms of retailing because:

1. Inventory turnover is considerably higher. Therefore less inventory is needed for a given sales volume.

2. Cash sales reduce the time for one merchandising cycle, namely, the movement from inventory, to receivables, to cash, and back to inventory. The speed of the merchandising cycle also is increased by high inventory turnover in supermarts.

3. Consigned merchandise from rack jobbers is used frequently in the nonfood area. The super then not only has no merchandising problems but also has no funds tied up in nonfood items.

4. Relatively stable sales from week to week or month to month can lower working capital needs and simplify its control. Seasonal inventories are much less of a problem than in most other forms of retailing, so that peak working capital needs are less. In addition, the predictability of sales, inventory, and working funds is simpler, so that supers can work on narrower cash requirements.

Therefore the current assets needed, compared with other forms of retailers doing the same volume, can be substantially less. A steady cash flow from sales reduces cash requirements and makes budgeting problems simpler. Thus management can center its attention on inventory and its control. A retailer is a merchandiser, and profits are made from merchandising operations—buying and selling. However, because of rising food costs and more diversified inventories, members of this industry have found it necessary to gradually increase working capital over the years.

Investment bankers who have assisted this industry in its financing problems by selling securities to the general public have indicated that working capital needs for a smaller concern should be 150 per cent of total debt and for large chains at least 125 per cent of total liabilities.[7] An examination of the balance sheets of representative industry members indicates that this ratio varies by size

[7] These statistics are from an address by Al Donohue, Kidder Peabody and Co., at the Twentieth Annual Meeting of the National Association of Food Chains held in Washington, D.C., on December 5, 1953.

of concern and is also a function of the number of buildings owned, the current expansion plans, and the method of financing. Colonial Stores, Incorporated, as of December 31, 1958, had a ratio of working capital to debt of 125 per cent; Fisher Brothers Company, a Cleveland chain, had a ratio of over 200 per cent on the same date; and Daitch Crystal Dairies, Incorporated, a New York chain, had working capital approximately equal to indebtedness.

EQUIPMENT NEEDS IN A SUPERMARKET

Next consider the specific equipment needed in a modern supermarket. Basically it takes as much capital to equip a store as to stock it. The substantial investment becomes apparent when the costs of specific items are considered: [8]

1 check-out stand and register	$1,775
1 double-decked dairy case	1,360
1 gondola for display	675
1 shopping cart	22
1 ice cream freezer	2,100
1 frozen food case	1,475
1 coffee grinder	375
Refrigerated display space for produce and meat, per linear foot	150
Air conditioning cost for a single store, 20,000-sq ft building	17,700
Compressor for the same size building	6,850

In a modern market with 14,200 sq ft of selling space and total space of 24,200 sq ft, the following layout specifications for meat, produce, and dairy displays were established: [9]

	Lin ft
Produce	170
Fresh meat	70
Processed meat	20
Delicatessen items	20
Floral	15
Dairy and cheese	60
Total	355

[8] "The Cost of a Supermarket," *Chain Store Age*, Grocery Executive Edition, October, 1953, p. 197.

[9] "How Three Get More for Their Construction Dollar," *Super Market Merchandising*, Vol. XXIII, no. 5, May, 1958, p. 86.

At a cost of $150 per linear foot, this equipment alone cost approximately $53,250. In addition, the market required 144 ft of frozen-food display space.

Furthermore, behind-the-scenes equipment must be considered. In a 20,000-sq ft market built in the 1950's, these expenditures necessitated (1) $1,300 for mechanical handling of merchandise, (2) $2,200 for a built-in overnight produce refrigerator, and (3) $8,500 for a built-in meat-storage room.[10] A cork cooler room in a 10,752-sq ft market built in 1958 cost $11,225.[11]

Outside equipment also must be considered. Furr's, a supermarket operation in Lubbock, Texas, paid $5,225 for neon display signs in a modern market.[12] Parking lot lights can vary from $800 to $2,500, depending on the size of lot and type of equipment. An advertising pylon or tower used to differentiate the stores of a Midwest chain cost $15,000.

Although smaller supers do not require as much in fixtures on a dollar basis, it is important to recognize the costly and specialized equipment required to operate a supermarket. In addition, the equipment needs continue to grow both in dollar cost and in absolute amounts.

LAND AND BUILDING

The direction taken by investment in assets plays a vital role in supermarket earnings. On the one hand, supers need to locate in areas where operations can be profitable. This may involve real estate commitments in order to have a place to do business. On the other hand, supers are in business to make money on merchandising, not real estate.

To erect a supermarket building is costly. Vice-President Meyer Marcus of Food Fair Stores indicated that a 12,000- to 15,000-sq ft building and land in a suburban location would cost about $200,-

[10] "The Cost of a Supermarket," *Chain Store Age, op. cit.*
[11] "How Three Get More for Their Construction Dollar," *Super Market Merchandising, op. cit.*
[12] *Ibid.*, p. 100.

000.[13] Carl Teutsch, architect and engineer of supermarkets in the Midwest, estimated that a 1954 one-story supermarket cost $9.00 to $10.00 a square foot plus the land.[14] He quoted the cost just prior to World War II at about $5.00 a square foot. John A. Logan, president of National Association of Food Chains, reported the average modern chain supermarket cost $25,000 for the land and $192,000 for the building.[15]

Specific building costs vary by areas. Eagle-United Supermarkets, Rock Island, Illinois, reported the following building cost figures for a 10,752-sq ft building built in 1958: [16]

General contract	$ 86,310
Steel	17,573
Gypsum roof	6,800
Floor covering	1,820
Electrical contract	37,460
Plumbing	12,230
Painting	1,202
Acoustical ceiling	5,896
Heating and air conditioning	22,500
Magic doors	3,391
Miscellaneous	2,184
Total	$197,366

H. W. Underhill, Los Angeles architect, reported the following building costs for a one-story stucco building with 27,800 sq ft of space all on one floor: [17]

Structure finish and plumbing	$204,000
Electrical work	37,000
Air conditioning	16,500
Fire sprinklers	14,250
Cooler rooms	8,200
Total	$279,950

[13] "Food Fair Supermarkets," *Fortune, op. cit.*

[14] These estimates were made in an interview on December 10, 1954. Mr. Teutsch had designed and constructed many of the buildings for the National Tea Company.

[15] John A. Logan, *Progress in Food Distribution, op. cit.*

[16] "How Three Get More for Their Construction Dollar," *Super Market Merchandising, op. cit.*, p. 101.

[17] *Ibid.*, p. 95.

The average 1957 super, as reported by the Super Market Institute, required building costs of $11.24 per square foot, exclusive of land, parking lot, coolers, and sprinklers but including air conditioning.[18] Costs were slightly lower ($9.83 per square foot) if all construction was on one floor. The industry figure for all equipment, land, and building for the year 1957 was $19.98 per square foot of building space.

INTANGIBLE ASSETS

Two intangible assets commonly appear on the records of supermarkets. One results from improvements or alterations made to property controlled by the super under lease—leasehold improvements. Such improvements become a part of the real estate and revert to the owner of the real estate at the expiration of the lease. Leasehold improvements include remodeled store fronts, electronic doors, and loading platforms. These assets are of value to the super in the conduct of its business in leased quarters, but they are subject to amortization over the period of the lease. The extent of improvement put in by a lessor is related to the rental charge, the value of the real estate, and the length of the lease.

The other intangible asset that appears is good will. This occurs in the outright purchase of a unit or group of units by another supor. Selling price is predicated on earning power, not the book value of the assets. For example, one supermarket chain in the Midwest paid $100,000 for a market that constantly earned $25,000 yearly profit before taxes. Assets were carried on the sellers books, however, at $80,000. The buyer recorded on its records $80,000 in tangible assets and $20,000 in good will. The recent strong trend toward acquisition and merger that developed in this industry in the 1950's has led to the rapid appearance of this intangible asset on supermarket balance sheets. Good will can be written off to a $1.00 value at the discretion of the purchaser.

[18] From an address, "Facts About New Supers Opened in 1957," given by Curt Kornblau, Director of Research, Super Market Institute, at the annual convention in Cleveland, Ohio, in May, 1958.

LEASING OF FIXED ASSETS

Supermarkets are merchandising organizations that thrive on a large volume of fast-moving inventory. Profits result from selling merchandise—the cash-to-inventory-to-cash cycle. In order to achieve this objective in a dynamic industry, supers have been forced to pioneer new locations with modern stores that require a substantial investment in equipment.

There are two methods by which supers can obtain the necessary fixed assets needed for their operation, namely, lease or purchase. Under the lease arrangement, the fixed assets used do not appear on the balance sheet nor do the lease payments contracted for appear as a liability, even though the rental obligation over a long period of years is there. Supers, in effect, are able to have their long-term financing provided by others. Under a purchase arrangement, the fixed assets and such indebtedness as results from financing appear on the records. This financing of fixed assets also can be furnished by others or by the supermarket itself through equity capital; or the financing can be furnished jointly by others (creditors) and the operators (owners). Therefore the method of acquiring fixed assets, either leasing or purchasing, significantly affects the ratio of profits to total assets used by supermarkets and makes analyses and comparisons among firms difficult. In addition, the method of acquisition has a bearing on profits related to net worth. If the fixed assets are leased, ownership capital can be used for current operations. If fixed assets are owned and can be financed 100 per cent by creditors, the equity capital can still be used entirely for current operations. Thus the ratio of net profit to net worth will not be changed. If fixed assets are owned and a portion of these assets must be financed from equity capital, which is generally the case, then one of two things must happen. Either more equity capital is needed (in which case the ratio of net profit to net worth decreases) or creditors' funds must be obtained to finance part of current operations (in which case the ratio of net profit to net worth remains the same as in the first case).

To compare companies that (1) own fixed assets, (2) lease fixed assets, or (3) both own and lease fixed assets, the long-term lease payments should be capitalized at some rate depending on real estate market conditions in order to get a true picture of debt in relation to controlled assets. This capitalized figure can be considered as debt when making comparisons, to put all concerns on a comparable basis.

Theory of Leasing versus Owning Store Buildings

Should a supermarket invest in land and buildings? The "cheapy" supers looked for abandoned factories or warehouses to rent. But the supers followed the population shift. As supermarkets mushroomed, particularly in outlying areas, new buildings and parking lots have been required. Many of these structures are specialized as to size, arrangement, and location. Alternate uses of the property frequently are limited, which increases the risk. Although some locations have been available for rent in shopping centers and in new suburban buildings, the supermart operators frequently are required to finance buildings in new locations. Is this the best alternative use of capital?

Assume the super shown by the statistics in Table 7-1 could lease the property. Then the balance sheet of the super would be as follows:

Cash	$ 30,000	Accounts payable . . .	$ 40,000
Inventory	75,000	Accruals and payments . .	20,000
Equipment	75,000	Long-term debt	31,500
Deferred charges . . .	3,000	Net worth	91,500
Total assets	$183,000	Total liabilities . .	$183,000

The changes from Table 7-1 are predicated on the following assumptions: Building, land, and parking lot are eliminated from the records. Assume that the real estate of $145,000 was financed equally by the operator and an insurance company; both long-term debt and net worth would be reduced $72,500 each to $31,500 and $91,500, respectively. No change in the current position would be involved. On the reasonable assumption that the rental expense of the property to the super would be approximately the same as the building expense involved under ownership of the property (under ownership the super faces depreciation, interest, insurance, and taxes), the net profit would remain 3 per cent of sales. With the volume unchanged, the net profit would remain at $33,000.

Profit on total assets of $328,000 for the company shown in Table 7-1 would be

$$\frac{\$33,000}{\$328,000} \times 100 = 10.06\%$$

Profit on total assets of $183,000 for the same company but with the real estate leased would be

$$\frac{\$33,000}{\$183,000} \times 100 = 18.03\%$$

Simply, leasing the real estate instead of owning it requires less equity capital and results in a substantially larger profit related to total assets owned. Yet, in effect, the super is controlling $328,000 in assets although only $183,000 appear on the financial records. The lease payments could be capitalized and considered as debt and the real estate regarded as an asset in order to compare assets used.

Profit on ownership capital of $164,000 for the super in Table 7-1 that owns the building would be

$$\frac{\$33,000}{\$164,000} \times 100 = 20.12\%$$

But if the building were leased, the percentage profit on ownership capital of $91,500 would be

$$\frac{\$33,000}{\$91,500} \times 100 = 36.07\%$$

Inventory versus Real Estate

Continue this analysis in terms of an alternative of investing either in real estate or in merchandise. The representative balance sheet in Table 7-1 indicates that real estate totaled $145,000. Assume this property commands a rental equal to 1 per cent of sales of $1,100,-

000, or $11,000, per year. Furthermore, assume taxes and insurance of $1,500 and neglect depreciation and repairs. The yearly net return on this asset bearing no mortgage would be

$$\$11,000 - \$1,500 = \$9,500$$

On an investment of $145,000, this $9,500 would furnish a return of 6.6 per cent.

To make an even better percentage showing on the investment in real estate, introduce leverage. Assume the property to be mortgaged for 70 per cent of its value at 5 per cent yearly interest. The owner would tie up only 30 per cent of his equity in the property, or

$$\$145,000 \times 30\% = \$43,500$$

Interest per year on the balance would be

$$(\$145,000 - \$43,500) \times 5\% = \$5,075$$

Therefore total yearly expense would be

$$\$5,075 \text{ interest} + \$1,500 \text{ taxes and insurance} = \$6,575$$

This would leave a yearly net profit of

$$\$11,000 \text{ rental} - \$6,575 \text{ expense} = \$4,425$$

A return of $4,425 on an investment of $43,500 would be 10.2 per cent. This would leave $101,500 of the original equity capital of $145,000 still available for other purposes.

If the $145,000 capital were placed in merchandise and the property leased at a comparable rate, the added inventory of $145,000 divided by the gross margin of 81 per cent would bring sales of

$$\frac{\$145,000}{(100\% - 19\%)} = \$179,000$$

Net profit of 3 per cent on that volume would be $5,370. But inventory is turned over 12 times per year, thus offering a phenomenal advantage in favor of merchandise instead of building ownership. Or, if the minimum investment in the building of $43,500 is used as the addition to merchandise, this will result in yearly sales at a turn-over of 12 times

$$\frac{\$43,500}{(100\% - 19\%)} \times 12 = \$644,000$$

The net profit on the $644,000 volume at a 3 per cent rate would be

$$\$644,000 \times 3\% = \$19,320$$

There is thus a substantially greater profit possibility of $19,320 from merchandising versus the $4,425 earned on the building investment, with $101,500 of the original equity capital of $145,000 still available for other purposes. The $19,320 profit is equivalent to a rate of 44.4 per cent return on the $43,500 placed in merchandise.

Obviously the addition of a larger stock totaling $43,500 as assumed above would require a larger market or an additional market and make exact comparisons difficult. If the same market were used, conceivably turnover could drop. But generally there is a comparative advantage of inventory over fixed assets. While a super must have a place in which to transact business, management must realize that greater profits can accrue from skillful merchandising than from investment in real estate.

Leasing New Locations

The major difficulties with owning store buildings are: first, tying up capital in fixed assets; and second, using capital in a less profitable alternative, namely, real estate activities and not merchandising. Several plans have been used to finance real estate requirements with no capital needed or with funds tied up for only a short period of time.

The first is to have the building erected and financed by outside interests. The super in turn leases the premises. Private individuals who own suitable land or concerns who develop shopping centers negotiate with supermarkets. On the strength of a lease, perhaps 10 years, private sources erect the building for the supermart. Frequently small satellite stores are included in the plans, or the project is designed as a regional shopping center housing several supers and a department store. If the property is developed by a concern specializing in that field, it is generally sold in turn to private and institutional investors.

The second plan is to have a supermart concern purchase the land, erect the building, and then sell the property to private investors. The supermarket leases the premises over a period of 10 to 25 years, generally with an option to renew at a stipulated increased rate. Funds are tied up in the property until sold. This leaseback method has developed into a widely used vehicle for financing real estate inasmuch as it offers the merchant a "tailor-made" market, frees capital, enables rental paid to be a legitimate tax expense, and furnishes a market to the merchant over a long period of years in an inflationary era. In addition, many leases contain a negotiation clause which will permit the lessee to terminate the lease should the location prove undesirable. Most real estate departments of large chains have developed properties they desire to sell.

A modification of the leaseback method used particularly by larger chains is the organization of real estate holding affiliates. An affiliate is a corporation related to another by owning or being owned by a common management or by any other control device. The concerns involved are separate legal entities; to the owner of the property (the lessor), the supermarket operating concern (the lessee) is simply a tenant. The supermarket chains execute long-term leases with their affiliates at going market rental rates. The affiliates in turn have been able to obtain financing, sometimes up to 100 per cent of cost, by offering as security not only the properties but an assignment of the rentals under the leases. The lender in this instance bases the appraisal not on the cost of the property but on the value under terms of the lease. This value is determined by market surveys which predict expected sales volume related to the rentals to be paid under the lease. Frequently these leases require a fixed obligation plus a percentage of sales above a prearranged amount.

The use of subsidiary corporations to finance real estate properties is examined later in this chapter in the section Sources of Capital—Debt.

Lease of Equipment

The arguments advanced for leasing real estate properties also can be used as reasons for supers to lease equipment. While the rental amount of equipment has nowhere near attained the proportions of real estate leasing, there has been a movement in this direction by either the straight-lease plan or the rental-purchase agreement. The latter has the advantage in that the lessor has an option to buy the equipment at some time during the term of the lease, receiving credit against the purchase price for any rental payments made. The rental-purchase plan may meet with objections of the Internal Revenue Bureau. The key as to what constitutes a bona fide lease is the option price to the lessee-purchaser. Where this price runs considerably lower than a reasonable market value for the equipment, tax authorities may reverse the claim. Operators who contemplate leasing equipment should bear in mind the annual cost of owning equipment, which in 1958 averaged 1.38 per cent of sales.[19] These costs include all charges for taxes, insurance, interest, repairs, and depreciation.

SOURCES OF CAPITAL—DEBT

Two sources of capital in a business enterprise appear on the credit side of a balance sheet, namely, ownership funds and indebtedness. In the preceding section, Leasing of Fixed Assets, it was shown that a super can control certain assets needed for the operation of the business without legally acquiring title to them. The asset and such accompanying financing do not appear on the balance sheet. Indebtedness, considered in this section, generally is classified by length of maturity as either a short- or long-term obligation. The usual accounting practice is to regard all obligations due within one year as a short-term liability; all others are long-

[19] Wilbur B. England, *Operating Results of Food Chains in 1958* (Cambridge: Harvard Business School, Bulletin No. 156, 1959), p. 2.

term. A list of sources of capital for the supermarket industry is shown in Table 7-2.

Supermarket management must borrow on the most favorable

TABLE 7-2 *

Sources of Capital for the Supermarket Industry.

Unsecured short-term loans	Commercial banks
Unsecured long-term loans (debentures)	Commercial banks Insurance concerns Public
Secured real estate loans	Commercial banks Savings banks Building and loan associations Mortgage bankers Investment trusts Pension funds Insurance concerns Universities U.S. Government corporations Investment bankers
Secured equipment loans	Finance concerns Factors Commercial banks
Inventory loans	Suppliers Commercial banks
Invested equity capital	Private Public sale of stock Customers

* Arthur H. Richland, "How to Raise Cash and Influence Bankers," *Super Market Merchandising*, XX, no. 8, August, 1956, p. 42.

terms possible in this narrow-profit industry. To do this, it is necessary to maintain a satisfactory financial condition and operating record. In addition, management (especially of the smaller firms) should make certain that: [20]

[20] This check list is from an address, "Essential Factors in Sound Financing," given by Henry Shaffer, Shaffer Stores Co., Inc., at the 20th Annual Meeting of Food Chains in Washington, D.C., on December 5, 1953.

1. The chief officer delegates authority and spends time on policy making and its direction.

2. A good No. 2 man is in the company.

3. A financial policy man is on the staff working with the top executives.

4. The accountant has set up a good system of records including cost control measures.

5. A personnel and training director is on hand.

6. An organization chart has been set up.

Short-Term Indebtedness

Supers sell on a cash basis. Stock turns over about once a month. It would seem possible for the trade debt to be large and for creditors' money to be used to finance the inventory. However, credit terms vary from daily or weekly for some lines (such as bread and dairy products) to monthly for others (such as coffee and certain canned goods). In addition, it is imperative that supermarkets take advantage of the 2 per cent cash discount frequently offered by food product manufacturers or distributors; the operating profit as a percentage of sales has averaged only 3 per cent of sales before income taxes. Thus the shortness of the selling terms and the necessity for taking cash discounts has mitigated to some extent in the use of suppliers' funds to finance the inventory. However, the super that gets into an overstocked inventory position frequently is aided financially by a wholesaler who has some control over the inventory. Banks find it inconvenient to make loans secured by the inventory in such a situation because it is difficult to supervise and control merchandise on a shifting-stock basis. Unsecured loans are possible in the right credit environment.

Supermarkets have found bank loans, in the form of short-term notes payable, to be of significant help in financing many activities. These short-term loans have been used: (1) in the purchase of an existing store by a larger organization with large cash flow from sales so that the loan can be paid off shortly, (2) as down payment on land, (3) for the start of construction pending the raising of long-term capital, (4) for purchase of equipment, and (5) for working capital. The expanding supermarkets have been wide users of bank credit. There is a trend toward increased current indebtedness in the form of notes payable, including current payments on long-term indebtedness.

Long-Term Indebtedness

Most indebtedness contracted for by members of the supermarket industry has been of a long-term nature in the form of:

1. Long-term notes payable
2. Debentures
3. Chattel mortgages
4. Real estate mortgages

Sources of long-term borrowing are shown in Table 7-2. Insurance companies and investment bankers have been the two major lenders to the large supermarket chains. For the small operators, insurance companies have been the main source of real estate financing; commercial banks and finance companies have been the principal lenders for the purchase of equipment. One source of long-term financing available to the small supermarket concern with annual gross sales less than $2,000,000 is the Small Business Administration. This governmental agency was organized to make loans to small business if no credit is otherwise available from private sources at reasonable rates of interest. These loans, which can run for a maximum of 10 years, generally require a real estate and chattel mortgage on all capital assets of the business. From 1953 to 1957 the Small Business Administration granted 409 loans to food retailers totaling $12,855,000.[21] The main reasons for the denial of loans by the Small Business Administration were (1) the earning ability of the firm was not demonstrated and (2) the collateral was insufficient.

[21] "Government—Its Role in Financing," *Cooperative Merchandiser*, August, 1958, p. 17.

Long-term notes payable. A *note payable* is a term applied to a promissory note with reference to its maker.[22] The classification *long-term liability* refers to an obligation which will not become due within a relatively short period, usually a year. Supers have borrowed for expansion on long-term notes from institutional investors or banks. It has been a common practice for supermart concerns, particularly the chains, to borrow sizable funds from a private source such as an insurance company or pension fund. The funds obtained have been used for general corporate purposes, including additions to working capital, purchase of another concern, or expansion. Examples of promissory notes payable, outstanding as of December 31, 1958, include notes totaling $453,316 of the Evans Grocery Company with 13 supers in West Virginia, Ohio, and Kentucky, and note indebtedness of $1,375,000 owed by Fisher Brothers Company with 87 supers in the Cleveland area.

Debentures (bonds). Debentures are securities not protected by collateral or tangible assets but only by the general credit of the issuer. The underlying indenture may require certain protective measures such as the maintenance of a specified working capital ratio, limitations on the amount of any additional funded debt, and restrictions on dividends to stockholders.[23] There is no clear-cut distinction between a bond and a note other than the fact that the latter generally means a relatively short-term obligation, one maturing not more than 10 years after issuance.[24]

While this method of financing has been used sparingly by one- or few-unit operators, many of the larger supermarket concerns have sold debentures both publicly and privately. Some concerns have offered several different issues of debentures. In addition, other operators have used successfully the subordinated debenture with conversion or warrant privileges. These privileges permit the holder

[22] Eric Kohler, *Dictionary for Accountants* (New York: Prentice-Hall, Inc., 1952), p. 285.

[23] *Ibid.*, p. 136.

[24] B. A. Graham and D. L. Dodd, *Security Analysis* (New York: McGraw-Hill Book Co., Inc., 1953), p. 83.

to convert the bond to capital stock at certain specified dates and at specified prices. Certain insurance concerns have loaned on debentures totaling as little as $500,000, but they may require an operator to furnish detailed financial statistics for a period of at least 10 years. On December 31, 1958, the previously mentioned Evans Grocery Company had $84,162 outstanding in 10-year debentures issued to employees. One of the largest users of debentures is Food Fair Stores, Incorporated. As of January 1, 1959, this concern had outstanding the following long-term obligations:

3 per cent debentures due January 1, 1965	$ 5,562,000
3⅜ per cent debentures due September 1, 1974	$18,750,000
4 per cent convertible, subordinated debentures due April 1, 1979	$21,203,200

Chattel mortgages. These are mortgages on personal property—equipment in a super. Financing by chattel mortgages has been used extensively in this industry, particularly by smaller chains or supers with one store or a few outlets. The large chains in the main have generated funds for equipment through normal cash flow operations or have borrowed from banks or institutions on a note basis.

Two principles of equipment financing are: (1) A particular fixed asset should "pay for itself" during its useful life; and (2) Ownership capital should provide a portion of the required financing. The different types of equipment in a supermarket vary in their useful life, but the operators and lenders alike report the maximum financing terms should not exceed 10 years, preferably 5 to 7 years. Some progressive banks that have become familiar with the supermarket industry have shown a willingness to extend loans longer than the traditional 36 months, considered to be a rule-of-thumb maximum for equipment financing by banks.

Repayment rate for chattel mortgages can be (1) a fixed amount payable monthly or quarterly or (2) a declining rate with a rapid payoff in the early years and nominal payments toward the end.

The latter plan has become more popular since tax authorities have approved accelerated depreciation. The two approved methods of computing rapid depreciation are the "sum-of-the-years-digits" and the "declining-balance method." Equipment manufacturers and dealers have given wide publicity to the "pay-as-you-depreciate" plans.

Real estate mortgages. These are liens on land or buildings given by a borrower to the lender as security for his loan. When a mortgage constitutes the security against which bonds are issued, the lien is conveyed by what is ordinarily known as a *deed of trust.* Mortgages can be secured by a specific piece of real estate or all the real estate property.

The basic method by which a supermarket finances and owns a new location is simply to acquire the land, erect the building, and mortgage the property for about two-thirds of the total cost. On the average, for a new $200,000 location a super would tie up $70,-000 of its funds and mortgage the balance for $130,000. In some cases, mortgage money only up to one-half of land and building costs is available.

A refinement of this fundamental method of financing real estate employed by some supermarket chains is the use of a subsidiary corporation. The stock of the subsidiary is owned partially or entirely by the parent supermarket. The subsidiary issues first mortgage bonds secured by mortgages on all the properties and by assignment of the lease rentals. These bonds are legal investments for a number of institutional investors who otherwise are not interested in single property financing. This plan also has the added attraction of more diversified security behind the bonds since the security consists of a number of properties with geographical spread. Furthermore, the insurance companies, which are an important source of long-term funds for the supermarket owner, are limited in most states by law as to the amount of fee-owned real estate they can hold. This limits their capacity for direct leasebacks. Institutional investors also are limited as to the mortgages they may hold both as to amount and location. The first-mortgage bonds of a real estate subsidiary are not limited to these extents and also make available to the operator 100 per cent financing of the cost of a store.[25]

SOURCES OF CAPITAL—OWNERSHIP

Many of the growing regional chains that started as one-store units back in the 1930's entered the capital markets in the postwar period to procure funds for expansion. As a result of public sale of securities, their financial records were revealed. This was the case for many of the concerns included in Table 7-4. The equity securities sold included both preferred and common stock. The quest for equity funds for expansion has taken many forms and has been a constant problem in expansion.[26] The sale of equity securities also has broadened the base for borrowing by supermarket operators.

The sale of preferred stock, generally offering 5 and 6 per cent cumulative dividends and preferable as assets in case of liquidation, has been widely used by over 60 per cent of the larger members of the industry. In fact, two issues of preferred stock were sold by six of 37 firms studied. However, preferred-stock financing is not limited to large firms. One enterprising operator sold preferred stock to his customers in the store literally "over the counter." Not only did he obtain funds, but he more or less tied his customers to the market. Care must be taken in this kind of operation to make certain the laws governing security sales are not broken.

The larger concerns that have sold stock publicly still have managed to maintain control of the business. This is possible because, with a large and widely held stock offering, a small active management minority can control the operation. Some of the smaller concerns, perhaps fearful of losing control, have issued several forms of common stock. The public on occasion has been sold nonvoting securities.

[25] Donohue, *op. cit.*
[26] "Methods of Financing Store Construction," *Super Market Merchandising,* XIII, no. 6, June, 1946, p. 66.

PROFITS ON EQUITY CAPITAL

Net profits expressed as a percentage of sales for the supermarket industry were found in Chapter 6 to be about a modest 3 per cent of sales before taxes. Then how can this industry flourish with such a relatively low profit rate, especially since it has tended to decline in the postwar era? The analysis of sales, cost, and profit relationships at various levels of volume of the representative supermarket given in Table 7-1 furnishes the key to one of the most vital supermarketing financial principles. The results of this analysis are found in Table 7-3.

(Assume the representative supermart illustrated in Table 7-1 is a successful venture with yearly sales of $1,100,000, profits of $33,-000, ownership capital of $164,000, net profit of 3 per cent of sales, and return on ownership capital of 20.12 per cent. Statistics contained in Table 7-3 indicate what the operating results of this store would be at various volume levels. Fixed costs (basic rent, depreciation, utilities, etc.) are assumed at 6 per cent of the $1,100,000 volume, or $66,000.[27] Merchandise cost and variable operating expenses fluctuate with sales; and in Table 7-3 these items are 81 per cent and 10 per cent, respectively. The variable expenses include such items as wages, stamps, and merchandise handling. The breakeven point for this store is $733,000, at which level the sales dollar equals merchandise cost plus all operating expenses.)

Basically the supermarket has a low fixed cost and a low breakeven point as compared with those of heavy industry. These, along

[27] The 6 per cent fixed expense figure was established jointly with Everett Mann, C.P.A., and former professor of accounting, Emory University, afer an analysis of operations at different levels of volume for several supermarket firms. This figure involved certain assumptions in classifying expenses as either fixed or variable. Fixed expenses are not absolutely constant in a supermarket inasmuch as certain expenses listed in this category, such as utility expense, could be curtailed if the volume shrank materially. In addition, all variable expenses do not vary absolutely with sales. Discontinuities develop in certain production services; for example, an additional check-out stand may be needed but yet may not be used at maximum efficiency when added. By allowing for these factors and assumptions, the relationships established are believed accurate for use in the analysis of breakeven operations.

OVER ←

25,000
52
_____
50000
125060
_____
$13000000.00

20,000
52
_____
40000
100000
_____
1040000.00

TABLE 7-3 *

Sales, Cost, and Profit Relationships for the Representative Supermarket at Various Levels of Volume.

Sales	Fixed cost	Cost of merchandise, 81% of sales	Variable LABOR expense, ONLY 10% of sales	Total cost	Profit or loss	Profit as a % of sales	Profit as a % of net worth
$ 100,000	$66,000	$ 81,000	$ 10,000	$ 157,000	-$57,000		
200,000	66,000	162,000	20,000	248,000	— 48,000		
300,000	66,000	243,000	30,000	339,000	— 39,000		
400,000	66,000	324,000	40,000	430,000	— 30,000		
500,000	66,000	405,000	50,000	521,000	— 21,000		
600,000	66,000	486,000	60,000	612,000	— 12,000		
700,000	66,000	567,000	70,000	703,000	— 3,000		
733,000	66,000	594,000	73,000	733,000	0	0	0
800,000	66,000	648,000	80,000	794,000	+ 6,000	0.75	3.66
900,000	66,000	729,000	90,000	885,000	+ 15,000	1.67	9.15
1,000,000	66,000	810,000	100,000	976,000	+ 24,000	2.40	14.63
1,100,000	66,000	891,000	110,000	1,067,000	+ 33,000	3.00	20.12
1,200,000	66,000	972,000	120,000	1,158,000	+ 42,000	3.50	25.61
1,300,000	66,000	1,053,000	130,000	1,249,000	+ 51,000	3.92	31.10

* Calculations based on relationships set forth in Table 7-1.

with other factors, allow concerns to pioneer markets in new, growing locations. At the outset, the market can still be profitable if the sales result is considerably below the future expected volume or if the actual volume is considerably in error on the low side from the sales forecast. As volume at a location rises, the profit percentage increases substantially. From a breakeven point at $733,000 sales, the results in Table 7-3 show that at a $1,300,000 volume, the margin is 3.92 per cent of sales. In turn, as a competitor encroaches on the market of a store, the original super still can suffer a considerable volume decline and remain profitable.

A business with high fixed expenses, like the steel industry, desperately needs added sales. Why then has the supermarket striven for large volume per store, since its fixed expenses are low and since the net profit tends to increase at a decreasing rate? As sales rose from $800,000 to $900,000, according to the figures in Table 7-3, the profit rose from $6,000 to $15,000, an increase of 150 per cent. As sales rose from $900,000 to $1,000,000, net earnings rose from $15,-000 to $24,000, an increase of only 60 per cent.

The answer commonly advanced is that even though the profit margin is modest, it becomes a sizable dollar amount when related to a large volume. This is true as evidenced by the data in Table 7-3 for the representative super at its $1,100,000 volume. However, this is only a partial answer to the super's success. Actually, for a given market, the profit margin and the absolute dollar profit rise with an increase in sales and will continue to do so until some added fixed expense is incurred, which may result eventually because the market could outgrow its present facilities. The market shown by the data in Table 7-3 earns $33,000, or 3 per cent, at a volume of $1,100,000; but at the $1,300,000 level, profits increase to $51,000, or 3.92 per cent. Furthermore, profit expressed as a percentage of net worth rises consistently and rapidly with volume. Profit as a percentage of net worth was 20.12 per cent at the $1,100,000 level; but at the $1,-300,000 volume, the rate rose to 31.10 per cent. Profit as a percentage of net worth is further aided by the high degree of leverage in the industry and by the policy of leasing fixed assets. Herein lies the key to financial success of supermarket operation.

From the viewpoint of management and store personnel, this increase in volume, with the resulting increase in net profit percentage on sales and equity, is vital. For example, consider the data of the representative super in Table 7-1. If one additional family that spends $1,000 per year can be induced to shop at that super as a result of the promotional effort, that marginal family will reflect the following changes in operating results:

Sales	$1,101,000
Fixed cost	66,000
Cost of sales	891,800
Variable cost	110,100
Total cost	1,067,900
Net profit	33,100
Profit as a % of sales	3.01
Profit as a % of net worth	20.18

Simply, this marginal family to the store is worth 0.01 per cent increase in net profit on sales and 0.06 per cent increase in net profit on equity. The marginal family appears highly significant and can have a double-edged effect. A loss of a customer can drop profits just as the addition of one can increase return.

RESULTS OF THE ANALYSIS OF CERTAIN FINANCIAL STATEMENTS OF SUPERMARKET CHAINS

The preceding discussion has indicated the large financial requirements of a single supermarket, the risk involved in pioneering new locations, the relatively specialized type of equipment and building, and the problem of obtaining capital. These appear as deterrents to expansion. However, the industry has grown. Profits as a percentage of sales have been modest. But what have the earnings on the investment been for actual concerns?

Inasmuch as balance sheet statistics based on an industry study are not available, the financial statements of selected supermarket chains, which operated 6,379 stores out of the 17,024 units in 1956, were studied. These revealed certain common characteristics. It is not to be inferred that these results were typical of the entire industry. The findings from this study presented in Table 7-4, when related to the previous financial discussion, revealed the following data:

1. (A large rate of return on the investment was realized by the owners. For the year 1950 the highest return was that for Colonial Stores, with a net profit before taxes of 34 cents on every dollar of owner's equity. In 1956 Market Basket earned 44 per cent on its equity. In the postwar years the rates of return on ownership funds have been consistently large. A high rate of return has been reported typical of this industry but has not been regarded excessive in view of the risks involved.[28] A favorable profit showing has been held essential for expansion financed from earnings and creditor's funds.)

2. The trend has been toward larger indebtedness as compared with the net worth. In many cases studied, owners and creditors in the postwar era had almost equal funds invested. The owners tended to "trade on the equity" fully.[29] By this policy of profitably controlling and using larger resources than their own funds permitted, supermarket operators were able to get large returns on their investment. The relative stability of this type of business, food, enabled large borrowing.

3. There was a limited use of suppliers' funds to finance the inventory, although the trend is toward a heavier current debt as compared with the inventory. The increase in current debt is accounted for largely by borrowing on a short-term note basis for current expansion funds.

4. The bulk of the debt has been of a fixed nature in connection with the acquiring of new outlets, the remodeling of existing units, and the rising equipment needs.

5. There has been a trend toward financing new store buildings by many of the companies. Inventory represents less of the total assets, and a greater percentage of fixed assets to total assets has been

[28] "Methods of Financing Store Construction," *Super Market Merchandising, op. cit.*

[29] Use of borrowed funds or stock with a limited return is known as *trading on equity.* See Harry G. Guthmann and Herbert E. Dougall, *Corporate Financial Policy* (New York: Prentice-Hall, Inc., 1955), p. 99.

TABLE 7-4 *

Results of Financial Ratio Analysis of Certain Major Supermarket Chains for the Years 1950 and 1956.

Company	Inventory to current liabs.		Net profit to tangible net worth, in %		Total debt to tangible net worth		Inventory to total assets, in %	
	1950	1956	1950	1956	1950	1956	1950	1956
American Stores Co.	2.34	1.44	13.73	23.40	0.64	0.70	48.39	37.93
A. J. Bayless Markets, Inc.	—	1.42	—	40.43	—	0.70	—	44.47
Century Food Markets Co.	1.08	0.71	15.28	16.51	1.13	1.18	45.60	27.35
Colonial Stores, Inc.	1.60	1.51	34.00	32.40	0.88	1.12	44.19	44.44
Daitch Crystal Dairies, Inc.	—	1.17	—	18.42	—	1.14	—	29.93
Fisher Bros., Co.	1.63	1.76	30.13	21.66	0.56	0.48	33.00	40.16
Food Fair Stores, Inc.	1.30	1.44	32.70	36.95	1.22	1.09	29.07	27.18
Food Mart, Inc.	—	1.56	—	27.11	—	0.64	—	40.59
Grand Union Co.	1.60	1.01	30.12	28.18	0.72	1.23	50.97	33.66
Jewel Tea Co., Inc.	1.09	1.02	31.99	31.68	0.58	0.92	39.10	32.49
Kroger Co.	1.36	1.15	27.86	26.52	0.63	0.99	51.65	40.95
Lucky Stores, Inc.	1.10	0.99	26.00	34.71	0.81	0.98	32.65	31.88
Market Basket	1.52	1.22	28.00	44.09	0.53	1.53	46.98	41.87
Purity Stores, Ltd.	—	0.84	—	19.19	—	1.13	—	24.72
Safeway Stores, Inc.	0.85	1.13	25.08	27.35	1.25	1.01	37.74	38.20
Shaffer Stores Co.	2.88	0.67	7.33	14.73	0.18	1.96	42.06	32.34
Shopping Bag Food Stores	0.83	0.77	31.28	30.59	1.98	1.52	40.60	32.02
Sunrise Supermarkets Corp.	—	1.06	—	25.29	—	0.98	—	31.64
Thriftimart, Inc.	—	1.17	—	24.27	—	0.96	—	47.41
Weingarten, J., Inc.	1.86	1.39	—	20.66	—	0.79	41.38	34.83

* Calculated from data in *Moody's Industrial Manuals.*

noted. Most concerns in the postwar era had larger net asset holdings in equipment and buildings than in merchandise.

SUMMARY

In summary, a modern supermarket is not a small business. The trend has been toward larger assets per store. Even the minimum-volume supers require a sizable outlay compared with that of the economy stores of the late 1920's. Rising equipment needs and costs plus the trend toward building in outlying locations have necessitated larger investments in fixed assets. Finding suitable quarters to rent has been a problem, particularly in the postwar period. Capital for expansion has been needed and obtained from many sources including the capital markets. These issues were met when the sizable profit possibilities of the industry were discerned. However, the trend toward real estate acquisitions has militated against profits to some extent, and management must assess whether supers are in the merchandising or real estate business. Finally, once a given location is established, there is a wide latitude in volume over which a store can operate and still be profitable. However, the sales and cost structures in this industry are such that increased volume augments considerably the profit rate expressed as a percentage of sales and enhances substantially the profit rate expressed as a percentage of net worth.

8 | EARLY SUPERMARKET IMPACT ON THE FOOD STORE INDUSTRY

INTRODUCTION

The development of the supermarket industry and the factors responsible for its innovation and growth have been presented in the seven preceding chapters. It is the purpose of this and the subsequent three chapters to examine the influence that the supermarket industry has tended to exert on the food and allied industries. The approach is to

1. Study qualitatively the early supermarket impact on small combination markets and grocery stores in the Los Angeles area and the East.

2. Follow quantitatively the movement of the large food chains toward supermarket operation, with special reference to the Great Atlantic and Pacific Tea Company.

3. Measure the strong trend within the supermarket industry toward horizontal integration in the post-World War II era.

4. Measure statistically the changes in the over-all pattern of food store sales in the year 1958 as compared with that of 1929.

This chapter examines qualitatively the early supermarket impact and the movement of the large food chains toward supermarket operation. The importance of early impact is that (1) it offers a key to shifts and trends in the pattern of food store sales that were to follow, and (2) it furnishes a better understanding of the statistical analysis in which the 1958 pattern is compared with 1929.

LOS ANGELES AREA SUPERMARKETS

Supermarts conforming to our definition in this book were in operation in the late 1920's in California, particularly in Los Angeles. One source estimated the number of supermarkets in the Los Angeles area as follows: [1]

1929	25
1930	39
1931	51
1932	79
1933	103

From 1929 to 1933 the estimated volume for these stores rose from $3,500,000 to $22,000,000, an increase of nearly 600 per cent.

Another source indicated as follows:

No attention was paid to the first super market in the Los Angeles area about five years ago (1928) or the increase in the number of such markets up to nearly 250, including about 200 large "drive-ins." Returning travelers now say they are amazed at the size and beauty of the super markets in Southern California, at their attractive methods of display and their clever merchandising stunts. They are crowded all day, drawing trade from a radius of eighty blocks away and do approximately 40 per cent of the total grocery business of the territory. Leaving 30 per cent each to the chains and independents has made pretty hard going for the chain stores.[2]

A third source is quoted as follows:

One of the directing heads of a large food company recently showed *Printers Ink* some figures received from an authentic source in Los Angeles. These show that a year ago (1932) there were 160 market stores in Los Angeles, while today (1933) there are 260 such stores. It is estimated these stores are doing about 35 per cent of the food volume of Los Angeles. . . . The 500 chain stores are getting about 21½ per cent. The remaining 44½ per cent is going to about 3300 independent stores, which

---

[1] M. J. Rowaldt, "Inside Figures of a Los Angeles Super," *Progressive Grocer,* XVI, no. 1, January, 1937, p. 43.

[2] H. M. Foster, "Threat of the Supermarket," *Sales Management,* XXXII, no. 9, April 20, 1933, p. 436.

is approximately close to the volume that those independents have been doing right along.[3]

This same source also indicated that several years earlier only 14 per cent of the food store sales had been transacted by supers, while the small independents transacted about 44 per cent of the total food store volume. These statistics indicate the sales these "market stores" gained at the expense of the chain stores.

Another writer indicated the presence of 104 large drive-in "market stores," as they were called in the Los Angeles area, on January 1, 1929.[4] People drove to these outlets in such numbers that the development of these "market stores" had a depressing effect on the chains. In an effort to join the movement, chain stores took over some of the departments in these large drive-in markets.[5]

In summary, writers at this time were of the opinion that these large "market stores" captured in a relatively short time a noticeable portion of the grocery and combination market sales in the Los Angeles area. This was largely at the expense of the chains. While other rough estimates on the depth of penetration varied, they judged that by 1933, supermarket sales were about 35 to 40 per cent of the available grocery store and combination market volume.

INVASION OF THE EAST BY THE "CHEAPY" SUPERMARKET

The wide publicity and uproar that accompanied the opening of the Big Bear Market in Elizabeth, New Jersey, led independent grocers and chains alike to recognize this menace.[6] Although the super was considered a depression product, they sought to eradicate it. But the Big Bear fought back and made headline news,

[3] C. B. Larrabee, "Grocery Manufacturers Condemn Supermarket Price Cutters," *Printers Ink*, CLXII, no. 9, March 2, 1933, p. 41.

[4] Walter Van de Kamp, "An Innovation in Retail Selling," *Magazine of Business*, July, 1929, p. 28.

[5] S. L. Brevit, "Drive-In Department Store Gaining Popularity in the West," *Sales Management*, XXX, no. 3, January 17, 1931, p. 118.

[6] M. M. Zimmerman, *Super Market Spectacular Exponent of Mass Distribution* (New York: Super Market Publishing Co., 1937), p. 27.

while Giant Tigers, Big Chiefs, and a host of other similarly named "cheapy" supers multiplied in many parts of the country.[7]

Briefly, the following tactics were used to oppose the Big Bear Market, with pressure originating from both independents and chain operators: [8]

1. A local drive was initiated to license all retail stores, with the implication of refusing to license supermarkets.

2. Parking limitations were imposed against the supers.

3. Many annoying small local ordinances were imposed against the Big Bear.

4. Union pickets had relatively free play.

5. Newspapers were coerced into refusing to carry Big Bear ads.

6. The State Retail Association attempted to push through legislation in New Jersey that would curb Big Bear and other supermarkets.

7. The Associated Manufacturers of America of Grocery Products drafted a bill to be introduced in all state legislatures against price cutting. Provisions of this bill, "An Act to Protect Intrastate Commerce Against Unfair Price Competition," included the following:

> *a.* The term *unfair price competition* means the advertisements or offer of an article of merchandise at or below its purchase price in the course of intrastate commerce.
>
> *b.* Unfair price competition is unlawful and violators shall be guilty of a misdemeanor and if convicted, suffer penalty.
>
> *c.* The Attorney General's duty is to prosecute in the proper state courts.
>
> *d.* Any person injured by unfair price competition which is outlawed by this act may sue and shall receive three-fold damages sustained plus costs of the suit.

But all these legal maneuvers were in vain. Supermarkets mushroomed; nationally advertised brands continued on sale in the stores; known brands of merchandise were purchased in many instances directly from the manufacturers. Even wholesalers started to sponsor

[7] *Ibid.*
[8] Foster, *op. cit.*, p. 437.

their own supermarkets or to work in close relationship with supers on narrow cost-plus arrangements.[9]

THE SMALL INDEPENDENT GROCER VERSUS THE "CHEAPY" SUPERMARKET

The "cheapy" supermarkets in this early period did not exist in sufficient numbers to affect appreciably the national sales of the small independent grocers as a group. Data for the years 1929 and 1935, as shown in Table 8-1, indicate that (1) the number of large-

TABLE 8-1 *

Statistics on the Number and Volume of Sales of Large Combination
Markets in the United States for the Years 1929 and 1935
(in thousands).

Dollar sales volume classification	1929		1935	
	Number	*Sales volume*	*Number*	*Sales volume*
300,000 to 499,999	58	$21,492	264	$ 97,253
500,000 to 999,999	20	13,083	100	66,915
1,000,000 and over	2	6,641	25	39,119
Total †	80	$41,216	389	$203,287

* U.S. Bureau of Census, *Census of Business, 1935, Retail Distribution Part II*, Vol. 1, Government Printing Office, Washington, D.C., pp. 2–21.

† These figures give the closest census statistics on the number of supermarkets existing in this period. No other statistics, even from private sources, were available. These data underestimate slightly the number of supermarkets, inasmuch as the accepted definition in this thesis includes markets with $250,000 sales volume and up.

volume combination markets increased from 80 to 389, and (2) their sales volume rose from $41.2 million to $203.3 million. Yet this $203.3 million volume of the large combination markets was only 2 per cent of the total food store sales of the country, which totaled $9.71 billion in 1935.[10]

In the many sections of the country where "cheapies" failed to

[9] Zimmerman, *op. cit.*, p. 29.
[10] U.S. Bureau of the Census, *1951 Statistical Supplement, Survey of Current Business*, Government Printing Office, Washington, D.C., 1952, p. 25.

open, the battle of the chains versus the independents still waged. The widely publicized supermarket was regarded as a depression product which would soon disappear.[11] But in the areas adjacent to operating supermarkets, independent grocery stores and small combination markets suffered losses in volume. Some independents, after the advent of the supermarket, reported losses of 30 to 40 per cent of sales volume.[12] It was in these areas that grocers reviewed their operating policies.

Certain of the choices open to the independent grocers were to

1. Join the movement toward supermarket operation.
2. Control expenses closely.
3. Switch to self-service or partial self-service.
4. Improve the service and try more to please the customers.
5. Add meats and switch to combination market operation.
6. Join cooperatives or buying associations for the purchase of staples at low prices in order to compete with the supers and the chains.
7. Work with wholesalers closely on a variety of plans in order to cut distribution costs.
8. Shift the hours of operation.

In reviewing the early impact of the "cheapy" supermarket, it can be concluded that the small independent grocer lost in sales volume upon competition with a nearby supermart. Generally, the closer the independent was to the super, the greater the loss; and some "cheapy" supers drew customers from as far as 50 miles away.[13] Not only did the independents covered here lose upon competing with nearby supermarkets, but the chains which are reviewed in the next section also lost.

FOOD CHAINS VERSUS THE "CHEAPY" SUPERMARKET

To review briefly the history of the supermarkets, the chain stores were not the innovators of the supermart, according to Malcolm

---

[11] Foster, *op. cit.*, p. 436.
[12] Zimmerman, *op. cit.*, p. 44.
[13] *Ibid.*

P. McNair.[14] In fact they were slow in adopting its format. Chains had developed a system of economy stores located close to the customer; these stores, except for differences in color and layout, were modeled after each other. Gradually in the late 1920's chains began to add meats; some offered services such as credit and delivery, did local advertising, and maintained all-day operations. These attempts at differentiation were quickly limited by competing chains.[15] The dominant chain, the Great Atlantic and Pacific Tea Company, boasted 13 per cent of all grocery store and combination market sales in 1929.[16]

Suddenly their price advantage was stolen from them by the "cheapy" supermarket. The alacrity with which the large super chains rallied to shift operations varied among the leaders. In 1935 the Kroger Company met competition in its home town of Cincinnati from the Albers Supermarkets by operating supers under the name of Pay'n Takit. On the Pacific coast, Safeway Stores, Incorporated, closed more than 70 of the Piggly Wiggly units purchased several years previously, abandoned more than 250 of its other smaller units, and replaced them with supermarkets. First National Stores in the New England region started toward supermarket operation in 1937.

Statistics on the total number of stores of the five largest volume food chains for the years 1934 to 1940 are included in Table 8-2. Each company reduced the number of stores it operated. During the same interval the total dollar volume for these concerns increased, as shown by the statistics in Table 8-3. While the figures do not specifically indicate the number of supermarkets, they represent an over-all movement to close small economy stores and replace them with fewer but larger units of the supermarket type.

[14] Testimony given at the trial, *United States* v. *The Great Atlantic & Pacific Tea Company*, U.S. Circuit Court of Appeals, 7th district, Docket 9221, Records and Briefs, Vol. II, p. 194.

[15] T. N. Beckman and H. C. Nolen, *The Chain Store Problem* (New York: McGraw-Hill Book Co., Inc., 1938), p. 137.

[16] Sales for A & P in 1929 were $1.04 billion; grocery store and combination market sales in 1929 were $7.4 billion. See Table 8-5.

TABLE 8-2 *

Number of Stores in the Five Largest Food Chains for the
Years 1934 to 1940.

	1934	1935	1936	1937	1938	1939	1940
A & P	14,716	14,610	14,446	13,058	10,671	9,021	7,073
Kroger Co.	4,352	4,250	4,212	4,212	3,992	3,958	3,727
Safeway Stores	3,228	3,330	3,370	3,327	3,227	2,967	2,671
American Stores	2,859	2,826	2,816	2,620	2,416	2,272	2,157
First National Stores	2,623	2,556	2,473	2,350	2,244	2,137	1,923

* *Moody's Industrial Manuals,* 1935, 1936, 1937, 1938, 1939, 1940, and 1941.

TABLE 8-3 *

Sales for the Five Largest Volume Food Chains for the
Years 1934, 1937, and 1940 (in millions).

Company	1934	1937	1940
A & P	$820	$907	$990
Safeway Stores	242	381	399
Kroger Co.	221	242	258
American Stores	114	115	124
First National Stores	105	120	131

* *Moody's Industrial Manual,* 1941.

The remainder of this chapter is concerned with the detailed reaction of the Great Atlantic and Pacific Tea Company to the supermarket development. The general practices adopted by this industry leader have appeared to be in line with those of the other large
food chains. All the food chains were confronted by the supermarket
development; all followed the same common policy of eliminating
small stores and opening supermarkets; they differed only in the
speed of change-over. In this respect A & P tackled the problem of
conversion at a rate more accelerated than that of any of the big
concerns.

THE CASE OF THE GREAT ATLANTIC AND PACIFIC TEA COMPANY

In the subsequent text, an examination of A & P's reaction to the supermarket invasion is presented in detail.

Initial Attention Given Supermarkets by A & P

John A. Hartford, president of The Great Atlantic and Pacific Tea Company, testified that his attention was first brought to supermarkets by the operation of King Kullen in the East Division [17] of A & P.[18] In February, 1934, the Central Division Executive Committee minutes reported the opening of a supermarket in Columbus, Ohio, by a former A & P employee.[19]

In the New England Division between 1930 and 1934, a great many independent supermarkets were organized. These independents operated at a much lower expense rate than the A & P stores, and their lower operating costs were reflected in lower prices.[20] During 1935 the Great Bear and Giant Tiger supermarket chains were expanding in the Southern Division.

In the Central Western Division of the A & P structure, sales had fallen, and the gross profit rate was considerably higher than the gross margin of the supermarket competitors according to Division President Toolin.[21] He took John A. Hartford on a tour of Detroit in 1934 and showed him what competition had done in the way of opening supermarkets. Toolin convinced President Hartford that A & P should change its mode of operation; but others in high authority still thought the supermarket was temporary. They further believed that the outstanding operating record of the supers was obtained by selling under cost and that A & P should not sell below cost; therefore they opposed this type of operation.[22]

---

[17] In order to facilitate control of this food giant, the management divided the company into six regional operation divisions.

[18] *U.S.* v. *The Great Atlantic & Pacific Tea Co., op. cit.,* p. 194.

[19] *Ibid.,* p. 195.

[20] *Ibid.,* p. 196.

[21] *Ibid.,* p. 198.

[22] *Ibid.*

Number of Unprofitable A & P Stores in the 1930's

That the management of the world's largest food retailer was cognizant of the supermarket is evident. At first the wide-scale operations of the A & P mitigated the supermarket influence; but as the supers increased, the number of unprofitable A & P stores steadily mounted, as shown by the figures in Table 8-4. The peak number of unprofitable units in the history of the A & P was reached in 1937 when one-third, or 4,382 stores, of the 13,264 outlets were in the red. But the substantial change in operation that took place from 1937 to 1941 literally wiped out small unprofitable units.

TABLE 8-4 *

Total Number of Stores and Number of Unprofitable Units of the A & P Co. for the Years 1933 to 1941.

Year	Number of stores	Number of unprofitable stores	% of unprofitable to total
1933	15,095	3,060	20.0
1934	14,995	3,871	25.8
1935	14,885	3,651	24.7
1936	14,697	3,467	23.6
1937	13,264	4,382	33.3
1938	10,827	2,354	21.7
1939	9,088	1,619	17.5
1940	7,143	889	12.4
1941	6,165	639	10.3

* *United States* v. *The Great Atlantic and Pacific Tea Company*, U.S. Circuit Court of Appeals, 7th district, Docket 9221, Records and Briefs, Vol. 1, p. 291.

A & P Loss in Relative Sales Position Among the Food Stores

The economy store operation of the A & P reached its zenith in 1930, at which time the company operated 15,422 stores in the United States. Volume attained a peak of $1.049 billion, as shown by the statistics in Table 8-3. From then until the company converted to supermarket operation, the trend in volume of sales was downward. For example, the vice-president of the Eastern Division indicated that prior to 1930, A & P had a very profitable operation in the Brooklyn unit.[23] But from 1930, when supermarkets were first opened by independents, there began a steady downward trend in the competitive position which was a direct result of supermarket competition. Sales in the Brooklyn unit dropped from $39,400,000 in 1930 to $25,400,000 in 1937; during the same period profits dropped from $1,200,000 in 1930 to a $400,000 loss in 1937.

In the Central Western Division, Albers, a supermarket chain, started about 1934. After two years Albers, with only eight supermarkets, enjoyed 9.5 per cent of the food store business in Cincinnati; the A & P volume transacted by 50 stores had dwindled to 7.7 per cent of the food store sales.[24]

The statistics in Table 8-5 further evidence the loss of the A & P competitive position. These figures indicate that the sales of A & P dropped from $1,039,000,000 in 1929 to $864,000,000 in 1937, a decrease of 17 per cent; total grocery store and combination market sales in the nation decreased from $7.35 billion to $7.25 billion, a reduction of 1.4 per cent. In terms of total food store sales, which include the specialty food shops as well as the grocery stores and combination markets, the A & P loss in relative position also was pronounced.

A & P Experimental Supermarkets

One of the unsolved questions that confronted the management of this mighty food chain was the true operating costs of a supermarket. A & P had adhered to the principle of not selling merchandise at a price less than cost; and the management questioned whether the competing independent supers could actually sell merchandise at such cheap prices and still obtain a profit.

In the spring of 1935 the Central Western Division opened a supermarket in Paducah, Kentucky, and attempted to operate at a gross margin of 13 per cent and a net profit of 2 per cent.[25] Next, 14 stores were opened in Nashville, Tennessee, and offered lower

[23] *Ibid.*, p. 195.
[24] *Ibid.*
[25] *Ibid.*, Vol. VI, p. 240.

TABLE 8-5

Total Sales of A & P, All Grocery and Combination Markets
and All Food Stores for the Years 1929 to 1943.

Year	Number of stores *	Dollar volume * (in billions)	Total grocery and combination store sales † (in billions)	Total food store sales † (in billions)
1929	15,150	$1.04	$ 7.4	$11.0
1930	19,422	1.05	—	—
1931	15,371	0.99	—	—
1932	15,108	0.85	—	—
1933	14,818	0.80	—	—
1934	14,716	0.83	—	—
1935	14,610	0.86	6.4	8.4
1936	14,446	0.89	6.8	9.0
1937	13,058	0.86	7.3	9.7
1938	10,671	0.87	7.2	9.5
1939	9,021	0.98	7.7	10.2
1940	7,073	1.10	8.3	10.9
1941	6,042	1.35	9.6	12.6
1942	5,821	1.38	12.1	15.8
1943	5,751	1.47	13.3	17.5

* *U.S.* v. *Great Atlantic and Pacific Tea Company*, U.S. Circuit Court of Appeals, 7th district, Docket 9221, Records and Briefs, Vol. I, p. 322.

† U.S. Bureau of the Census, *1951 Statistical Supplement, Survey of Current Business*, Government Printing Office, Washington, D.C., 1952, p. 8.

prices than other A & P economy stores in that city on the entire line of merchandise. This division expanded experimental operations to Cincinnati where competition raged between independent Albers and Kroger's Pay'n Takit stores.

In 1935 the A & P Eastern Division experimented with 100 stores known as Baby Bears in the Pittsburgh area.[26] Prices were cut in these stores on merchandise that was directly delivered from carload lot purchases. These Baby Bears emphasized in their advertising the lowest prices in town on this carload lot merchandise.

[26] *Ibid.*, Vol. II, p. 162.

The available evidence from the testimony indicated that these experimental stores were for the most part developed independently by the separate divisions with little or no support from the central management. In 1937 the central management reviewed the situation and decided to switch to supermarket operation. Its aim was to operate each super at a gross margin of 12 per cent, expenses of 10 per cent, and a net profit of 2 per cent.[27]

A & P Joins the Supermarket Industry in 1937

The success of the divisional experimental supers, coupled with the loss of sales, profits, and competitive position in the conventional stores, finally resulted in a decision by top management to shift the operational policy. The data in Table 8-6 indicate the complete re-

TABLE 8-6 °

Statistics on Total Number of A & P Stores, Number
of Supermarkets, Total Sales and Supermarket
Sales for the Years 1936 to 1943
(sales in millions of dollars).

Year	Number of stores	Number of supers	Total dollar sales	Super sales
1936	14,446	20	$ 889	$ 00
1937	13,058	282	864	53
1938	10,671	771	866	220
1939	9,021	1,119	976	401
1940	7,073	1,396	1,099	594
1941	6,042	1,594	1,348	846
1942	5,821	1,633	1,435	934
1943	5,751	1,646	1,259	761

° *United States* v. *The Great Atlantic and Pacific Tea Company*, U.S. Circuit Court of Appeals, 7th district, Docket 9221, Records and Briefs, Vol. 1, p. 323.

versal of policy and the rapid conversion to supermarket operation that this giant food chain made within six years. At the close of 1937, A & P was already operating 282 supermarkets. Yet, President Hartford expressed concern over the pace of supermarket develop-

[27] *Ibid.*, p. 196.

ment and urged that everything possible be done to speed up the program. He suggested the advisability of having special men concentrate on the search for new locations.

In addition to concentrating on supermarket expansion, the management endeavored to ascertain whether the larger or smaller supers were more profitable. Statistics from the Central Western Division indicated that the larger type of supermarket with weekly sales of $10,000 and over had an operating expense advantage over the stores with $6,000 or less weekly volume.[28]

Data in Table 8-6 indicate that by 1941, the 1,594 units (or about 29 per cent) of all A & P stores were supermarkets; and these units, with sales of $846,000,000 accounted for 63 per cent of the total sales. However, following 1941, supermarket expansion by the A & P was handicapped because of World War II. The management reported operations were hampered by gas rationing, food rationing, and man power shortages. Furthermore, some customers switched to stores where they could establish personal relationship with the owners.

Effect of A & P Supermarket Operation on Its Gross Margin, Expense, and Profit

Once the supermarket independents became important in the food store field, the operation of the industry giant was adversely affected. From 1932 until A & P joined the supermarket operation, the average A & P store was forced to operate on a smaller gross margin in order to meet price competition. Even though expenses were reduced through close control, profits dwindled. However, after 1937 company operations improved because of its switch to supermarket activity. By 1941 the supermarket division of A & P was working on a gross margin of 12.4 per cent, an expense of 10.51 per cent, and a net profit of 1.96 per cent as indicated in Table 8-7. This was a vastly superior showing compared with the economy stores that still remained in operation in 1941. A & P gained in its relative sales posi-

[28] *Ibid.*

tion in the grocery store and combination market industry after it switched to supermarket operation; whereas A & P had only 11.7 per cent of the total grocery store and combination market sales in 1937, it increased its position to 14.1 per cent of the industry sales by 1941.[29]

SUPERMARKET ADVANTAGES FOR LARGE FOOD CHAINS

The numerous red-front A & P units scattered throughout the country were the leaders in food store retailing prior to 1930. Other large chains had a similar type of operation.[30] Then, almost simul-

TABLE 8-7 *

Operating Results of the A & P Detailed into Economy Stores and Supermarkets for the Year 1941 (sales in thousands).

	4,448 Economy stores		1,594 Supers	
	Dollar sales	*% of sales*	*Dollar sales*	*% of sales*
Weekly sales	$6,276	100.00	$17,336	100.00
Cost of sales	5,208	82.99	15,169	87.53
Gross margin	1,068	17.01	2,167	12.47
Expenses	966	15.39	1,820	10.51
Net profit	$ 102	1.62	$ 347	1.96

* *United States* v. *The Great A & P Tea Co.*, U.S. Circuit Court of Appeals, 7th district, Docket 9221, Records and Briefs, Vol. I, p. 323.

taneously, the A & P and its brethren had to meet the challenge of the supermarket, the NRA, the Robinson Patman Act, and chain store tax laws. The supermarket was underpricing the food chains; the NRA forced the chains to raise wages; the Robinson Patman Act

[29] Statistics to make these calculations are contained in Table 8-5. The 1937 A & P sales were $864 million, and grocery store and combination market sales were $7,300 million. In 1941 A & P sales were $1.348 billion, and grocery and combination market sales were $9.6 billion.

[30] Paul H. Nystrom, *Retail Store Operation* (New York: The Ronald Press Co., 1937), p. 466.

restricted the buying advantages of the large operators; and the progressively heavier chain store taxes levied on the number of units operated stifled large multi-unit expansion.

Actually, the supermarket type of operation adopted by the A & P and other large chains aided them to meet successfully the existing price competition. The advantages of supermarket operation stemmed from the following:

1. Fewer stores resulted in reduced chain taxes per store.

2. The total cost of opening new stores was reduced since fewer stores were opened.

3. Reduced operating costs as a percentage of sales were realized.

The principal disadvantage lay in the larger investment per store with its accompanying risk.

SUMMARY

The independent operators were the innovators of supermarkets. Unlike David versus Goliath, they tackled two adversaries, namely, the food chains and the host of small independent food store operators. The supermarket methods of merchandising and store operation proved so successful that they rapidly spread consternation among the chains and small independents. The supers captured substantial portions of the volume in the trading areas they invaded. The small independents, in the main, either became supers or gradually disappeared from the scene. The chains successfully competed by joining the supermarket movement. Chains substantially revamped operations and soon became dominant in the industry volumewise. This change-over by the chains, as evidenced in this chapter by the record of the Great Atlantic and Pacific Tea Company, was revolutionary in nature.

9 | SUPERMARKETS BECOME BIG BUSINESS— INTEGRATION

INTRODUCTION

In the preceding chapter, the initial impact of the supermarket on the field of food store retailing was presented. The reaction of both small independent merchants and giant food chains, with special emphasis on the Great Atlantic and Pacific Tea Company, was measured. Through rationing restrictions beyond its control, the supermarket showed little growth and impact during the World War II years. The only exception was the addition of nonfoods to the line in order to sustain or build volume.

This chapter measures the impact of the supermarket in the postwar era when the industry literally came of age. Food retailing became big business, not only in the sense that larger and larger stores requiring substantial investments were built in new locations, but also through a strong trend toward concentration in the hands of fewer and larger concerns.

CHAINS DOMINATE SUPERMARKET INDUSTRY

In the early 1930's all supermarts were independents. In the early 1940's chains began to make inroads. These chains were not necessarily the big food concerns of the 1920's. Shrewd and capable merchants who started with one unit built empires as exemplified by Food Fair Stores and Albers Supermarkets. By 1950, according to *Progressive Grocer,* about 37 per cent of the supermarkets with less

168

than 37 per cent of the volume were still individual operations at one location; by 1958 only 20.7 per cent of the supermarkets transacting 18.2 per cent of the industry volume were one-unit operations in an industry that now dominated all food store sales.[1] Chain stores in 1958 operated 66.6 per cent of the stores and transacted 69.1 per cent of the supermarket industry volume.[2]

INTEGRATION

The entire supermarket industry has mushroomed in the postwar era as indicated by statistics in Table 1-2; yet the chain members have outstripped the independent operators in this aura of growth. Integration has played an important role in the drive of the chains to dominate this field since they used this device more frequently than the independents. Although all chains have not grown at the same rate, the most rapidly growing concerns generally have been the principal users of integration.

Integration, which means the bringing of parts into a whole, has taken two directions, namely, horizontal and vertical combinations. In marketing parlance, horizontal or lateral integration occurs with consolidations of two or more similar concerns performing the same functions in the same stage of distribution. This occurs when one supermarket concern purchases the store or stores of another supermart firm. Vertical integration refers to the operation by a firm of the processes and functions in two or more stages of distribution or production.[3] Simply, a supermarket firm that operates its own bakery and distributes the products through its outlets is integrated vertically. Also, the supermarket concern that performs wholesale functions by operating its own warehouse is integrated vertically. Inherent in a successful combination is the reduction in expense that results from the coordination of the various parts of the integrated concern.

[1] See Table 1-3.
[2] *Ibid.*
[3] Paul Converse and Harvey Huegy, *The Elements of Marketing* (New York: Prentice-Hall, Inc., 1958), p. 243.

Supermarkets generally have employed both horizontal and vertical integration. The usual practice has been for the smaller concerns to integrate horizontally until they are large enough (have sufficient outlets) to assume the major part of wholesale operations. The assumption of the wholesale function is vertical integration of marketing activity. Supermarkets obtain 81 per cent of their groceries through their own central warehouses and an additional 10 per cent through retailer-owned cooperatives.[4] Supermarket chains or retail-sponsored cooperatives design and operate their wholesale integration at different levels of volume. Some need about 12 to 14 retail outlets doing from $15 million to $20 million in yearly volume to make the entire operation a success. Certain larger chains may require as many as 25 stores doing at least $30 million in sales to be serviced by the wholesale division in order to make the integration profitable.

As the concerns attain sufficient size, they can extend vertical integration by entry into certain manufacturing operations and can thus perform all the consecutive processes in food manufacture and distribution. The extent of food manufacturing performed by food chains is shown by the data in Table 9-1. In 1958 the 62 major chain supermarkets owned 326 factories that produced and shipped $1.304 billion in products. Chain-branded products of $1.304 billion at manufacturer's prices or $1.630 billion at retail prices (adjusted for a 20 per cent markup) are slightly under 10 per cent of total chain food store sales of $18.589 billion in 1958. The coffee and bakery areas are two of the most frequently entered fields. Generally a supermarket operation needs about $30 million in volume to make the vertical integration into the bakery operation profitable. Other areas invaded by supers include dairy products, mayonnaise, preserves, and confections. Certain of the larger supermarket operations are experimenting with or have entered into the meat-packing field with 22 packaging and preparing plants in operation. Food processing in the form of storing green bananas and tomatoes until they

[4] "How the Super Markets Get Their Groceries," *Super Market Industry Speaks* (Chicago: Super Market Institute, 1956), p. 14.

TABLE 9-1 *

Number of Food Manufacturing Plants Operated by 62 Major
Food Chains and the Value of Shipments from These
Establishments for the Years 1954 and 1958.

Kind of establishment	Number of establishments		Value of shipments (in thousands)	
	1954	1958	1954	1958
Meat packing	9	9	$ 94,500	$ 149,000
Prepared meats	11	13	38,200	78,100
Poultry dressing	2	4	3,400	7,100
Dairy products	32	41	34,700	54,800
Concentrated milk	12	12	46,800	57,200
Fluid milk	22	27	57,500	95,900
Canning and freezing	11	13	77,000	99,100
Bread and related products	126	147	289,500	379,500
Confectionery	6	7	31,000	43,200
Miscellaneous food preparation	16	14	85,700	105,300
Coffee, roasted or concentrated	38	39	316,700	234,400
Total	285	326	$1,075,000	$1,303,600

* Federal Trade Commission, *Federal Trade Commission Economic Inquiry into Food Marketing—Interim Report*, Government Printing Office, Washington, D.C., June 30, 1959.

are ripe is performed on a large scale. The ultimate in vertical integration is exemplified currently by the Great Atlantic and Pacific Tea Company with its widely known Ann Page, Jane Parker, Iona, Red Circle, Bokar, and Whitehouse lines of products.

While the statistics in Table 9-1 indicate that the supermarket industry is expanding into the meat packing area through vertical integration, a battle with the giant packers may be in the offing. The meat-packing industry, one in which there is a high degree of concentration of power in a relatively few firms, has been hamstrung by the Consent Decree of 1920. This decree resulted from action taken by the federal government under the Sherman Anti-trust Act and listed more than 100 products which the packers were not allowed to make, sell, or transport. In addition, the packers involved agreed to divest themselves of businesses considered to be unrelated to the preparation and wholesale distribution of meat products. In November, 1956, the Cudahy Packing Company filed a petition in the United States District Court in Chicago, Illinois, seeking release from certain provisions of the 1920 Decree. Two other parties to the decree, Armour and Company and Swift and Company, also filed petitions asking for similar relief. Extensive evidence demonstrating the significant changes in the distribution of food products at all levels since 1920 has been presented to the court; a decision is expected in 1961. Some of the possible areas of expansion for the meat packers include diversification into allied food products, integration through acquisition of common stock in supermarket chains, expansion into the area of frozen and prepackaged meats for the retail trade to be sold under an identifying label, and development of new operating methods.

CONCENTRATION AMONG MAJOR FOOD CHAINS

The major food chains currently dominate the supermarket and food store industries volumewise. The sales statistics of ten of these chains are recorded in Table 9-2 and show a phenomenal $10.1 billion increase between the years 1945 and 1958. The industry giant, the Great Atlantic & Pacific Tea Company, had a sales rise from $1.435 billion to $5.095 billion in this 13-year period, or an increase of 355 per cent. Food Fair Stores, Incorporated, experienced a phenomenal sales boost during this interval from $61 million to $734 million, or over 1,200 per cent.

Further evidence of this high degree of concentration in the retail food industry is indicated by the statistics in Table 9-2. Ten of the largest volume concerns with sales of $13.4 billion transacted about one-fourth of all food store sales in the country in 1958.

It is not solely in the number of stores where strength of the large chains lies. Examine the trend toward fewer and larger stores with bigger investments per location, as shown by the statistics of American Stores Company in Table 9-4. The statistics of this company exemplify the direction the large supermart chains generally have

TABLE 9-2 *

**Dollar Sales of Ten of the Largest Food Store Chains
for the Years 1945 and 1958 (in millions).**

Company †	1945	1958
Great A & P Tea Co.	$1,435	$ 5,095
Safeway Stores	615	2,225
Kroger Co.	457	1,776
American Stores Co.	224	866
National Tea Co.	107	794
Food Fair Stores	61	734
First National Stores	182	531
Colonial Stores	99	437
Grand Union Co.	55	504
Jewel Tea Co.	62	444
Total	$3,297	$13,406

* *Moody's Industrial Manuals.*
† In 1958, Winn-Dixie Stores, Inc., transacted $631 million in sales. However, consolidated sales for this firm, which is the result of a merger in 1955, are not available for the year 1945.

TABLE 9-3

**Sales of Ten Major Supermarket Chains and
Total Food Store Sales for the Years 1945
and 1958 (in millions).**

	1945	1958
Sales of 10 major supermarket chains *	$ 3,297	$13,406
Total food store sales †	19,120	53,075
10 major supermarket chains as a per cent of total food store sales	17.24%	25.26%

* See totals Table 9-2.
† *Facts in Grocery Distribution* (New York: Progressive Grocer, 1959), p. F–17.

taken to dominate the food store industry. Between 1945 and 1958, American Stores followed a policy of integration while decreasing the number of outlets from 1,954 to only 844; but in the same interval, average sales per store rose from $118,000 to almost $1,000,-000, and net income per outlet rose from $1,005 to $12,432.

FOOD CHAIN DILEMMA—ACQUIRE OR EXPIRE

In the postwar era, the supermarkets became the largest class of food stores, according to volume. In turn, the food chains as a group gained volume and numerical superiority in the supermarket industry. They were able to attain superiority over the independent supers

TABLE 9-4 *

Number of Stores, Sales per Store, and Net Income per Store for American Stores Company for the Years 1945 to 1958.

Year	Number of stores	Average sales per store (in thousands)	Net income per store
1945	1,954	$118	$ 1,005
1946	2,012	156	2,237
1947	1,921	202	3,084
1948	1,833	227	3,089
1950	1,637	254	4,119
1951	1,505	312	4,727
1952	1,408	370	3,590
1953	1,289	421	3,948
1954	1,132	533	6,597
1955	1,076	581	6,520
1956	953	687	8,745
1957	903	864	10,731
1958	844	992	12,432

* *Moody's Industrial Manual.*

as to the number of stores and volume even though they eliminated many small outlets. The food chains attained dominance by the standard procedure of (1) continuously building and opening new large units and (2) integrating horizontally through the acquisition of going concerns. The Federal Trade Commission reported that 151 companies during the years 1953 to 1958 opened new stores and acquired existing outlets which had sales of $3.908 billion and $1.2999 billion, respectively, for the year 1958.[5]

[5] Federal Trade Commission, *Federal Trade Commission Economic Inquiry Into Food Marketing—Interim Report,* Government Printing Office, Washington, D.C., June 30, 1959.

Further evidence of the extent of acquisitions is shown by the data in Table 9-5. In the years 1949 to 1958, 83 supermarket concerns acquired 315 operating companies which owned 2,238 stores that transacted $1.916 billion in annual sales at the time of acquisition. The merger movement trend continues to increase. The year 1958 was the most active year for mergers, both as to the number of companies active in acquiring outlets and as to the sales of the stores purchased at the time of acquisition.

Among the food chains themselves, however, significant shifts had been taking place in the pattern of sales. Statistics in Table 9-2 indicate remarkable growth for all major members of the industry; but all concerns did not expand at the same rate. The fast-moving, medium-sized chains appear to have made inroads in the relative position volumewise at the expense of the giants in the industry and the small-chain operators.

In order to assess this development in supermarket chain sales, it is necessary (1) to measure changes in relative volume among the large, medium, and small chains; (2) to summarize recent acquisitions and mergers; (3) to examine the underlying forces behind the merger movement; and (4) to indicate the impact on food store distribution.[6]

Changes in Relative Position Among Food Chains by Size

Only for the purpose of showing approximate size are the food chains grouped into three classifications by volume. This grouping includes large concerns with sales of $1 billion or more, medium-sized chains with sales from $100 million to $999 million, and small companies with sales of less than $100 million as of the year 1957. This classification need not be sacrosanct in that large and small concerns bordering on the $100 million and $999 million boundaries have been active in mergers and could be considered for the purposes of analysis in the medium sized class.

[6] The author first presented these ideas in an article, "Food Chain Dilemma—Acquire or Expire," which appeared in the *Journal of Retailing*, XXXIV, no. 4, Winter, 1958–1959, p. 216.

TABLE 9-5 °

Number and Volume of Food Stores That Were Acquired
by Food Chains for the Years 1949 to 1958.

Year of acquisition	Number of acquiring companies	Number of concerns acquired	Number of stores acquired as a result of the merger	Annual sales of stores purchased at time of acquisition (in thousands)
1949	6	6	72	$ 66,180
1950	5	5	5	3,889
1951	10	12	69	27,829
1952	5	10	273	67,343
1953	11	12	71	86,617
1954	17	20	70	60,580
1955	23	48	455	434,166
1956	36	70	439	397,325
1957	34	54	363	322,520
1958	38	78	421	450,003
Total	83 †	315	2,238	$1,916,452

° Federal Trade Commission, *Federal Trade Commission Economic Inquiry Into Food Marketing—Interim Report,* Government Printing Office, Washington, D.C., June 30, 1959.

† This total represents the number of concerns that made acquisitions; it is not based on a column total inasmuch as some companies made acquisitions in more than one year.

The individual leader in the food chain field, by far, continues to be the Great Atlantic and Pacific Tea Company, which in 1957 transacted 27.44 per cent of all chain grocery and combination store sales, as shown by the statistics in Table 9-6. Yet, the A & P together with Safeway Stores suffered a loss in relative industry position among the food chains in recent years. Although they followed the standard practice of eliminating smaller stores and opening larger units, they were inactive in the merger movement with one notable exception, namely, Safeway's expansion in the Des Moines, Iowa, market.[7]

[7] *The Merger Movement in Retail Food Distribution* (Chicago: National Association of Retail Grocers, 1959), p. 15.

This does not mean, however, that these concerns are losing their share of total food store volume. For example, A & P had 9.1 per cent of the total food store sales in 1951 and 10.1 per cent in 1958.[8]

TABLE 9-6

Chain Grocery Store Sales Classified by Volume, Expressed in Dollars and as a Percentage of Total Chain Grocery Sales for the Years 1951 and 1957.

	1951		1957	
Number of outlets	*Millions of dollars*	*% of total*	*Millions of dollars*	*% of total*
Chains with $1 billion and over sales in 1957 *				
Great Atlantic & Pacific Tea Co.	$ 3,393	31.66	$ 4,769	27.44
Safeway Stores, Inc.	1,455	13.58	2,117	12.18
Kroger Co.	997	9.30	1,674	9.63
Subtotal	5,845	54.54	8,560	49.25
Chains with $100–999 million sales in 1957 †	2,922	27.26	6,267	36.06
Chains with sales less than $100 million in 1957 ‡	1,951	18.20	2,552	14.69
Totals §	$10,718	100.00	$17,379	100.00

* Compiled from statistics published in the Federal Trade Commission report entitled *Federal Trade Commission Economic Inquiry Into Food Marketing—Interim Report*, Government Printing Office, Washington, D.C., June 30, 1959.
† *Ibid.*
‡ Calculated by subtracting total chain food store sales of $100 million or more volume from total industry sales.
§ U.S. Bureau of the Census, *Statistical Abstract of the U.S.*, Government Printing Office, Washington, D.C., 1959, p. 834.

The other member of the billion-dollar volume classification, The Kroger Company, improved its relative position through opening new stores and the merger route. These three members of the billion-dollar classification group acquired 179 stores transacting $240 million in annual sales during the period 1955 to 1958.[9]

[8] Federal Trade Commission, *op. cit.*
[9] *The Merger Movement in Retail Food Distribution, op. cit.*

The greatest increase in volume from 1951 to 1957 was made by the medium-sized group of stores in the $100 million to $999 million volume class. In 1957 these stores commanded 36.06 per cent of the chain food sales as compared with only 27.26 per cent in 1951. Mergers and acquisitions were responsible primarily for this gain. This segment of chain food stores acquired 1,092 outlets transacting $1.220 billion in annual sales during the period of 1955 to 1958.[10]

The small chains of less than $100 million in annual volume have suffered a significant loss in relative position in recent years. They have dropped in volume from 18.20 per cent to 14.69 per cent of chain grocery and combination store sales. It was on this group, multi-unit operators of less than 11 stores and single-unit concerns, that the medium-sized chains made their raids. These inroads resulted even though the chains of $100 million sales or less in turn made acquisition among the smaller supermarket companies; these acquisitions included 392 stores that transacted $443 million in annual sales during the period 1955 to 1958.[11]

Acquisitions

The numerical record of mergers compiled by ten of the major supermarket chains for the years 1949 to 1958 is summarized in Table 9-7. All but the Great Atlantic and Pacific Tea Company have participated to varying degrees in this movement; the most active concerns in the merger movement have been the National Tea Company, Winn Dixie Stores, Incorporated, the Kroger Company, and the Grand Union Company.

Specifically, what acquisitions have the major supermarket concerns made? What marketing areas have they invaded? The A & P, the major operator among the food chains as to volume and number of outlets, has added no new stores through merger or acquisition in recent years. Safeway Stores, Incorporated, the second largest operation, has been a relatively minor factor nationally in the merger movement, with its only major acquisition activity in the Des

10 *Ibid.*
11 *Ibid.*

TABLE 9-7

Number and Volume of Food Stores That Were Acquired by
Ten Major Food Chains for the Years 1949 to 1958.

Name of company	Number of acquisitions	Number of of stores acquired	Annual sales of stores purchased at time of acquisition (in thousands)
American Stores Co.	5	93	$ 34,442
Colonial Stores, Inc.	10	99	121,906
Food Fair Stores, Inc.	6	67	107,731
Grand Union Co.	15	128	128,417
Jewel Tea Co., Inc.	2	43	56,234
Kroger Co.	5	130	174,064
Lucky Stores, Inc.	4	56	72,612
National Tea Co.	24	485	251,612
Safeway Stores, Inc.	25	67	33,016
Winn-Dixie Stores, Inc.	11	306	221,070
Total	107	1,474	$1,201,104

* Federal Trade Commission, *Federal Trade Commission Economic Inquiry Into Food Marketing—Interim Report,* Government Printing Office, Washington, D.C., June 30, 1959.

Moines, Iowa, market. Kroger, on the other hand, has been on a constant program of acquisition. It recently acquired control of the 26 Henke & Pillot Stores of Houston, Texas, and the 25-unit Krambo Food Stores, Incorporated of Wisconsin. Whereas Henke & Pillot Stores were in an entirely new marketing area, the other merger put Krambo and Kroger in direct competition with each other for more intensive market coverage. Then, in 1958, Kroger acquired the 44 stores of Wyatt and Evans Food Stores in Texas. On April 6, 1959, however, the Federal Trade Commission charged the Kroger Company with illegally acquiring since 1928 more than 40 corporations and their 1,900 stores. The commission charged the acquisitions violated the antimerger laws in that they may result in a substantial lessening of competition or a tendency toward monopoly in the processing, manufacturing, purchasing, and distributing of grocery products and in the sale of merchandise in retail grocery stores.

In the classification of chains with annual sales of $100 million to $999 million, the following changes occurred: Colonial Stores, Incorporated, captured the 73 stores of Albers Super Markets, Incorporated, of Ohio and 14 units of Stop and Shop Enterprise of Indiana. Food Fair Stores, Incorporated, after experiencing remarkable growth in the postwar era, added 16 Carl's Markets, Incorporated, of Florida and four stores of Budget Markets, Incorporated. American Stores Company purchased the 92-unit chain of the Market Basket Corporation of New York. Grand Union Company acquired 31 Carrolls' Limited Stores and certain Food Fair Stores in Washington, D.C.; Shirley Food Stores and certain Stop and Shop outlets in New Haven, Connecticut; six Food Center Supermarkets in New York; and two Value Markets and three Tanner Stores in Miami. Jewel Tea Company added 41 stores of Eisner Grocery Company of Champaign, Illinois.

The greatest forager of the medium-sized chains was the National Tea Company, which acquired C. F. Smith Stores Company, Northwest Piggly Wiggly Company, George T. Smith's Market Basket, Incorporated, Dale Supermarkets, 28 Food Center Stores in St. Louis, Missouri; 28 Capital Stores, Incorporated, of Baton Rouge, Louisiana; Ashton's Supermarket of Gulfport, Mississippi; and H. A. Smith Markets, Incorporated, and Montag's Supermarket Chain of Memphis, Tennessee. The most recent additions of National Tea Company include the Maker's Food Chain of Michigan and seven stores in Peoria, Illinois, from Illinois Valley Stores; seven units of Devan's Food Stores, Mobile, Alabama; nine Logan's Supermarkets of Nashville; and 85 Council Oak Stores in Minnesota and Iowa. Other recent additions include stores in Colorado, Michigan, Iowa, and Illinois.

In addition, National Tea Company may become part of a new major international company in the industry. George Weston, Limited, a Canadian biscuit manufacturer, controls Loblaw Groceterias Company, Limited, one of Canada's largest grocery chains. In turn, Loblaw Groceterias' assets include 56 per cent of the stock of Loblaw, Incorporated, and 33 per cent interest of National Tea Company. Both of the last two are classed as medium-sized chains. The George Weston group, which has been built in recent years, also has cast covetous glances at certain Safeway Stores. On March 31, 1959, the National Tea Company was charged by the Federal Trade Commission with illegally acquiring stores in violation of the Clayton Act's antimerger section and with unfair competition and business practices in violation of the Federal Trade Commission Act.

Two of the medium-sized group, Dixie Home Stores and Winn-Lovett Company, merged into the Winn-Dixie Stores, Incorporated, a chain of some 447 stores. Prior to the merger, Winn-Lovett Company had acquired eight Jitney Jungle Stores of Alabama and Edins Food Stores of Columbia, South Carolina. In 1956, Winn-Dixie acquired 24 stores in North Carolina from Ketner-Milner Stores, Incorporated, and 42 stores of H. G. Hill Stores, Incorporated, in the New Orleans area.

Perhaps the most revolutionary merger of the medium-sized chains was the formation in 1955 of ACF-Wrigley Stores, Incorporated. In this, ACF-Brill Motors Company and the 92 Wrigley Stores of Detroit, Michigan, were the principals. Also included in this and subsequent development were the 20-odd Big Bear Markets of Michigan, Incorporated, 33 Humpty Dumpty Stores of Oklahoma, 13 Foodtown Stores, Incorporated, and 10 Fred Rapp, Incorporated, stores of St. Louis, Missouri. This new company of about 177 stores is reported planning additional acquisitions and openings.

Mergers have taken place in the classification of chains with less than $100 million yearly volume, but these have been of substantially less importance volumewise in the industry as shown by the statistics in Table 9-6. Perhaps one of the most significant of these was the growth of Lucky Stores, Incorporated, from a 40-odd unit chain into a 96-unit operation as of December 31, 1956, through merger of Cardinal Stores, Incorporated, Serv-U-Meat Markets, and Dolly Madison International Foods, Limited. In this class, the trend is toward larger operation by the individual chain.

Underlying Forces Behind the Movement

While there are many evident causes for this merger movement, the following are advanced as the major reasons for this growing concentration in the food chain industry.

1. The food chains are the major factor volumewise in the supermarket industry, which in turn dominates retail food store distribution. The general supermarket movement has been characterized by an aggressive attitude by management toward growth. The supermarket industry has been one to adapt operations to meet the needs and requirements of the consumer. "Non progredi est regredi" (not to go forward is to go backward) or expand or die is the keynote.

2. Profits before taxes as a percentage of tangible net worth among food chains in the post-World War II era have been excellent. For example, Dixie Home Stores and Big Bear Markets of Michigan, Incorporated, have earned in some years as much as 50 cents on every dollar of owner's equity. In 1956, Food Fair Stores earned 39 per cent and Market Basket, Incorporated, earned 36 per cent on tangible net worth. Reinvestment in merchandising activity is necessary to continue this high level of earnings.

3. New locations constantly are being pioneered. However, as these are harder to find, management has turned to acquisition of existing locations. It is easier to estimate and evaluate the potential of a going operation than a new location.

4. The problems are fewer in acquiring existing locations than in pioneering new stores. There is no time delay in start-up expense, no financing of real estate and building, and less waiting for the location to pay off profitably.

5. The larger concerns are able to spread the risk of failure over a wider geographical area by acquiring outlets in new regions. This, plus the stability of the industry (food sales), has enabled many chains to enter the capital markets to "trade on equity." The ability to borrow more easily and cheaply because of size and diversified locations has benefited the larger firms. The rates paid for capital have been less substantial than the profits that accrued from the

use of these funds. Many of the firms studied in the postwar period have had consistently more creditors' funds than owners' funds in the business.

6. The larger firms have more marketable securities to exchange for the shares of the smaller companies than do those concerns under $100 million annual volume. This has given the larger concerns an advantage in acquisition through stock exchange.

7. A number of food chains were started in the 1930's by individuals as single-unit operations, many of which were supermarkets. These ventures have grown into multi-unit operations. Management now is nearing retirement and is selling out to larger operators.

8. Many of the local operators have found it difficult to secure outside capital and have been forced to rely to a large extent on retained earnings for expansion. The present tax rate reduces the amount available for reinvestment, especially since the cost of pioneering new locations has increased substantially. This has placed the independent at some disadvantage.

9. The estate tax also has influenced the merger movement. The small, family firms in which the owners have a large share of their wealth in the supermarket operation have been facing the prospect in recent years of paying the estate tax. The possibility that payment of this tax may jeopardize the financial stability of the firm and injure the heirs of the owner are factors that contribute to the mergers.[12]

10. Independents find it difficult to expand into shopping centers. The big insurance companies that do the bulk of the financing of the centers demand as tenants under long-term rental contracts the big regional and national chain outlets. The independent, in most instances, is prohibited by economic fact from expanding into shopping centers. The centers are changing the retail pattern of the United States.[13]

[12] *Ibid.*
[13] Testimony of Earl W. Kintner, Chairman, Federal Trade Commission, before a Subcommittee of the Select Committee on Small Business, United States Senate, Eighty-sixth Congress, First Session, July 2, 1959. These hearings are published as *Mergers and Unfair Competition in Food Marketing,* Government Printing Office, Washington, D.C., 1960.

11. There are economies of large-scale operation in certain instances. Better utilization of warehouses, transportation equipment, and manufacturing facilities have been advanced as reasons for acquisitions. One of the supermarket successes has been in spreading fixed costs over a large volume. Large units can integrate vertically more easily. Certain buying and selling advantages accrue to the large-scale operator; for example, the Thursday newspaper advertising cost can be spread over more stores.

Trends in Mergers and Conclusions

This trend toward concentration among the food chains is a manifestation of a general trend in the economy—the big absorbing the small. The largest member of the food chain industry has had frequent bouts with the Department of Justice as to the size and scope of its operations. Safeway Stores, Incorporated, operating in 24 states and commanding from 12 to 13 per cent of the chain food store volume, likewise has been aware of the A & P versus the government. But the framework of operation and the advantages of integration and growth are such that the lesser lights in the industry will continue to gain on the top few. In the not-too-far future the data indicate definite trends toward fewer and larger food chains. Not only will the medium-sized concern capture the small but they will also join forces with other medium-sized chains. The expansion to new regions, such as the move of Kroger Company to the Southwest, will be continued. In fact, large international chains such as the aforementioned George Weston, Limited, organization, are more than a remote possibility. The main limiting factor appears to be fear of government interference.

As chains grow larger and outlets for investment of funds are needed, more emphasis may be placed on vertical integration. There seems to be a parallel between size of food chain and degree of emphasis on manufacturing operations. If vertical integration is followed, more products of the Ann Page or Jane Parker variety can be expected, although some of the actual manufacturing may be done by regular food manufacturers. This leads to what can be called "chain labels" as distinct from private labels or nationally advertised brands. "Chain labels" supported by strong advertising and promotion can make it more difficult for the national brands to gain shelf space. Brand competition will become keener with more emphasis placed on advertising and promotion.

Faced with large capital requirements and competition from large chains with diversified locations, the individual entrepreneur will find it more difficult to enter the food business successfully. There is a trend toward fewer and larger food stores in the economy.

The death knell of the service and limited-function wholesaler has been sounded for many years; yet, they continue to exist. However, increased concentration in the food chain industry, with emphasis on buying and shipping direct from the manufacturer to chain stores or warehouses, could affect adversely wholesalers' operations.

As a corollary to the above, important contracts may tend to be made to a great extent at chain branches or headquarters. This would make the position of many manufacturers' salesmen come under review in this battle for survival. Some salesmen possibly could be eliminated, or their functions could be changed to those of setting up displays and other merchandising activities, or both possibilities could occur.

In the past 25 years, developments in food store retailing have been almost revolutionary. How much further these changes will go depends primarily on governmental policy in curbing mergers. The economic forces in food chain distribution are marshaled in favor of bigness.

VOLUNTARY CHAIN GROWTH

Faced with the integration threat of the food chains in the postwar period, many independent supermarket operators have joined the voluntary chain movement. Voluntary chains are of two types, namely: (1) wholesale grocers sponsoring voluntary retail groups and (2) retailer-owned food cooperatives jointly owning the wholesale activity.[14] Both types have shown substantial growth in the post-

14 The activities of the voluntary chains are discussed in Chapter 5.

war period, as shown by the statistics in Table 9-8. While the data show wholesale sales of the two types of cooperatives, the statistics can be adjusted to retail figures by applying an approximate 20 per cent markup. Wholesale data are furnished inasmuch as this is one of the most feasible methods of collecting statistics to assess the importance of the numerous independent retail operators throughout the country.

TABLE 9-8 *

Wholesale Sales of Certain Voluntary Food Chain Groups in the United States for the Years 1948, 1954, and 1958 (in millions).

Type	1948	1954	1958
Wholesale-sponsored †	$746	$1,444	$2,096
Retailer-owned food cooperatives ‡	543	1,211	2,030

* Federal Trade Commission, *Federal Trade Commission Economic Inquiry Into Food Marketing—Interim Report,* Government Printing Office, Washington, D.C., June 30, 1959.

† Includes the data for 146 wholesale grocers sponsoring voluntary retail groups for each of the years.

‡ Includes the data for 141 retailer-owned food cooperatives for each of the years.

These voluntary groups not only have become powerful buying forces, but in addition, they are growing more and more important as manufacturers. In 1958 the voluntary chain wholesalers that participated in the Federal Trade Commission study reported operating 57 manufacturing plants that shipped $65.7 million in products.[15] The plants operated primarily in the coffee roasting, dairy products, baking, and canning areas.

SUMMARY

In the postwar era, the supermarket industry literally came of age. Volumewise, the supermarkets became the largest group of food retailers. In turn, the independent supermarkets that started and dominated the industry were surpassed by the chain supers, both as to number of stores

[15] Federal Trade Commission, *op. cit.*

and volume. The industry has become one of bigness—not only as to size of stores—but as to concentration among its members. The industry has followed a standard practice of closing small units and opening new and large locations in order to maintain relative competitive position. Except for the two largest concerns, A & P and Safeway Stores, the industry members have been on a shopping spree of gobbling up going concerns. As a result, the fast-moving, medium-sized chains have acquired a host of new outlets through merger and acquisition. The smaller chains in turn have been acquiring numerically the even smaller operators. The forces within the industry are marshaled toward bigness, with the only major deterrent being the action of the federal government through the Federal Trade Commission and the Department of Justice. Legal action has been taken by the government against certain of the major industry members for both horizontal and vertical integration. More legal action against the major concerns now active in mergers can be anticipated in the near future.

This move toward bigness is a result of many factors. Basically, management in this industry has been characterized by an aggressive spirit. The earnings of the industry have been excellent, and a source for reinvestment in merchandising activities is necessary to continue this high level of earnings. New locations are more and more difficult to find, and it is easier to estimate and evaluate the potential of a going operation than a new location.

In addition, the larger firms have more marketable securities to exchange for the shares of the smaller companies. Next, management of many supermarkets that were started in the 1930's is nearing retirement and is selling out to the larger operators. Finally, there are economies of large-scale operation in certain instances that benefit the large supermarket chains.

This trend toward concentration among the supermarket members is a manifestation of a general trend in the economy—the big absorbing the small. Faced with large capital requirements and competition from large chains with diversified locations, the individual entrepreneur will find it more difficult to enter the food business successfully. The trend toward fewer and larger food stores in the economy will continue.

CHANGES IN THE
NUMBER OF FOOD STORES
AND THEIR SALES VOLUME

INTRODUCTION

The preceding chapter examined the movement of the large food chains toward domination of the supermarket industry in the postwar era. Integration policies and practices of the large food chains were examined. The purpose of this and the following chapter is to discern changes in the pattern of food store sales between 1929 and 1958. To do this, it is necessary to examine data at three points in time—1929, 1954, and 1958.

The year 1929 was selected because (1) for all practical purposes, supermarkets were nonexistent at the time, and (2) it was a year for which the Bureau of Census published Retail Distribution Statistics. The year 1954 was included because it was the closest year to date for which Retail Trade Statistics were given by the Bureau of the Census. The changes that are measured statistically at these points in time are shifts in the absolute and relative positions. These include:

1. Number of different types of food stores
2. Dollar sales of different types of food stores
3. Sales of the major product lines transacted by different types of food stores

The first two issues are examined in the remainder of this chapter.

Product-line sales by type of food store outlet are analyzed in Chapter 11.

CHANGES IN THE NUMBER OF FOOD STORES

The era of the "roaring twenties" was also the heyday of specialty food stores. This is evidenced by data in Table 10-1 which indicate

TABLE 10-1

**Number of Food Stores in the United States by Type
of Store for the Years 1929, 1954, and 1958.**

Type	1929 stores *	1954 stores †	1958 stores ‡
Grocery stores (without meat)	191,876	000 §	72,300
Combination markets	115,549	279,440	188,700
Meat and seafood markets	49,865	27,354	22,500
Fruit and vegetable markets	22,904	13,136	12,000
Confectionery stores	63,265	20,507	20,000
Bakery product stores	12,013	19,034	18,500
Delicatessen stores	11,166	8,132	8,000
Other food stores	15,253	13,777	15,000
Country general store	104,089	17,701	16,000
Total	585,980	399,081	373,000

* U.S. Bureau of the Census, *Retail Distribution Part I*, Vol. 1, Government Printing Office, Washington, D.C., 1933, p. 47.

† U.S. Bureau of the Census, Retail Trade, *Summary Statistics*, Vol 1, Government Printing Office, Washington, D.C., 1957, p. 2–3.

‡ *Facts in Grocery Distribution* (New York: Progressive Grocer, 1959), p. F–5.

§ Grocery stores without meat were not classified separately in the 1954 census and are contained in the combination markets classification.

the large number of stores (62.8 per cent) handling specific food lines. However, the trend toward the combination of at least the grocery and meat departments was under way. In the year 1929, 115,549 grocery stores handled meat and were thus in the combination market class. These represented 19.8 per cent of all food stores. The major industry class was the neighborhood grocery store without meat, representing about one-third of all food stores.

While not classified as a food store by the Bureau of the Census, the country general store did approximately 60 per cent of its volume in food products in 1929. Therefore it is included in the study.

By 1958 the major shifts in the number of food stores can be summed as follows:

1. The most startling change was the passing of the country general store. The decline by more than 88,000 units from a total of 104,089 was a decrease of 85 per cent.

2. The next significant shift was the sharp increase in the number of combination markets (the classification for supermarkets). These increased by 73,151 units to become the dominant member of the food store group. Supermarkets, which numbered 20,413 in 1958, accounted for 27 per cent of the increase in the combination market class.

3. The group of grocery stores without meat lost its major relative and absolute status. However, an undisclosed number of this class added meats and became combination markets. This change-over was also true of the meat market, which added groceries and joined the combination movement. The exact number of both types that shifted to combination operation is not known. But grocery stores without meat and meat markets as specialty stores decreased numerically between 1929 and 1958 by 146,941 units; combination markets increased numerically only 73,151 units in this 29-year period, and a growing number of these were new supers under chain ownership. Therefore a substantial number of limited-line stores under individual ownership permanently closed their doors.

4. Of the specialty food group members, the produce stores, delicatessens, meat markets, and confectionery outlets suffered losses in numerical position. Only the bakery product stores improved their numerical status.

5. Supermarkets, classified under combination stores in Table 10-1, for all purposes were nonexistent in 1929. As of 1958 their total was estimated at 20,413, a mere 5.5 per cent of all the food stores and 10.8 per cent of all the combination markets. Numerically the dominant class of food stores in 1958 comprised the nonsuper combination markets with an estimated 168,287 units or about 45 per

cent of all food stores in the country as compared with the supermarkets, which represented only 5.5 per cent of all food stores.
However, a true appraisal of the supermarket movement is not ob-
tainable from an examination of the number of supermarkets alone.
Their basic operating practice of developing a large volume of sales
per store must be considered along with their relatively insignificant
but growing numerical status.

6. There had been a trend toward fewer small combination markets. This movement had been quite pronounced in the past decade.
The combination market class numerically declined from 223,662
units in 1948 to 188,700 outlets in 1958.[1] The supermarket made
impressive numerical gains in this decade, as shown by the statistics
in Table 1-2. However, the superette, a combination market that
transacts a yearly volume of possibly several hundred thousand dollars, had become an important factor in the food store group during
this period. Superettes, which numbered 59,700 units in 1958, had
been growing in numerical importance along with the supermarket
to the detriment of the small combination market with yearly sales
under $75,000.[2]

CHANGES IN THE SALES BY TYPE OF FOOD STORE

Total food store industry sales, including statistics for the country
general store, increased from $12.589 billion in 1929 to $50.263 billion in 1958, as shown by the statistics in Table 10-2. This gain of
400 per cent in food store sales included a rise in price plus an improvement in over-all tonnage. But all membership classes by type
of store did not experience the same relative growth. The statistics
on the distribution of sales by type of store, shown in Table 10-2,
indicate the following salient changes:

1. Grocery stores without meat commanded 28 per cent of all food
store sales in 1929. By 1948 this group had slipped to 13 per cent of

[1] U.S. Bureau of the Census, *Retail Trade-General Statistics*, Part I, Vol. 1,
Government Printing Office, Washington, D.C., 1952, p. 104.
[2] *Facts in Grocery Distribution* (New York: Progressive Grocer, 1959), p.
F–9.

TABLE 10-2

Food Store Sales in the United States by
Type of Store for the Years
1929, 1954, and 1958.

Type	1929 sales (in millions) *	1954 sales (in millions) †	1958 sales (in millions) ‡
Grocery store (without meat)	$ 3,449	$ 000 §	$ 000 §
Combination markets	3,904	34,421	44,547
Meat and seafood markets	1,337	2,128	
Fruit and vegetable markets	308	485	
Confectionery stores	572	568	
Bakery product stores	201	862	
Delicatessen stores	195	480	
Country general store	1,622	707	
Other food stores	1,001	818	5,716 ¶
Total	$12,589	$40,469	$50,263

* U.S. Bureau of the Census, *Retail Trade-General Statistics*, Part I, Vol. 1, Government Printing Office, Washington, D.C., 1952, p. 104.

† U.S. Bureau of the Census, *Statistical Abstract of the United States*, Government Printing Office, Washington, D.C., 1959, p. 840.

‡ *Ibid.*, p. 833.

§ Grocery stores without meat were not classified separately in the 1954 census or in the 1958 estimates. Statistics for this group are contained in combination markets.

¶ For 1958 the other food stores classification contains all food stores with the exception of combination markets. The data were not reported separately and are grouped as specialty food stores.

all food store sales, and the trend continued downward.[3] By 1958 this class had only 72,300 stores, compared with 154,277 outlets in 1948, and the volume was considered under $4 billion. The Bureau of the Census no longer considers it essential to report this dwindling group.

2. Combination markets were last reported separately in 1948, at which time they had captured almost 66 per cent of all food store

[3] In 1948 there were 154,277 grocery stores without meat that transacted $4.027 billion in sales. Combination markets of that year numbered 223,662 units and transacted sales of $20.743 billion. These data are from the U.S. Bureau of the Census, *Retail Trade-General Statistics, Part I*, Vol. 1, Government Printing Office, Washington, D.C., 1952, p. 104.

sales, compared with 31 per cent in 1929. Combination store sales in 1958 were estimated to transact at least $40 billion of the total grocery and combination classification volume of $44.547 billion or over 80 per cent of all food store sales, as shown by the statistics in Table 10-2.

3. The supermarket group is contained in the combination market classification in Table 10-2. This division had sales of $28.7 billion in 1958 and had become the major factor in both the combination market class and the food store industry. From 1929 to 1958 the supermarket classification raised its share of food store sales from zero to 57.1 per cent. Not only had the supermarket made vast inroads in the volume of food store sales, but the superettes also had captured $11.85 billion of the food store sales in 1958.[4] The small grocery and combination stores as a group in 1958 numbered 195,400 outlets and yet transacted a mere $3.75 billion in food store sales.[5] The small combination markets (nonsupermarket combination stores with sales under $75,000 per year) suffered a severe loss in relative industry position between 1929 and 1958.

4. Sales of food products by the country general store had fallen to an insignificant amount of total food store sales.

5. Among the specialty food store group, the only one to show significant progress and improve its relative industry position was the bakery products group.

CONCLUSIONS ON CHANGES IN THE NUMBER OF FOOD STORES AND THEIR SALES VOLUME

If the preceding analysis is viewed in its broadest aspects, three major features stand out:

1. The passing of the country general store as a significant medium for the sale of food products.

2. The attainment of major status by the combination market in the food store industry coupled with a noticeable loss in relative

---

[4] *Facts in Grocery Distribution, op. cit.*
[5] *Ibid.*

position by the single-line stores.[6] (The supermarket was the major exponent of multiline operation in the food group.)

3. The successful combating of the trend toward multiline operation by the bakery shops.

These three aspects are reviewed in the following section to establish the major underlying forces that brought about these changes and to discern what role, if any, the supermarket played.

Passing of the Country General Store

The country general store, which at one time held an important place in the retailing pattern, dwindled to a position of insignificance. As late as 1929, 12.7 per cent of the food store sales were transacted by this type of outlet; by 1954 sales were reduced to 1.7 per cent. This decline can be traced to both internal and external factors. A list of the important internal failings includes: [7]

1. Lack of capacity to buy in quantity
2. Small size of stores preventing specialization
3. Unskilled buying because of wide lines handled
4. Incomplete assortments
5. Inadequate records

Externally, the most important factors have been: [8]

1. The farm-to-city movement
2. Improved roads and transportation
3. Increased importance of fashion merchandise
4. Development of rural mail delivery

Most of the internal factors could be lumped under one heading—poor management. To this can be added changes in the buying

[6] A single- or limited-line store is used here to indicate a food store in which the sale of one type of merchandise, such as bakery products, groceries, or confections, predominates. These are distinguished from the multiline outlets, exemplified by the combination market which handles groceries and meat plus any number of other lines. The supermarket is perhaps the best example of an exponent of multiline operation among the food store group.

[7] C. F. Phillips and D. J. Duncan, *Marketing Principles and Methods* (Chicago: Richard D. Irwin, 1956), p. 159.

[8] *Ibid.*, p. 177.

habits of the rural people plus their ability to travel great distances to shop. Supermarkets have attracted farm and rural patronage.[9] The ability of the super to operate as a low-cost marketer of food and its ability to merchandise farm produce have earned the respect and support of many of the farm folks.[10] Although the number of supers in rural areas is small, the trend has been toward locating in these rural and small communities. The location of many new supers on or adjacent to arterial highways has attracted rural trade. These data indicate that the supermarket development added to the decline of the general store; but in view of other factors, the specific influence of the supermarket cannot be assessed.

Rise of the Combination Market and the Decline of the Limited-Line Food Store

In 1931 the trend toward competition among different types of retailers in selling the same commodity was indicated. Malcolm P. McNair wrote:

It is an era of scrambled merchandising. Grocery stores sell cigarettes; drug stores sell grocery products; and tobacco stores sell razor blades. Grocery stores are on the way to becoming food department stores.[11]

The theory that limited-line stores move toward multiline operation and then back again in a cyclical nature has been advanced.[12] However, after World War I, there was a pronounced trend of grocery stores to widen their lines; this continued on a larger scale, with impetus given by the success of the supermarket.[13]

[9] B. A. Durrant, "Why Go After the Small Town Market," *Chain Store Age,* Grocery Executive Edition, April, 1945, p. 171.

[10] L. L. Clovis, "What the Farmer Expects from the Operator," *Super Market Merchandising,* XII, no. 11, November, 1947, p. 81.

[11] Malcolm P. McNair, "Trends in Large-Scale Retailing," *Harvard Business Review,* X, no. 1, Fall, 1932, p. 31.

[12] Paul D. Converse and Harvey W. Huegy, *The Elements of Marketing* (5th ed.; New York: Prentice-Hall, Inc., 1952), p. 399.

[13] "50 Years—1888 to 1938," *Printers Ink,* Vol. 184, no. 4, July 28, 1938, p. 309.

Specifically, the causes of intertype competition among retailers were: [14]

1. The large pool of overhead or common costs
2. Interrelated demand among several products
3. Changing consumer shopping habits
4. Development of new products; improvement and standardization of old ones

The economic consequences of such a movement had important effects on the structure of retail trade and on the economy at large. Ostensibly, improvement was realized in the market position of the multiline distributor at the expense of the limited-line dealer. There were possible shifts in the relative importance of price competition and nonprice competition in various lines. There was encouragement of further legal restrictions. [15]

This pattern of scrambled merchandising is exemplified by the record of the food store industry. The 1920's were largely an era of specialty stores that handled limited-line merchandise. However, the trend toward multiline operation had started with the growth of the combination market. By 1958 the combination market had gained major status in the food store industry—both numerically and as to volume—at the expense of all limited-line stores except bake shops. The movement was given impetus by conversion to combination markets of many limited-line outlets. The combination market movement was one manner in which the small merchant could attempt to combat the spectre of the supermarket.

The reasons for this were two: (1) The small combination mart generally was able to reduce substantially the costs of products purchased. [16] (2) The small combination market alert to new trends also could reduce operating expenses. The nonsuper combination market was able to reduce purchase costs largely through the media of buying associations or cooperatives. Many wholesalers sponsored dealer

[14] Richard N. Alt, "Competition Among Types of Retailers in Selling the Same Commodity," *Journal of Marketing*, XIV, no. 3, January, 1948, p. 442.

[15] *Ibid.*, p. 446.

[16] Robert Mueller, "Detroit Dealers Thrive on Modern Plan," *Progressive Grocer*, XXIX, no. 2, February, 1950, p. 40.

plans.[17] The methods varied, but usually they enabled the small merchant to purchase grocery products at a small percentage above the cost to the buying association plus a percentage for cartage to the store.

The reduction in the operating expenses for the small combination market enabled many of them to compete with the supers insofar as expense as a percentage of sales is considered. Lower operating expenses were effected through adoption of self-service, displays, and reduced credit and delivery.[18] The owner of the small combination market of 1958 generally was considered to have more knowledge of how to run a store than did his counterpart in the 1920's. He was able to observe the supermarket techniques, and buying associations furnished valuable service on operations to its members.

Despite the fact that the nonsuper combination markets were able to lower both the cost of goods purchased and expenses, they appeared at a disadvantage in the intraclass struggle with the supermarket. The latter opponent generally had facilities and resources to adopt operating practices more in line with the changing desires of the shoppers. The super was able to exploit more fully than the nonsuper combination market the customer attractions of one-stop shopping, new suburban locations, diversified lines of merchandise, and other buying preferences.

Position of the Bakery Shops

The bakery products outlets successfully challenged the trend toward scrambled merchandise and the desire for one-stop shopping. The bakery stores were at the same time the beneficiary and the victim of cross-currents in the economy. On the one hand, people reduced their per capita consumption of bakery products in favor of other types of food.[19] On the other, the population grew numeri-

[17] R. D. Tousley, "Reducing Distribution Costs in the Grocery Field," *Journal of Marketing*, XII, no. 4, April, 1948, p. 40.

[18] Godfrey Lebhar, "Self-Service Marches On," *Chain Store Age*, Grocery Executive Edition, September, 1952, p. 67.

[19] Charles Slater, "Statistical History of the Baking Industry," *Baking Industry*, Vol. 97, no. 1219, April 12, 1952, p. 264.

cally. In addition, a decided change in the past twenty years reflected the consumer's demand for convenience in the preparation of meals; this brought about a decided shift to store-bought bakery products.[20] Yet, above all, consumers demanded freshness in their bakery products; and freshness was associated with purchase near the point of manufacture—the bake shop. This single-line type of food store actually improved its industry position in regard to sales. However, this group is not removed from supermarket competition inasmuch as many members of the latter have attained sufficient size to open their own bake shops and compete on both a price and quality basis.

SUMMARY

In 1929 supermarkets were for practical purposes nonexistent. By 1958 this member of the food store industry claimed only 5 per cent of all food stores but 57.1 per cent of all food store sales. The supermarket became a highly successful exponent of scrambled merchandising to the detriment of the limited-line retail food merchant. The only limited-line store to improve its relative industry position in this 29-year period was the bakery products store. While the latter was subject to cross-currents in the economy, these stores succeeded in satisfying consumer demand by emphasizing freshness of their products as well as offering convenience in the serving of meals. The small combination market has followed the supermarket's technique of multiline operation, but as a class it has not been able to withstand the competition offered by the supermarket industry, which has more resources at its command.

20 *Ibid.*, p. 47.

11 CHANGES IN THE SALES OF MAJOR PRODUCT LINES BY TYPES OF FOOD STORE OUTLETS

INTRODUCTION

This chapter continues the analysis of changes in the food store sales pattern between 1929 and 1958. In the preceding chapter, significant changes in number and sales of different types of food stores were discerned. The purpose of this chapter is to examine shifts in the sales of certain major product lines transacted by different types of food stores.

Analysis is made at the same points in time—1929, 1954, and 1958—and for the same reasons advanced in Chapter 10. The major product classes selected for study include:

1. Meat, poultry, and seafood
2. Fresh fruit and vegetables or produce
3. Confections
4. Bakery products
5. Canned goods, grocery items
6. Nonfood lines

SALES OF MAJOR PRODUCT CLASSES IN SUPERMARKETS

The 1958 supermarket handled 5,600 separate items.[1] These can be grouped primarily by departments under eight major headings. Three separate studies recently were completed which measure the relative importance of various product classes; these findings, expressed as a percentage of sales, are shown in Table 11-1. Individual

TABLE 11-1

Results of Three Recent Studies on the Percentage of Sales of Major Product Classes Transacted by Supermarkets.

Product class	Food Town * study, %	Super Valu † study, %	Food chain ‡ survey, %
Meats	28.11	22.42	25.10
Dairy products	8.61	11.51	10.30
Bakery products	2.67	5.76	4.30
Frozen foods	4.14	4.78	4.50
Confections	1.48	1.85	1.60
Produce	12.76	8.79	9.90
Grocery items	38.01	37.14	36.10
Nonfoods	4.22	7.75	8.20
	100.00	100.00	100.00

* "The Food Town Study," *Progressive Grocer*, XXXV, no. 1, January, 1955, p. 49.

† "How an Average Customer Spends Her Super Market Dollars—Super Valu Markets," *Facts in Grocery Distribution* (New York: Progressive Grocer, 1959), p. F-20.

‡ "What Do Food Chain Stores Sell," *Chain Store Age*, Grocer Executive Edition, July, 1959, p. 47.

markets may have product statistics that vary from these data as a result of size, finances, facilities, location, competitive factors, and policy. But approximately 25 per cent of a supermarket's sales is in meat, 10 per cent each in produce and dairy, 4 to 5 per cent in frozen

[1] *Facts in Grocery Distribution* (New York: Progressive Grocer, 1959), p. F-3.

foods, about 4 to 5 per cent in bakery products (exclusive ⟨
aged cookies and crackers), and from 4 to 9 per cent in nonfood
lines. Confections, which average between 1 and 2 per cent of sales,
normally are considered part of the grocery line, but this class is
recorded separately since the impact of the super on confectionery
stores is assessed later in this chapter.

A breakdown of sales of the multitude of grocery products is given
in Table 11-2. The gross margin percentage for these grocery items

TABLE 11-2 °

**How an Average Customer Spends Her Supermarket
Dollars for Grocery Products and the Percentage
of Gross Margin on Sales of These Items.**

Product group	% total supermarket sales	% gross margin of sales
Beverages	5.42	12.1
Household and laundry supplies	2.59	28.3
Vegetables, canned	2.48	21.4
Cookies and crackers	2.20	25.3
Paper products	2.11	23.4
Soaps and detergents	2.01	10.5
Fruit, canned	1.82	21.6
Baking needs, flour	1.45	16.5
Breakfast foods	1.44	18.1
Soups	1.41	15.0
Baking, batter mixes	1.36	17.5
Fish, canned	1.09	19.4
Jams, jellies, and spreads	1.04	23.6
Sugar	1.04	8.0
Snack and party foods	1.01	23.9
Baby foods	0.99	14.1
Juices, canned	0.86	19.4
Pet foods	0.70	20.2
Salad dressings, mayonnaise	0.68	15.5
Shortening	0.66	9.7
Condiments, sauces	0.56	18.4
Pickles, olives, relishes	0.55	26.7

Table 11-2 (*Continued*)

Desserts	0.54	16.7
Prepared foods, canned	0.42	20.8
Salt, seasonings, spices	0.39	24.6
Milk, canned and dry	0.38	13.5
Macaroni products, dry	0.36	18.8
Meat, canned	0.31	21.0
Fruits, dried	0.30	22.1
Vegetables, dried	0.25	25.4
Syrups and molasses	0.23	17.9
Chinese foods	0.16	24.3
Diet foods	0.15	27.0
Pet supplies	0.02	29.8
Misc. grocery items	0.16	25.9
Total grocery products	37.14	18.2
Total all others	62.86	
	100.00	

* *Facts in Grocery Distribution* (New York: Progressive Grocer, 1959), p. F–20.

also is included. Again, individual markets may have sales that vary from these findings inasmuch as this industry is so diverse. In the wide range of products handled by a super, the importance of beverages, household and laundry supplies, paper products, and soaps and detergents is apparent.

SALES OF MEAT PRODUCTS, POULTRY, AND SEAFOOD BY TYPE OF FOOD STORE

(This category includes the sale of all fresh meat, poultry, fresh fish, and other fresh seafoods, plus meat provisions such as cured hams, bacon, and sausage.)

In 1929 the meat market, a limited line store, was the principal outlet for meat and related products, as shown by the statistics in Table 11-3. By 1954 total food store sales of meat in the United States soared to more than $10 billion. The rise was due in part to an increase in population and to a higher per capita consumption of meat products—from 139 lb in 1929 to 164 lb of meat per inhabitant

TABLE 11-3

Estimated Meat, Poultry, and Seafood Sales by Major Type of Food Store Outlet for the Years 1929 and 1954.

	1929		1954	
Type of store	*Sales* * *(in billions)*	*% total*	*Sales* † *(in billions)*	*% total*
Meat markets	$1,245	54.4	$ 2,128	19.9
Nonsuper combination markets	1,045	45.6	4,547 ‡	42.6
Supermarkets	0	0.0	3,995 ‡	37.5
Total	$2,290 §	100.0	$10,670 §	100.0

* U.S. Bureau of the Census, *Retail Distribution—Food Retailing,* No. R-83, Government Printing Office, Washington, D.C., 1934, p. 82.

† U.S. Bureau of the Census, *Retail Trade,* No. R-2-2, Government Printing Office, Washington, D.C., 1957, pp. 2–333.

‡ Total grocery and combination market sales of meat products for 1954 were estimated at $8.542 billion in *What the Public Spends for Grocery Store Products* (New York: Topics Publishing Co.). Supermarket sales for 1954 were estimated at $15.980 billion in Table 1-2. On the assumption that 25 per cent of a supermarket's sales are in meat products, supermart sales of meat in 1954 were estimated at $3.995 billion. Nonsuper combination market sales of meat are the difference between total grocery and combination market sales of meat and the meat sales of supermarkets.

§ These totals do not include the sale of meat products in other food stores such as country general stores and delicatessens. Sales through these channels are considered relatively insignificant.

in 1954.[2] In addition, the wholesale price index for meat products (1947 to 1949 equals 100) rose from 48.1 in 1929 to 91.5 in 1954.[3] Among the stores, the nonsuper combination market became the major retailer of meat, followed closely by the supermarket, which made substantial progress during this period, rising from negligible sales of meat in 1929 to 37.5 per cent in 1954.

[2] Data on meat consumption are found in Table 3-2.

[3] Changes in the wholesale price of meat are considered generally to indicate changes in the same direction in the retail price of meat. Statistics are from the U.S. Department of Commerce, reported in "Meat and Dairy Products," *Standard and Poor's Industrial Surveys,* Section 3, October, 1959, p. 4. This same source reported that consumption of meat per capita rose 3.7 per cent between 1954 and 1958 and that the wholesale price index for meat products rose 18 per cent, or from 91.5 to 107.9, during this same four-year interval.

In the years 1954 to 1958, further shifts in the pattern of meat sales resulted, to the detriment of the limited-line stores and the smaller combination markets. Statistics of the approximate 1958 sale of meat products by major food stores were: [4]

Meat markets	$2.128 billion
Nonsuper combination markets	$4.917 billion
Supermarkets	$7.175 billion

The supermarket became the dominant factor in the sale of meat products, grossing more than 50 per cent of the volume. Small meat markets and combination markets seemed destined to becoming the new "Vanishing American."

SALES OF FRESH FRUIT AND VEGETABLES BY TYPE OF FOOD STORE

(This category includes all items classed by the Census as fresh fruits and vegetables. It does not contain frozen or canned produce.)

For the year 1929 the "big three" in the sale of fresh fruit and vegetables among the major food stores, as indicated in Table 11-4, were: grocery stores without meat (claiming 32.5 per cent of total U.S. fresh fruit and vegetable sales), nonsuper combination markets (34.8 per cent), and fruit and vegetable stores (22 per cent). The country general store also was significant, with about 11 per cent of the produce sales by major food outlets for fruits and vegetables.

In the 25 year interval, produce sales among the food stores increased to over $4 billion. The price level rose; the population in-

[4] The 1954 meat market had average sales of $77,700 per outlet. In 1958 this same market would have its sales raised to $94,600 as a result of a 3.7 per cent increase in the per capita consumption of meat and an 18 per cent rise in the price index of meat products. However, by 1958 there was a decrease in the number of units to 22,500 which, when multiplied by the new average sales per store, gave the $2.128 billion estimate for meat markets.

Total grocery and combination market sales of meat products in 1958 were estimated by the Topics Publishing Company in its yearly study at $12.092 billion. Supermarket sales in 1958 were $28.7 billion, of which 25 per cent were estimated to be in meat products. Thus supermarket sales of meat products were estimated at $7.175 billion. Nonsuper combination market sales of meat products is the difference between total grocery and combination market sales of meat and supermarket sales of meat.

TABLE 11-4

Estimated Fresh Fruit and Vegetable Sales by Major Type of
Food Store Outlet for the Years 1929 and 1954.

	1929		1954	
Type of store	Sales [a] (in millions)	% total	Sales (in millions)	% total
Fruit and vegetable	$ 285	22.0	$ 485 [b]	10.8
Grocery stores without meat	421	32.5	000 [c]	—
Nonsuper combination markets	451	34.8	2,416 [d]	53.7
Supermarkets	0	0	1,598 [d]	35.5
Country general store	139	10.7	— [e]	—
Total	$1,296 [f]	100.0	$4,499 [f]	100.0

[a] U.S. Bureau of the Census, *Retail Distribution—Food Retailing*, No. R-83, Government Printing Office, Washington, D.C., 1934, p. 82.

[b] U.S. Bureau of the Census, *Retail Trade*, No. R-2-2, Government Printing Office, Washington, D.C., 1957, pp. 2–333.

[c] This class has become relatively insignificant, and the data are included under nonsuper combination markets by the Bureau of the Census.

[d] Total grocery and combination market sales of produce for 1954 were estimated at $4.014 billion in *What the Public Spends for Grocery Store Products* (New York: Topics Publishing Co.). Supermarket sales for 1954 were estimated at $15.980 billion in Table 1-2. On the assumption that 10 per cent of a supermarket's sales are in produce, supermarket sales of fruit and vegetables in 1954 were estimated at $1.598 billion. Nonsuper combination market and grocery store sales of produce are the difference between total grocery and combination market sales of produce and the produce sales of supermarkets.

[e] This type of outlet became relatively insignificant in the sale of produce by 1954, with sales estimated well below $100 million.

[f] These totals do not include the sale of fresh fruits and vegetables in other food stores such as delicatessens. Sales through these other channels are considered relatively insignificant.

creased; but most significantly, changes took place in the dietary habits. There was a shift from consumption of bulky, lower-cost produce of the potato type to greater consumption of the higher cost leafy green vegetables and citrus fruits.

The 1954 sales pattern of produce differed substantially from that of 1929. The country general store became almost extinct. Grocery stores without meat had lower fresh fruit and vegetable sales than those of 1929 and had become insignificant in this area.[5] Both non-super combination markets and supermarts gained substantially in absolute and relative positions in the sale of produce during this 25-year era.

In the years 1954 to 1958, further shifts in the pattern of produce sales resulted, to the detriment of the limited-line stores and the smaller combination markets. Statistics on the approximate 1958 sale of produce by the three major food stores were: [6]

Fruit and vegetable stores . . . . $ 510 million
Grocery stores and nonsuper combination
    markets. . . . . $2,020 million
Supermarkets . . . . $2,870 million

The supermarket has become the dominant factor in the sale of fresh fruit and vegetables with more than 50 per cent of the volume. Small fruit and vegetable markets, grocery stores without meat, and small combination markets are suffering substantially from the stepped-up activities of the supermarket in the merchandising of produce in the past few years.

[5] In 1948 there were 154,277 grocery stores without meat that transacted $346 million in sales of produce. These data are from the U.S. Bureau of the Census, *Retail Trade—General Statistics, Part I,* Vol. 1, Government Printing Office, Washington, D.C., 1952, p. 104. By 1954 the number of grocery stores without meat dwindled to an estimated 119,000 units, according to *Progressive Grocer.*

[6] The 1954 fresh fruit and vegetable market had an average sales volume of $37,000. In 1958 this same market would have its sales raised to $42,500 as a result of a 15 per cent increase in the value of produce consumed at retail prices during this four-year interval, as reported by Topics Publishing Company in its annual reports on *What the Public Spends for Grocery Store Products.* However, by 1958 there was a decrease in the number of units to 12,000 which, when multiplied by the new average sales per store, gave the $510 million estimate for fruit and vegetable markets.

Total grocery and combination market sales of produce in 1958 were estimated by the Topics Publishing Company in its yearly study at $4,890 million. Supermarket sales in 1958 were $28.7 billion, of which 10 per cent were estimated to be in produce. Thus supermarket sales of fresh fruits and vegetables were estimated at $2,870 million. Nonsuper combination market and grocery store sales of produce are the difference between total grocery and combination market sales of produce and supermarket sales of fresh fruits and vegetables.

SALES OF CONFECTIONERY PRODUCTS
BY TYPE OF FOOD STORE

(Included in the category of confectionery products are bar candy, gum, packaged confections, bulk candy, candy specialties, and nuts.)

Although candy and confections can be bought in many types of retail establishments, the custom of the 1920's was to buy them largely in the little neighborhood candy store. In 1929 confectionery stores transacted 67 per cent of all confectionery sales in the food store group and 45 per cent of the total $512 million sales retailed by both food and nonfood outlets.[7] The nonfood trio of restaurants, drugstores, and variety shops also was significant in the retailing of confections.

But from 1929 to 1954 many changes in the marketing of confections resulted in taking more and more of the candy sales away from the specialty confectionery store. The confectionery group suffered a 68 per cent reduction in the number of outlets in 1954, compared with the number in 1929.[8] Dietary changes over the 25-year interim influenced the purchase of confectionery products; per capita consumption increased only from 15.7 to 16.1 lb between 1929 and 1954.[9] Retail dollar sales rose with the growth of population and with an increase in the average price of confections from 20.5 cents to 37.5 cents per pound during this same interval.[10] There was, however, an important change in the type of confections produced, namely, a shift to the branded, prepackaged candy bar. These nickel and dime bars together with gum and related items were regarded as convenience goods and were given wide distribution in a variety of new outlets. Vending machines became large sellers of confections. Theaters discovered additional revenue from the sale of con-

---

[7] U.S. Bureau of the Census, *Retail Distribution—Food Retailing*, No. R-83, Government Printing Office, Washington, D.C., 1934, pp. 82–86.

[8] See Table 10-1.

[9] U.S. Department of Commerce, *Confectionery Sales and Distribution*, Government Printing Office, Washington, D.C., 1957, p. 49.

[10] *Ibid.*

fections. The small candy store next to the theater became a rare phenomenon.

By 1954 three new outlets for confections, namely, vending machines, theaters, and supermarkets, transacted a total volume larger than the confectionery store, as shown by the data in Table 11-5.

TABLE 11-5

Sales of Confections by Certain Major Retail
Outlets for the Years 1929 and 1954.

Outlet	1929 * (in millions)	1954 (in millions)
Confectionery stores	$230	$568 †
Grocery stores and nonsuper combination markets	87	177 ‡
Supermarkets	—	240 ‡
Vending machines	—	165 §
Theaters	—	160 ¶

* U.S. Bureau of the Census, *Retail Distribution—Food Retailing*, No. R-83, Government Printing Office, Washington, D.C., 1934, pp. 82–86.

† U.S. Bureau of the Census, *Retail Trade*, No. R-2-2, Government Printing Office, Washington, D.C., 1957, pp. 2–333.

‡ 1954 supermarket sales were $15,980 billion, as shown by data in Table 1-2. On the assumption that 1.5 per cent of a super's sales are in confections, the 1954 figure for supermarket sales is $240 million. Total grocery and combination market sales were $417 in 1954, according to the Topics Publishing Company. Therefore grocery store and nonsuper combination market sales are $417 million less $240 million supermarket sales, or $177 million.

§ U.S. Bureau of the Census, *Retail Trade Summary Statistics*, Government Printing Office, Washington, D.C., 1957, pp. 1–6.

¶ U.S. Bureau of the Census, *Retail Trade-Selected Service Trades*, Government Printing Office, Washington, D.C., 1957, p. 16.

Since 1954, both supermarkets and vending machines have increased their relative market shares, as have the theaters, which have been aided by the expansion to outdoor movies; yet, the confectionery store group decreased numerically by more than 500 units according to estimates by *Progressive Grocer*. Supermarkets merchandise candies at the check-out counter where they utilize little display space and are ideal as an impulse purchase; supers sell candies in volume at a narrow gross margin and on a low price basis. If a statistic of

1.5 per cent is used to represent candy sales in a supermarket as a percentage of total super volume, the 1958 supermarket industry sold over $400 million in confections and is closing in rapidly on the confectionery store.

SALES OF BAKERY PRODUCTS BY TYPE OF FOOD STORE

(This category of bakery products includes bread, bread products, pastries, doughnuts, and related items. It does not contain crackers, packaged cookies, and pretzels.)

The principal outlet for the $614 million food store volume of bakery products in 1929 was the neighborhood bake shop (with 31.4 per cent of U.S. sales of baked goods), followed closely by the combination markets (30.7 per cent) and grocery stores without meat (26.2 per cent). These statistics are found in Table 11-6. The figures do not separately list house-to-house sales of bakery products; these are estimated to have been negligible during this period (well under 5 per cent of the total bakery product sales in food stores) although their importance to the industry in recent years has increased.[11]

During the interval between 1929 and the 1950's, there was a decided shift from baking at home to the purchase of store products.[12] This was attributed to women's demand for greater convenience in the preparation and serving of food. This change in buying habits, the population increase, and the rise in the price level of bakery products more than compensated for the decrease in per capita consumption of bakery goods.[13] Major food store sales of bakery products, reported in Table 11-7, increased substantially in this period. However, the bake shops were able to prosper and had sales rocket-

---

[11] This estimate was made in an interview on March 1, 1954, by Charles Slater, Research Economist, Bakery Industry Study conducted at Northwestern University.

[12] Charles Slater, "Statistical History of the Baking Industry," *Baking Industry,* Vol. 97, no. 1219, April 12, 1952, p. 266.

[13] *Ibid.*

TABLE 11-6

Estimated Bakery Product Sales by Major Type of Food Store Outlet for the Years 1929 and 1954.

	1929		1954	
Type of store	Sales *a* (in millions)	% total	Sales (in millions)	% total
Bakery products	$170	31.4	$ 862 *b*	29.6
Grocery without meat	142	26.2	000 *c*	
Nonsuper combination markets	166	30.7	1,343 *d*	45.9
Supermarkets	0	0	719 *d*	24.5
Country general store	63	11.7	000 *e*	—
	$541 *f*	100.0	$2,924 *f*	100.0

a U.S. Bureau of the Census, *Retail Distribution—Food Retailing,* No. R-83, Government Printing Office, Washington, D.C., 1934, p. 86.

b U.S. Bureau of the Census, *Retail Trade,* No. R-2-2, Government Printing Office, Washington, D.C., 1957, pp. 2–333.

c This class has become relatively insignificant, and therefore the data are included under nonsuper combination markets by the Bureau of the Census.

d Total grocery and combination markets sales of bakery products for 1954 were estimated at $2.062 billion in *What the Public Spends for Grocery Store Products* (New York: Topics Publishing Co.). Supermarket sales for 1954 were estimated at $15.980 billion in Table 1-2. On the assumption that 4.5 per cent of a supermarket's sales are in bakery goods, supermarket sales of bakery items in 1954 were estimated at $719 million. Nonsuper combination market and grocery store sales of bakery products are the difference between total grocery and combination market sales of baked goods and the bakery sales of supermarkets.

e This type of outlet became relatively insignificant in the sale of bakery items by 1954 with sales estimated well below $100 million.

f These totals do not include the sale of bakery products in other food stores such as delicatessens and home delivery. Sales through these other channels are considered relatively small.

ing to $862 million. The supermarket by 1954 also became a major factor in this field by capturing 26.5 per cent of the volume for baked goods. Country stores, grocery stores without meat, and the small combination markets appear to have suffered substantially because of the supermarket.

In the years 1954 to 1958, further shifts in the pattern of sales for bakery products resulted, to the detriment of the smaller combination markets and even to some extent in the relative position of the limited-line bake shops. Statistics on the approximate 1958 sale of bakery goods by the three major food stores were: [14]

Bakery shops	$ 981 million
Grocery stores and nonsuper combination markets	$1,120 million
Supermarkets	$1,292 million

The supermarket became the dominant factor in the sale of baked goods in 1958 with approximately 38 per cent of the volume transacted by the major outlets. Supermarkets intensified activities in this area inasmuch as a growing number of chains reached sufficient size to manufacture and market their own packaged bakery products. These items were sold under the chain brand as a good value in terms of price, size, and quality, and thus attracted shoppers. This policy of merchandising by stressing good value of the frequently purchased baked goods has overcome to some extent the desire on the part of the consumer to purchase oven-fresh products at or near the point of manufacture. Thus baked goods form an integral part of marketing strategy by a super and offer an important source of profit to the integrated firm of proper size. Supermarket activities in this area also have intensified competition with the large bakery manufacturers who market packaged goods regionally or nationally.

[14] The 1954 bake shop had an average sales volume of $45,000. In 1958 this same market would have its sales raised to $53,000 by an 18 per cent increase in the value of bakery products consumed at retail prices during this four year interval as reported by Topics Publishing Company in its annual reports on *What the Public Spends for Grocery Store Products.* However, by 1958 there was a decrease in the number of units to 18,500 which, when multiplied by the new average sales per store, gave the $981 million estimate for bakery product stores.

Total grocery and combination market sales of bakery products in 1958 were estimated by the Topic Publishing Company in its yearly study at $2.412 billion. Supermarket sales in 1958 were $28.7 billion, of which 4.5 per cent were estimated to be in baked goods. Thus supermarket sales of bakery products were estimated at $1.292 billion. Nonsuper combination market and grocery store sales of baked goods are the difference between total grocery and combination market sales of bakery products and supermarket sales of baked goods.

SALES OF CANNED GOODS AND GROCERY ITEMS
BY GROCERY STORES AND COMBINATION MARKETS

The term *grocery items* has been used as a catch-all classification.
Its definition has been complicated and subject to change by the
wide assortment of food and nonfood lines added by the grocery
stores and combination markets. The items listed in this classification are found in Table 11-2.

A variety of retail stores today handles canned goods and grocery
items. However, only the major outlets for the years 1929 and 1958
are contained in the data of Table 11-7. In 1929 the grocery stores
without meat were the major retailers of canned goods and grocery
items. From then until 1958, the grocery store without meat suffered

TABLE 11-7

Sales of Grocery Product Items by Major Food
Store Outlets for the Years 1929 and 1958.

Type of outlet	1929 Sales * (in billions)	% total	1958 Sales † (in billions)	% total
Grocery stores without meat	$2.853	54.9	000 ‡	—
Nonsuper combination markets	2.347	45.1	$ 6.531	37.9
Supermarkets	0	0	10.659	62.1
Total	$5.200	100.0	$17.190	100.0

* U.S. Bureau of the Census, *Retail Distribution—Food Retailing*, No. R-83,
Government Printing Office, Washington, D.C., p. 82.

† Total grocery and combination market sales of grocery items for 1958 were
estimated at $17.190 billion in *What the Public Spends for Grocery Store Prod-
ucts* (New York: Topics Publishing Co.). Supermarket sales for 1958 were estimated at $28.7 billion in Table 1-2. From Table 11-2, grocery items are repre-
sented as 37.14 per cent of total supermarket sales. This percentage applied to
total supermarket sales furnished the $10.659 billion estimate for supermarkets.
Nonsuper combination market and grocery store sales of grocery items are the
difference between total sales of $17.190 billion and supermarket sales of
$10.659 billion.

‡ This class has become relatively insignificant as to volume, and the data are
included under nonsuper combination markets by the Bureau of the Census.

a severe loss, in relative numbers and volume, to both the nonsuper combination market and the supermarket. Again, the shift in buying habits, price competition from more efficient marketers of food, and the ability of the large multiline outlet to spread overhead costs over a wider line enabled supermarkets to attain major status in this area.

SALES OF NONFOOD PRODUCTS IN GROCERY STORES AND COMBINATION MARKETS

Nonfood products in grocery stores and combination markets do not include food or food products for consumption. But the classification also excludes commonly carried items such as soap, cleanser, household supplies, and paper products.

Growth of Nonfoods in Supers

Supermarkets were not the innovators of the sale of nonfood merchandise among the food stores. In the 1920's some combination markets handled nonfoods before the supers were in existence. H. C. Bohack in 1929 operated a chain of 512 service grocery stores which sold razor blades, drug items, and even automobile tires.[15] However, the tendency to scramble merchandise among the grocery stores and combination markets in the 1920's was not common. In fact, the 1929 retail census did not have a separate category for nonfoods.

The early supermarkets concentrated on merchandising food products. During World War II, supers added nonfoods in order to supplement their reduced lines of food items. In 1949 nonfood items continued to be no novelty to supermarkets, but health and beauty aids were the only major items universally stocked.[16] Since then, sales of nonfoods have increased steadily in supermarkets through broadening the product line until they have currently reached about 5 per cent of total sales.[17] The middle half of the companies report-

[15] "Diversified Lines Give Bohack Chain $60,000 Yearly Unit Sales," *Sales Management*, XXIX, no. 10, March 8, 1930, p. 441.

[16] Curt Kornblau, *Facts and Figures About Non-Foods in Super Markets* (Chicago: Super Market Institute, 1959), p. 1.

[17] *Ibid.*, p. 4.

ing volume statistics to the Super Market Institute in 1958 achieved nonfood sales between 3 and 8 per cent of their total sales. While there is no clear-cut pattern in the proportion of nonfood sales to total sales according to volume groups, the largest companies with sales of more than $50 million average the highest nonfood sales; these were reported at 6.3 per cent of total volume. One of the major exponents of nonfoods among the giants is Grand Union Company which in recent years has opened a series of combined supermarkets and junior department stores under the same roof.

The two principal nonfood lines generally carried by supermarkets, however, are health and beauty aids and housewares. Statistics on the major nonfood lines carried by supermarkets in 1958 are shown in Table 11-8 along with the relative percentage of supers carrying these products. In addition, the major source of supply for each of the 21 classifications is listed. The method of procurement differs widely for the various kinds of products.

Much diversity exists among individual operators as to the extent of nonfood lines carried. In order to conform with supermarket operating techniques, normally merchandise must: [18]

1. Have rapid turnover.
2. Require little space.
3. Need no technical selling or readily lend itself to self-service.
4. Have no high-styling of goods.
5. Lend itself to simplified purchasing and reordering, since the supermarket operator is not normally an expert in the wide line of nonfoods.

For the smaller concerns, the rack jobber has simplified the problem of merchandising items that do not conform strictly to the above prerequisites. Larger companies are becoming strong advocates of separate nonfood departments. Approximately 27 per cent of all supermarkets have a separate department with at least one full-time employee in charge; the majority of supers with separate depart-

[18] Milton Alexander, "Where We Stand in Non-Food Merchandising," *Progressive Grocer*, XXXI, no. 10, October, 1952, p. 197.

TABLE 11-8 *

Estimated Percentages of Supermarkets That Handle Nonfood Lines
Together with Major Source of Supply for the Year 1958.

	% super markets handling	Typical number of items	% Major source of supply		
			Rack jobber	Whole-saler	Manu-facturer
Health and beauty aids	98	325	52	31	17
Housewares	87	200	78	16	6
Women's hosiery	81	10	48	25	27
Stationery	74	25	48	34	18
Children's books	73	35	55	29	16
Magazines (general line)	71	75	55	42	3
Glassware	69	40	43	20	37
Baby needs	68	25	47	34	19
Toys	66	75	80	13	7
Men's socks	64	10	59	21	20
Pet supplies	63	50	73	20	7
Phonograph records	62	75	87	9	4
Hardware	58	75	73	22	5
Garden supplies	58	25	24	43	33
Children's socks	55	10	63	19	18
Underwear	47	12	60	20	20
Photographic supplies	37	10	42	50	8
Greeting cards	35	150	56	18	26
Notions and sundries	33	50	60	30	10
Other soft goods	33	35	61	19	20
Electrical appliances	11	20	31	54	15

* Curt Kornblau, *Facts and Figures About Non-Foods in Super Markets* (Chicago: Super Market Institute, 1959), p. 6.

ments are larger concerns.[19] The titles given to the nonfood specialist include nonfood buyer, nonfood supervisor, and director of nonfood division.

[19] Curt Kornblau, *op. cit.*, p. 7.

Impact of Nonfoods in Supers

Generally the supermarket exploited nonfoods ahead of small grocery stores and combination markets. Therefore the sales penetration by the supermart in nonfoods has been at the expense of other than food store retailers. The success of the supermarket in these areas resulted in the grocery store and small combination market imitating the supers in an effort to increase sales and profits. Data in Table 11-9 indicate the extent to which all grocery stores and

TABLE 11-9 *

Sales of Nonfood Items in Grocery Stores and
Combination Markets, in Dollars and as a Percentage
of Total Consumption for the Year 1958.

Product	Sales (in millions)	% total domestic consumption †
Tobacco products	$1,774	29
Packaged medications	220	23
Health aids	80	26
Oral hygiene products	182	48
Hair products	171	40
Shaving products	84	38
Cosmetics and lotions	52	16
Other toiletries	34	26
Greeting cards	10	3
Magazines and newspapers	60	3
Toys	21	1
Phonograph records	50	12
Housewares	265	—

* *What the Public Spends for Grocery Store Products* (New York: Topics Publishing Co., 1959).

† Total domestic consumption includes all consumption, even at the farm level, or by institutions, restaurants, or government, at the value of retail store prices.

combination markets, including supers, have invaded the nonfood field. Tobacco products and certain health and beauty aids almost universally are distributed through grocery and combination stores.

However, the activities of the small merchant are dwarfed by the supermarket with its large and diversified assortment of nonfoods.

Specific merchandising practices of supermarkets in the nonfood area and the extent of penetration in some lines can be assessed. The Toilet Goods Association reported in 1957 that supermarkets had captured 20.3 per cent of the retail business in toilet goods.[20] Drugstores still were the main outlet, with 28.6 per cent of the sales; but the supermarket has been making inroads on this lead. Furthermore, these figures are distorted since they include high-priced perfume normally not handled in supers. Margins for toilet goods in supers range from 25 to 40 per cent, with an average of about 30 per cent, and turnover ranges from 12 to 25 times per year. Total 1957 sales of toilet goods in supers were $600 million.

Dollarwise, apparel has taken over the No. 3 position in non-food supermarket sales; the most important item is nylon hosiery.[21] The markup for apparel averages from 30 per cent to 35 per cent. The bulk of the merchandise is sold on impulse and is priced at $1.00 or less. Purchases are made largely from the manufacturer, and many of the items are branded and presold through advertising. In 1957 supermarkets sold $240 million in women's hosiery, or 33 per cent of total industry sales of $720 million.[22] More than 85 per cent of the larger supers carry hosiery, which sells on impulse; hosiery is conveniently displayed, attractively packaged, requires a small amount of floor space, and turns over rapidly (up to 25 times per year). With regard to complete lines of apparel, few stores have attained the position of Grand Union, which has at least three specialized apparel buyers and in some stores has up to 14,000 sq ft of space devoted to nonfoods, mostly clothing. The new Grand Union stores for the most part are junior department stores along with the food departments.

The 1957 retail sale of cigarettes was about $3 billion; of this

---

[20] *Supermarket News*, May 5, 1958, p. 54.
[21] *Ibid.*, March 10, 1958, p. 58.
[22] *Ibid.*, March 31, 1958, p. 36.

total, 60 per cent, or $1.8 billion, was sold in supers.[23] Cigarettcs are ideal for supermarkets since they have a turnover of as high as 52 times per year, require small display space, and need little advertising or promotion since they are presold by the manufacturer and sell in volume by the carton. Disadvantages of cigarettes are that pilferage is high, markup is low, and recently so many lines are needed that increased display space is required. However, supermarket operators have found cigarettes an ideal product to attract both men and women shoppers.

Housewares, including pots, kitchen gadgets, and brooms and mops, in 1957 had supermarket sales of $385 million, whereas in 1951 they amounted to only $16.5 million.[24] Houseware retailing is considered specialized merchandising, and many operators are willing to use service jobbers and pay slightly higher prices to get service and consigned merchandise.

Hardware items carried by supers range from 125 to 950 items.[25] These mainly include convenience goods purchased primarily by women, such as batteries, light bulbs, extension cords, paint, brushes, and small tools. These items, which carry from 25 to 40 per cent margin, have been growing in importance each year since 1950; however, they are still a relatively small portion of industry sales.

Phonograph records sold by supers in 1957 totaled $40 million or 10 per cent of the total industry sales of $400 million.[26] Records are handled primarily through rack jobbers. On the average, only 5 sq ft of space is needed for display, the records carry a 35 per cent margin, and turnover of as high as 30 times per year has been experienced. Pilferage has been low. The main difficulty is that a recording may be a hit one day and not sell the next. That is why rack jobbers are the major supplier in this field.

Toy sales in 1957 were $1.25 billion nationally, of which supermarkets transacted 2 per cent or $25 million.[27] Supermarkets were

[23] *Ibid.*, April 14, 1958, p. 52.
[24] *Ibid.*, April 21, 1958, p. 34.
[25] *Ibid.*, May 26, 1958, p. 80.
[26] *Ibid.*, June 2, 1958, p. 50.
[27] *Ibid.*, July 14, 1958, p. 42.

well behind variety stores and department stores, which transacted about 24 and 23 per cent, respectively, of toy sales. Supers have on the average devoted less than 5 sq ft of display space to toys. This display space is expanded slightly at Christmas time when half of the volume is attained. The best sellers are plastic items selling under $1.00, with the most important price line being 39 cents. On the average a super carries approximately 75 items procured primarily through rack jobbers. Whereas the sale of toys has experienced steady growth, supers have not merchandised toys effectively; and this line remains a small item in total supermarket sales and total industry sales of toys.

Cameras and sports equipment are stocked by relatively few supermarkets; only the biggest department store type of super offers a selection in these categories.[28] The reasons for this include low turnover, high price, seasonal sales, and need for many items to make a complete line. Only two photographic items provide an exception; these are film and flash bulbs, which enjoy from 33 to 40 per cent margins, require little display space at the check-out counter, and are ideal for impulse purchases.

Most supers have stayed clear of appliances.[29] Those that have succeeded in this area have done so with small items such as radios, toasters, and blenders, which sell for under $50. The reasons for not handling this type of merchandise are (1) too much display space is needed, (2) a large number of items must be carried, (3) the appliances are bulky to display, (4) discount houses offer strong competition and (5) prices are too high to qualify as an impulse item. For the same reasons, few supers have been successful with power lawn mowers, auto accessories, and large garden items.

SUMMARY

The supermarket has become the dominant factor in every division of food store retailing. The super reigns supreme over limited-line stores in

[28] *Ibid.*, July 21, 1958, p. 30.
[29] *Ibid.*, July 28, 1958, p. 37.

such areas as fresh fruits and vegetables, bakery products, fresh meats, sea food, and grocery items. Supermarkets currently gross more than 50 per cent of the retail food store sales of meat, produce, and grocery items. Even the delicatessens have felt the impact of the supermarket, which has opened delicatessen departments in neighborhoods where products of that nature are sold readily. Supers are the major retail channel for such diverse items as cigarettes, ice cream, canned fruit, bread, soap, and bananas.

imp. *

In the nonfoods area, the supermarket, with its scrambled merchandising techniques, has become a nightmare to other retailers such as drugstores, variety shops, and department stores. The supermarket industry yearly continues to invade new areas in an effort to exploit customer traffic to the fullest. Products that are attractively packaged, require small display space, are relatively inexpensive, are purchased on impulse, carry good margins, experience a high turnover, and are subject to frequent purchase have become "must items" for the supermarket. The trend toward wider lines of nonfoods continues unabated, especially by the larger supers. Approximately 27 per cent of the supers now have separate nonfoods departments under the management of a nonfoods specialist who merchandises such items as apparel, toys, books, household supplies, phonograph records, and health and beauty aids. Currently about 5 per cent of a supermarket's sales are in nonfood lines; but the expansion in nonfoods is expected to grow over the years as the stores become larger.

To increase net profit margin.

Normal Sale of Supermkt. goods

+ 1) Non-Foods - Houneware, hardware, clothing, glassware, etc.
2) Delicatessen
3) Specialties

12 | MANAGERIAL POLICY AND PERSPECTIVE

INTRODUCTION

The preceding eleven chapters traced the development of the supermarket industry, examined external factors and internal policies that influenced its growth, and measured the impact of the supermarket movement on the food store industry. This final chapter sets forth industry trends and conclusions of this study written from a managerial viewpoint. The major topics to be considered are the dynamic nature of the industry, the position of the supermarket in its growth cycle, the trend toward "bigness," organizational concepts, the science of decision making in management, the use of research, the relationship of profit to volume, fixed expense and promotion, merchandising policies, store operations, financing growth, deterrents to progress, and the illusiveness of good will. The purpose of these discussions is to facilitate the making of present and future policy and decisions.

DYNAMIC NATURE OF THE SUPERMARKET

Management must realize that change is the cornerstone on which a successful supermarket operation is based. If management stops its quest for a better way of merchandising food and related products in line with the desires of the consumer, then growth will cease and the supermarket will become just another mature retailer.

The record of this industry is one of astute and capable management. No other segment of retailing has demonstrated greater dynamism in the past 30 years. The super, a marketing innovation, came into national prominence because it pursued an unusual practice with regard to the sale of food store products. It featured large volume, narrow margins, and reduced expenses through self-service and a variety of other economies. In a period of depression it established itself as a low-cost marketer of food as compared with existing food store retailers, and it passed on some of its savings in lower prices to the consumer.

Once the movement started amidst much controversial publicity, it continued its dynamic policy of constant change. With the rise in national income, supers switched from the "cheapy" form to a better-equipped, better-located and better-housed type of market. During World War II when food rationing was in effect, the supermarkets added nonfoods.

Supers continued to capture more of the business in older, densely populated areas where the price appeal was important. But in the postwar period, they followed the trend to the suburbs and stressed locations in these new areas where purchasing power was higher and opportunity for growth was greater. These new units featured such customer services as parking facilities, air conditioning, music, and rest rooms.

When the trend toward one-stop shopping developed, supers exploited this preference to the fullest with their wide lines of merchandise. As new products were introduced, supers in general had more facilities to handle them than the small grocer or combination market. The postwar trend of supermarkets was to build larger stores to handle greater varieties of stock.

These changes increased both gross margins and expenses of the supermarket. Margins were forced upward because there was a tendency to expand into wide lines, including nonfoods, which earned a higher markup than grocery items. Gross margins also increased as a result of higher expenses because of the trend to "trade up" the store and to increase customer services. In addition to the rise in expenses attributed to improving customer shopping facilities, there was an increase in the percentage of sales expended for salaries and wages.

The supermarket management attempted to combat this rise in wages with an increase in self-service. The wider use of self-service was in line with the wishes of the customers; and the trend towards complete self-service continues to grow.

Chain brands, manufacturing and food processing activities, and prepackaging are more recent areas of investigation by management. And the future offers promise for additional change for more effective and efficient marketing that ranges from electronic checkout stands to spirally designed stores.

More than any other type of food store, the super has adapted its operations and policies to meet changes in consumer buying habits. Management has been aware of economic trends and has shaped operations accordingly. The small stores frequently had neither the finances nor the business acumen to profit by the changing times. The ability of management generally to experiment, to adapt, and to take advantage of the circumstances must be continued if this industry is to grow in the future. Management of a specific supermart operation that lacks vision in setting forth its objectives and also the means and the ability to attain these objectives will cause that concern to become just another mature retailer.

POSITION IN ITS GROWTH CYCLE

The record of the supermarket industry is a story of growth. Normally an industry passes through four phases in its pattern of development or growth cycle. These stages include (1) the period of experimentation, (2) the period of rapid growth into the social fabric, (3) the period when growth continues but at a diminishing rate, and (4) the period of maturity or stability.

The supermarket, an innovation, invaded a mature or relatively stable business—the sale of food for home consumption—which is more or less geared to population growth. And in a short span of 30 years it revolutionized the food business and related industries. Currently the supermarket transacts about 65 per cent of grocery and combination market sales and 57 per cent of all food stores sales. While the industry currently continues to grow and command a larger share of the market, the rate of growth—not the absolute amount—tends to decrease. This would place the supermarket in the third stage of its asymptotic growth, but at no time to date has this industry evidenced maturity.

Underlying reasons for past and future growth are found in (1) operating practices and techniques, (2) the favorable economic and social climate in which to operate, (3) the basic philosophy of management, and (4) the composition of the industry. The operating techniques developed by management stand as a monument to retailing. The external factors of new developments from research, suburbia, and prosperity show no evidence of basic change in the immediate future. The original philosophy of management to seek a better way to market food and related products has remained in effect throughout. Like the New York Yankess in baseball, management has never stopped winning and will continue under the spirit of "success breeds success." Many grass-root operators—pioneers and innovators who were imbued with the desire to create and who fought their way to the top—are still with the industry. Many of these have developed large, even gigantic, operations. Others who have since joined the movement, including many chains, learned there is no such term as "status quo" in this field. Those who could not stand the pace any longer have left the industry. Inasmuch as there are advantages to large-scale operation in this field, it is no problem to sell an operation profitably to a larger competitor. This trend of "acquire or expire" will continue.

Chains have now come to dominate the supermarket industry; and yet no one concern ranks supreme. Competition prevails everywhere. The major battle is no longer a struggle among segments of the food distribution area; rather, it is an intra-industry battle among supermarkets. The small markets and limited-line stores are caught in the cross fire of supermarket operators who vie among themselves for new products, locations, and ideas to secure some marketing advantage. Intensive competition has kept and will continue to keep the industry alert. The growth in the foreseeable future will continue independently of the increase in population and in personal disposable income. The industry will continue in phase three of the growth cycle in the era of the "sizzling sixties."

While the industry as a whole is in phase three of the growth cycle, all members are not necessarily in this stage. All concerns are not experiencing the same rate of growth; some individual companies evidence maturity. Managements of individual concerns should assess their past rate of progress, set forth objectives, and plan for the future to attain these goals whatever they may be. In recent years, chains with 100 to 1,000 units as a class experienced the greatest absolute and relative growth. Concerns with one or a limited number of stores will continue to experience a more fluctuating pattern of development since the opening of one new super influences operations significantly. But the small members of the industry are not growing at the accelerated rate of the medium-sized chains and are becoming the more stable members of the industry. This also is the case of the largest industry members who must watch expansion closely, not for lack of resources, markets, facilities, and ability but for fear of governmental interference.

SUPERMARKET TREND TOWARD "BIGNESS"

The supermarket industry today is basically one of big business. Management must realize that forces within the industry no longer favor "large" but "larger" scale operation. This trend toward "bigness" reflects the investment in each store and the size of the concern that owns and operates the markets.

The "cheapy" supermarket investment was at a minimum. These stores rented abandoned buildings and used flimsy fixtures. Since then the investment in a supermarket has spiraled, particularly in the postwar period because of the trends toward (1) larger stores, (2) larger inventories, (3) more and better equipment, and (4) holdings in real estate. Larger stores are needed to handle the increased lines of merchandise and enable better display. Larger inventories reflect the growing lines handled including nonfoods and the host of convenience food products. Additional equipment is required to handle frozen foods, self-service meats, and food preparation and processing. Many pioneer locations require the erection of buildings and the development of parking lots. Since rented facilities are not always available, supers erect many of their own buildings or arrange for financing them in this postwar era of expansion. Today a modern supermarket requires a substantial investment at one location. The degree of risk inherent in pioneering a new location with a substantial investment limits entry into the industry to the large operator. And the long-range trend continues toward larger and better equipped markets with wider lines of merchandise.

Whereas the supermarket was an innovation of independent merchants, the industry received its main impetus when the chains joined the movement. By 1958 the local, regional, and national chains dominated the supermarket field with 67 per cent of the stores and 69 per cent of the sales. And these chains continue to capture more of the volume and to operate the larger markets. These trends will continue in the near future.

Management must realize that the industry has certain definite advantages for the big operator. In financing, supers have used retained profits as an important source of funds for expansion; yet, outside capital to a large degree also has been needed. The larger concerns have been able to acquire capital (sell stock or debentures) on a more advantageous arrangement since the degree of risk inherent in pioneering a new location or withstanding the inroads of an encroacher in a given market can be minimized by geographical diversification of the outlets. "Bigness" also has certain operational advantages in such areas as buying, warehousing, advertising, and promotion. The low, fixed expense of a supermarket accentuates territorial encroachment by the diversified large enterprise. Furthermore, horizontal and vertical integration practices benefit the larger concerns. When chains acquire a sufficient number of outlets as a result of horizontal expansion, they find it advantageous to integrate vertically by assuming some of the wholesale activities. Horizontal integration as a result of acquiring existing markets of smaller competitors furnishes the needed outlets rapidly and eliminates the risk and the increased costs of an untried location. After a chain attains a sufficient number of outlets, additional vertical integration is feasible by entry into manufacturing and food-processing activities. The chains are able to incorporate their own branded products in their marketing strategy in this highly competitive field where price and value are vital; and the manufactured products also can become an important source of profits to firms of the proper size in terms of retail volume.

The wave of horizontal integration that has taken place in recent years primarily through acquisitions is creating a growing class of medium-sized chains that wield a potent force in buying and selling operations. Furthermore, these medium-sized chains have branched out into manufacturing and food-processing activities that range from coffee to store fixtures. Manufacturers of food products, even the national advertisers with widely known brands, are finding growing competition with chain brands arising from vertical integration; and this trend is expected to continue.

The largest member of the industry, the Great Atlantic and Pacific Tea Company, for years was singled out by the federal government for antitrust action as a result of its broad line of manufactured products and its 4,500 plus outlets. Two other major concerns, the Kroger Company and the National Tea Company, recently have been charged with violation of the antimerger law resulting from extensive acquisitions. In the Kroger compaint, the Federal Trade Commission charged that 20 per cent of the supermarket concerns now transact 72 per cent of the sales. While these actions may deter the largest members of the industry from aggressive expansion, the smaller members (but large in their own right) continue on their merry pace of integration, both horizontal and vertical. The extent to which this industry becomes one of large-size chains depends solely on the policing action of the federal government.

Future possibilities for this industry that make for "bigness" are mergers of supermarkets with appliance, variety, drug, and department stores. This would enable expansion through mergers without running afoul of the antimonopoly provisions of the Clayton Act. Possibly, supermarket chains could be merged with discount houses.

Or the pattern established by the Grand Union Company in developing its Grand-Way stores may offer expansion in the junior department store area. All these developments point toward "bigness."

Individual company management must think in terms of "bigness." This must be inherent in its policy and perspective. Management must cope with these trends toward horizontal and vertical integration and all the ramifications of reorganization. It can join the movement in its own manner or sell out at the best possible price. It is difficult to swim upstream or fight against statistical odds favoring the opposition. Forces are marshaled in favor of "bigness," both in size of stores and size of concerns.

ORGANIZATION CONCEPTS

Brain-Storming

Management has come more and more to realize that "bigness" leads to complications in the operation of a supermarket. This fact of life requires that an organization—a team—be developed to achieve with the minimum of effort the goals of the enterprise, which, whatever they may be, are set forth by top management. Everyone in authority must know, endorse, and be imbued with these objectives. Otherwise friction, confusion, and disagreement can render ineffective the organization and operation of the business.

Top management of a large-scale operation must set forth the major functions of the business required to achieve the desired goals. For example, the selling operation is a major function in a supermarket; the number of individuals in the chain of command depends upon the size and scope of the concern. The chain of command for a large supermarket company runs from the president to the vice-president in charge of operations. Then it passes to the district managers and finally to the store managers from their respective district supervisors. In turn, the department managers in a super are responsible to the store manager, and the crews report to the department managers. Throughout, this organization must center responsibility with certain individuals; and it is imperative to give these individuals the specific authority that goes with their assigned responsibility and to make compensation accordingly. A staff of experts is required to offer technical information and assistance to the managers and other executives in the line operation. These staff members—experts in such areas as research and development, merchandising, personnel, advertising, promotion, and home economics —facilitate the work of the line executives. Finally a committee of major executives from both staff and line departments (or an outside management-consulting firm) should evaluate the organization to assure proper operation. Every supermarket organization should be subject to frequent review.

There has been a trend in the past decade in the supermarket industry toward this type of line-and-staff organization and away from the functional kind in which, for example, the store produce department managers in a division are responsible to a district or headquarters specialized produce manager. This suggested basic pattern of line-and-staff organization has been used successfully by large organizations. It centers the responsibility in the store, and it enables the market to operate under a line authority as a team effort. The supermarket is a big business, and management must have an organization geared for big business. The organization chart should be made available to all personnel so that enterprising employees can see avenues for advancement.

SCIENCE OF DECISION MAKING IN MANAGEMENT

Management problems of any business become more complex as the enterprise becomes larger and more diversified. Supermarket management faces added difficulties in decision making which result from the wide geographical dispersement of its operating units: that is, stores, warehouses, processing plants, and factories. Furthermore, the logistics problems of handling a large physical volume of bulky, diversified merchandise which is sold on a narrow margin of profit become exceedingly complex. This is no industry of apron-stringed men with strong backs. Supermarket concerns require capable management personnel who are able to make proper decisions at all levels of the organization. Decentralized management is essential.⟩

Decisions basically fall into three categories, namely: (1) policy, (2) operating, and (3) crisis.[1] Policy decisions as to the broad objectives of the concern, such as extent of integration or general product line, are set forth by the board of directors. Lesser policy decisions involving personnel or purchasing are made by the key executives in the concern. Operating decisions relating to the daily activities of the company, such as the purchase of a particular product or the pricing of an item, should be made by store managers and department heads to allow for maximum flexibility in taking advantage of local conditions. Crisis decisions are those made on the spur of the moment to solve an immediate problem without regard to existing policy or due to the lack of policy. These can be made at any level of management, but normally they appear at the operational level. Too often the danger of crisis decisions made to solve particular problems lies in the fact that they become company policy.⟩

Local management is confronted with the problem of making more and better operating decisions. These decisions should be predicated on a rational, systematic basis rather than on intuition or experience-based judgment alone. The process of decision making is not a substitute for judgment but is a systematic approach to the solution of problems. For the purposes of analysis, the elements of decision making can be reduced to:

1. Finding the problem
2. Analyzing the problem
3. Developing alternative solutions
4. Selecting the best solution
5. Making the decision effective

For example, consider two supermarkets in the same chain in adjacent trading areas. One store purchases perishables from local

---

[1] These categories were suggested by Dr. Robert Carney, Associate Professor of Management, Georgia Institute of Technology.

farmers and the other from the central warehouse. Friction exists between the two store managers, and there is resentment toward the division manager on the part of the one store manager who follows orders and purchases from the central warehouse. *(Problem Found.)*

The problem can be defined as (1) misinterpretation of policy by either or both local managers, (2) obedience to formal policy by one manager and disregard for it by the other, or (3) failure to include all stores in the policy. Next, in order to develop a solution, an analysis must be made as to what caused these two different practices to exist in the first place. Management must know where to find sufficient information; it must have the ability to draw to- *(Analysis)* gether data and set forth the necessary assumptions. Otherwise a sufficient number of alternatives will not be set forth, and the analysis will be made in too narrow a framework. The analysis must assess the information accurately by assigning the correct weights to the data. For example, if vine-ripened produce in season is demanded by the vast majority of customers of one store and this feature is known to differentiate the particular market and attract customers, then this factor that favors the practice of buying locally may outweigh many minor points favoring central purchasing. *(Alternative Solutions)*

As one solution to this dilemma in produce buying, management could inform all local managers to follow policy as set forth. A second choice would be to have formal policy followed except in special circumstances. Or, if the policy regarding outside purchasing is too rigid and needs to be made flexible, a third solution would be to permit decision making at the operating level. *(Solution)*

Circumstances in each case would determine what the specific solution to the problem should be. It is essential in good decision making that the solution not be made in a vacuum without regard for the human element. The goals of the individuals who will be affected by the choices must be considered. It is also necessary to anticipate the reaction of those affected by the solution selected because, in the final analysis, decisions will be ineffectual unless accepted by those who are to carry them out. Other factors to *(Making decision effective.)*

be considered are the cost, time, personnel, skill, equipment, and resources with which to do the job.⟩

The above problem could have evolved from lack of company over-all policy on outside buying, or it could have resulted from a crisis decision made by a division manager or store manager. This crisis decision may have become a precedent for the one store to follow. Management must organize and operate the concern so as to require the fewest number of crises decisions. Yet, policy should not be so rigid that store managers are prevented from making sound decisions affecting the operation of their respective stores.

USE OF RESEARCH

The small food store operator knows his customers; he can survey his domain daily, ascertain his requirements, and make his decisions on first-hand information.⟨Supermarket management is more re-moved from the customer. The business is larger and more complex, the operation is more widespread and diversified, and competition among the markets is rampant. These factors indicate the growing need in a supermarket for research to furnish reliable data to man-agement for decision making.⟩

Research activities in a supermarket are directed toward market-ing or merchandising functions and operating practices. Frequently the marketing and operating activities in a supermarket are difficult to separate.⟨By definition, marketing research is the gathering, re-cording, and analyzing of all facts about problems relating to the transfer and sale of goods and services from producer to consumer.[2] Operations research is the prediction and comparison of the values, effectiveness, and costs of a set of proposed alternative courses of action involving man-machine systems.[3]⟩Operations research uses a model of the action that has been developed analytically by a logical and, when feasible, mathematical methodology, the values for

---

[2] Harper W. Boyd and Ralph Westfall, *Marketing Research* (Homewood, Illinois: Richard D. Irwin, Inc., 1956), p. 4.

[3] Joseph McCloskey and Florence Trefethen, *Operations Research for Man-agement* (Baltimore: The Johns Hopkins Press, 1954), p. xxiii.

which are derived from past actions or designed operational experiments. While operations research normally has a broad connotation and overlaps the area of marketing research, the technique is used in supermarkets more narrowly to denote logistic problems in the physical movement of merchandise in performing buying, selling, warehousing, delivery, and handling functions.

Marketing research applicable to the supermarket industry includes activities pertaining to (1) markets, (2) products, (3) motivation, (4) internal sales analysis, and (5) advertising and display. Market research includes a study of the characteristics of the customers and their purchasing habits. It also embraces the detailed research needed for new store locations. Prior to sinking a substantial investment in a new outlet or contracting to make rental payments over a long period of years, management must make exhaustive studies of the past, present, and future possibilities of the location. Only too frequently markets have been opened in unsuitable areas. This practice is abetted by promoters who are willing to make deals and concessions to put the land into use and by supermarket operators who are willing to take on an outlet with low, fixed expenses so that a competitor won't get it, even though the location is questionable. Product research measures consumer preference for brands, types of products, packaging, size, and other physical attributes. Motivation studies measure why people buy a particular product or patronize a certain market. The store image in the minds of the customers can be depicted along with psychological attitudes held by consumers as to color and style of markets. Sales analysis furnishes information on the movement of particular products as well as profitability of departments and product lines. Advertising and display research measure the effectiveness of the types and kinds of strategy employed.

Of all the research designs available to perform the various marketing research studies, the experimental method offers supermarket management the most unusual opportunity to collect data as to permit clear and unconfused conclusions as to the correctness of an hypothesis which involves cause-and-effect relationships. The data obtained from experimentation can furnish management vital information for decision making. Supermarket concerns possibly have the best facilities of any business for conducting experimental research in the area of social science. Only those industries engaged in the physical sciences appear more favorably situated to conduct experiments. Supermarket management can use experimentation to check advertising effectiveness, display techniques, product preferences, pricing strategy, and packaging. Even small concerns can use the various experimental methods such as the before-after, the before-after-with-control group, and the after-only-with-control group designs. For example, the operator of only one store can measure for one week the sale of potatoes in the traditional package, introduce a new packaging method for the following week, hold all other factors unchanged, and measure the difference in sales. Consumer panels which can serve as a valuable adjunct to the buying committees should not be restricted to the large companies. To facilitate experimentation, concerns should designate certain stores for the purpose of conducting experimental tests. Necessary facilities for conducting tests can be maintained permanently.

Opportunities for the successful use of operations research exist in supermarkets in the physical movement of goods in all areas. There is only a specific amount of shelf space in a given market; each new item purchased takes its place only at the expense of some other product. Operations research can furnish quantitative aids in determining what to buy and how much to buy. This technique also can facilitate the warehousing and delivery of groceries. For example, one concern revamped its entire delivery system so that selectors at the warehouse loaded the trailers daily, drivers delivered them at night during periods of little traffic, and store managers assigned the correct number of grocery clerks to be available for unloading and stocking shelves on a predetermined morning. Operations research also can be of value in the area of selling by increasing efficiency of personnel in stocking shelves and operating check-out stands. For some concerns, it has led to the establishment of standards by departments for man-hours expended in relation to sales.

Produce and meat departments, for example, need not necessarily have the same ratio of sales to man-hours.

These illustrations indicate the types of opportunities that are available in a supermarket for operations research. The principal contribution of this technique is that it presents to management alternative opportunities or courses of action in quantitative terms. Management can use these data in making decisions.

Product research of the technical type involved in producing an item that will accomplish certain results has been passed on to the manufacturer by the supermarket industry. Expenditures of this type thus do not appear as a cost to the supermarket in performing its functions. Competition for shelf space has been so intense that food manufacturers have been forced to develop a multitude of new and improved products which are marketed in cooperation with supermarket concerns. This research involved in the creation of form utility rightfully belongs to the manufacturer. But, as the supermarket industry becomes more integrated and active in manufacturing, management may have to face the problem of product development and not depend so much on the research accomplishments of other manufacturers as it has in the past. Some compromise has appeared in which supermarkets and food manufacturers have engaged in joint research efforts.

In summary, the larger members of this industry have tended to do most of the research in the areas of marketing and operations. The total amount spent as a percentage of sales has appeared negligible for the industry as a whole. Management of some concerns has rationalized its position on limited research by contending that this activity is not needed, inasmuch as operations are flexible and the market is in constant contact with the consumer. Or, under the guise of research, management has used casual observation to substantiate ideas or concepts. Casual observation is not scientific in its approach because it is not objective, subject to accurate measurement, or conducted exhaustively. Managements of individual concerns must assess the benefits derived from true research versus the cost involved because of the narrow profit margin on which they operate. Money properly spent on research can more than pay for itself in economies of operation and better merchandising.

RELATIONSHIP OF PROFIT TO VOLUME, FIXED EXPENSE, AND PROMOTION

A supermarket is geared by management to transact a large volume on a narrow margin of profit. The industry has flourished even with a relatively low profit margin expressed as a percentage of sales since this rate can reflect a sizable dollar profit when related to a large volume. This concept has been expounded by management throughout as a basic financial tenet.

But, this truism is only a partial answer to the super's financial success. The factor of large variable costs and expenses, or of low, fixed expenses estimated at 6 to 7 per cent of sales, must also be considered as a factor in the profit picture. The low fixed expense of a supermarket and the ability of fixed expense to remain constant over a fairly wide range in sales accentuate the ability of a concern with territorial diversification to invade a new area. Stores for a particular location are planned to transact a certain predetermined present and future volume. The design is such, however, that a super can still operate profitably even though a considerable variation in actual volume from planned sales occurs. The absence of a large fixed expense is a beneficial factor for a store in which sales fail to materialize. On the other hand, the fact that the fixed expense remains constant, even with a considerable increase in sales over normal anticipated volume, benefits the volume-building market. Instead of the 2 to 3 per cent profit before taxes, some stores have earned 5 per cent on sales as a result of a high level of volume. Even though the investment in a new super is sizable, the fact that fixed expenses are low relative to sales is an added inducement to new territory invasion.

For an industry faced with this relationship of profit to volume and to fixed expense, the additional or marginal customer is of considerable importance. The marginal family that spends $1,000 to $1,500 per year in a super must be obtained and retained. The marginal family reflects a sizable increase in profits, both as a percentage of sales and of net worth for a supermarket operating at the normal volume for which it was designed. For example, if local management of a typical super operating at normal volume can induce an additional hundred families to shop regularly at the market, an increase in profits of 1 per cent as a percentage of sales for that market is possible. Retention of the consumer is vital since a loss of a customer can reduce profits just as the addition of one can increase return. This is why trading stamps and other promotional devices have met with such wide adoption by the industry. In the near future, increased competition will make for even wider use of promotional devices. Management easily could consider funds spent on continuous promotion as a short-term capital investment on which earnings now and in the very near future are possible. Some of the best creative brainpower should be devoted to the development of new promotion ideas.

The prize of profits is held out to all supermarket competitors in a trading area as a significant reward for attracting these marginal families. Unfortunately, most promotion tends to be transitory in effect. Other operators mimic the successful concern. Thus it is a constant race among the competitors to attract the customers. And while the profit prize may not be fully attained by any one market, the manager who doesn't advertise and promote to gain consumer patronage will be left literally "in the dust," with the remaining competitors still in the lead. As more supers are opened, the marginal families continue to be drawn away from the existing markets and detract from their earnings. However, new markets should be opened only after careful research has been performed to forecast the success of the venture. Yet, the wide range of volume over which a given market can operate and still be profitable is a lure to opening new outlets and will continue to make for highly competitive conditions. There is no lessening of it; the conclusion is that competition among the supermarket members will be more intensive in the years immediately ahead.

MERCHANDISING POLICIES

Executives in retail concerns basically must be merchandisers. This is especially true for all levels of supermarket management. All store personnel must realize they are part of a merchandising team. Their economic justification for employment is that the store in which they work adds value to the merchandise sold. Basically, a supermarket buys 81 cents worth of merchandise from its suppliers which it sells for $1.00 to its customers. Whether a consumer will pay this 19-cent differential is a direct function of the merchandising skill of the store management and the efforts of all employees.

The term *merchandising* was defined in this text as the practice of making certain that the products sold meet the needs and desires of the customers; at the same time the goods must be presented effectively. In the main, supermarkets have been effective merchandisers of food products. On a more limited scale, supers have been moderately successful in merchandising nonfoods. At the local level, skillful tactics in merchandising nonfoods have not always been demonstrated.

Supermarket executives merchandise when they screen the 100 to 200 new products presented weekly for their inspection and decide which ones will sell. Powerful buying committees have been established to help make the selection process more rational and free from personal prejudice. In cases of doubt, the marketing research techniques of test stores or consumer panels have been used. This selection of merchandise by management constitutes a major factor in determining the success of the venture. In an endeavor to please the consumer further, management has increased the number of lines handled almost yearly in the postwar era. The wide line of products in turn has forced manufacturers into a continuous battle both to attain and then retain shelf space.

Food manufacturers have become highly cognizant of product policy. They have developed through research a broad line of convenience goods and other new items such as pot pies, TV dinners, and instant hot cereals. The near future of food manufacturers depends on producing new convenience goods which meet the needs of the consuming public. In turn, these and related products must be pulled through the channels as a result of extensive advertising and promotion. As new and really improved products continue to come out of the research laboratories and into the markets, producers will of necessity need to cooperate with the supermarket operators to develop merchandising strategy that will move the goods. These new items are the life blood for the dynamic supermarket which strives for added volume and greater profit while retaining its basic competitive position in a trading area.

The use of chain brands as a part of merchandising strategy has been on the increase in recent years. Wider use of chain brands will continue as stronger and larger supermarket chains dominate more of the industry. The increased use of chain brands in canned goods, for example, will in time lower over-all margins on these items. Manufacturers may be forced to innovate pricing systems in which staples as price leaders compete with chain brands. The bulk of the profit will be earned by the manufacturer in new food specialties that the supermarket will not find suitable to manufacture. But the supermarket industry will become more powerful as it branches out into untried areas such as private branding in prepackaged meats. The pendulum of customer satisfaction that once favored the manufacturer is now swinging wider and wider over the area of the supermarket industry.

In the nonfoods area, the trend will continue toward increased sales of these products. The rapid growth of separate nonfood departments under a nonfoods specialist coupled with the building of larger stores able to handle more products pretells the story. While nonfood sales currently are about 5 per cent of total sales of a supermarket, this percentage can easily be doubled in the near future by adding general lines of merchandise. However, supermarkets must learn to do a more effective job of merchandising nonfoods. This includes better product plans and control of inventories. In addition, pricing policies more in line with those of food products must be employed; and merchandising techniques for the sale of seasonal products must be developed. Inasmuch as there is a strong organizational trend toward separate nonfood departments under a specialist, these merchandising prerequisites can be attained.

Merchandising also includes the effective presentation of goods to the consumer. The produce manager who trims the decay from the lettuce to make the head more salable is merchandising as is the manager who marks sale prices on all badly dented cans and places them in a cart near the check-out stand. Displays that create impulse sales also are part of the merchandising function. Supermarkets have been the innovator and proponent of self-service and impulse selling. As a result of mass display, which psychologically tends to make people buy, the supers have found an unusually prolific source of unplanned purchases. However, wider use of experimental research must be adopted in order to gain maximum benefit from display. For example, before-and-after studies should be used more widely to measure the impact of a particular display arrangement. Also, psychological tests of the consumer should be made to approach more scientifically the subject of display.

The display practices of the supers in turn have forced manufacturers to revamp their merchandising policies and to adopt better packaging, branding, and display practices. As supermart chains become more powerful through integration, manufacturers may be forced to establish tailor-made displays, promotions, and deals for different kinds and classes of stores. In turn, representatives of the manufacturers will be better merchandisers and devote less time to being only salesmen.

STORE OPERATIONS

Management must realize that the economic justification for a supermarket lies in the time, place, and ownership utility (or usefulness) the store gives the merchandise it sells. This measure of value imparted to the goods is measured by the gross margin. However, in order to perform its economic function, a super must have physical facilities and personnel with which to operate. These areas of store operations are growing in importance and complexity with the size of the markets and the unionization movement.

Management currently faces the problem of furnishing individual stores more and more selling space and larger parking facilities. One solution for additional selling space is better control of inventory and ordering procedures through use of electronic computers so that less storage is needed at the store. Also, processing activities conceivably could be centralized in many concerns; this would furnish additional display facilities. Thus, within limitations, management can remodel and offer a market some additional selling space. However, the added space from relocating processing activities in most instances will not offer sufficient space, and the markets will have to be relocated in the same area if possible in the near future. This change in location will have strong repercussions on the financial community holding mortgages on present supermarket properties that lack sufficient facilities. Furthermore, management must design new stores with an eye on costs, present and future requirements, and flexibility in the use of space. The importance of planning space requirements is exemplified in a recent study of 100 markets that were built in the year 1940.[4] Only 23 markets operate unchanged, whereas 26 were abandoned and 51 required major remodeling.

Another operating feature that may reward a chain organization with patronage loyalty is chain differentiation. With the trend toward fewer and larger concerns in this industry, the chains should take on more of an individualized appearance as to color, design of store fixtures, arrangement, and outside appearance. This familiarity will wed customers to the entire chain and not just one store.

As markets become larger and require greater investment, better management at the local level is required constantly. There has been an organizational trend in the industry in the past decade for each store to be under a general manager who is responsible for operations at the store level. Department managers report to him and not some central specialized supervisor. Store managers must

---

[4] "NAFC Looks into the Future," *Super Market Merchandising*, XIX, no. 12, December, 1955, p. 61.

be trained to be business executives with administrative prowess; they must be merchandisers, advertisers, and publicists as well. Executive development programs for middle management in decision making and case study are a must if this industry is to be successful in operating larger stores with greater varieties of merchandise in the future. Some companies have taken steps in this direction by sending key personnel to universities that offer programs in executive development; others have developed short-term clinics for their personnel. The Super Market Institute's program of executive training has drawn favorable response, but more positive action must be taken in this entire area of development and management training.

Many concerns have attracted young, capable future leaders, but the industry as a whole apparently has failed to draw its share of junior executives in competition with industry generally and department, drug, and variety stores in particular. Universities hear little about the supermarket industry. Supers have not made themselves competitive in search for the top talent needed because of the growing size of markets and the intense competition facing the stores. This does not mean to imply that hard work and long hours should be played down, but the rewards to management could be accentuated in salary, bonus, stock options, insurance, and retirement. Organization charts clearly showing paths for promotion should be publicized; opportunities for training programs and executive development must be made available.

No big business can operate without effective personnel. Workers are a vital part of the operation in a supermarket. Those who have daily contact with the public, from the grocery clerks stocking shelves to the check-out personnel, form a part of the store image. Supers should be a good place in which to work as well as to shop. Individuals must be trained, motivated, and made part of the store team to make them efficient. In this era of high labor costs, the supermarket stands today as a monument for all retailers and industry alike to envy. The supermarket and self-service are synonymous, and yet, 6 to 7 per cent of the sales dollar expended on labor is a substantially larger percentage of the sales dollar than that paid out by the pioneers in the field. Added services have been offered the consumer in "traded up" markets that necessitate additional personnel expenditures, but management must watch this expense so that the super does not lose its "claim to fame." Increased expense for personnel must be matched with increased output from the worker; and management must furnish the equipment and facilities for increased efficiency. Rising expenses generally will continue to be a constant threat for management, which must counter with increased productivity from the worker, more efficient methods and equipment, complete self-service, better use of resources, and the elimination of unnecessary frills.

FINANCING GROWTH

The aggressive expansion plans pursued by management in this industry have made financing a major issue. Dynamic growth over a protracted period of time cannot occur without adequate funds. Management has acquired assets to operate the business through (1) reinvesting of earnings, (2) selling of equity securities, (3) borrowing, and (4) leasing. All four methods are used widely.

Operations of the members of this industry in the main have been profitable. While the earnings as a percentage of the sales dollar have been a modest 2 to 3 per cent before taxes, profits on equity capital have appeared excellent. Over the years management has plowed back earnings into the business to finance growth and improvements. Dividend policies have been conservative, even for companies with widely held common stocks. Since the industry is expected to grow, no major change in this dividend policy for the industry appears imminent. Management of individual concerns must realize, however, that if growth diminishes, stockholders will insist on larger dividends.

Many of the supermarket chains that dominate the industry have sold equity securities in the capital markets. The investment attitude of the public toward the industry in general and specific concerns in particular is important if the industry is to obtain equity funds advantageously. Many investors are attracted to growth equities. The retail food business in itself is relatively stable and noncyclical. It faces gradual growth as the population rises; and it is influenced only slightly by changes in per capita family income. This also is the case of the electric power industry whose members generally have attained a high investment status for their equity securities as a result of the monopoly feature in their services. Supermarkets, the principal segment of the food store group, face strong competition in the market place. They have countered with aggressive practices that have imparted growth characteristics to their division of the food store group. But, as a class, supermarket shares are not likely to attain in the near future the status of a utility equity because of this turmoil in the market. On the other hand, the supermarket concerns lack the growth aura of companies in the fields of chemicals, missiles, and electronics. Stocks of these concerns traditionally sell at a high multiple of earnings and considerably above their net tangible book value per share. Equity financing for supermarkets generally will continue more on the basis of good-grade industrial concerns. The financial community is aware that the supermarket is not completely immune to recessions. Competitive pressures can force concerns to pass on to the customers reductions in the cost of merchandise. These pressures, coupled with the trend toward handling merchandise with higher margins, can squeeze gross profit in a period of economic turbulence, such as during a steel strike. Since the cost of handling food in a supermarket is tied more to the tonnage handled than to revenue, expenses in a recession can increase relative to sales and squeeze net profit. In addition, the growing trend toward more luxury items can make dollar sales more volatile.

Many individual members of the supermarket industry, primarily the medium-sized chains, have experienced remarkable sales and earnings growth resulting, in part, from acquisitions. The financial community has recognized these features and has placed a premium price on the common stocks of these concerns more in line with those of other growth equities. The very largest concerns, hamstrung by possible antitrust legislation, tend to have their common stocks sell on a more conservative basis. The small concerns or supers with one store are for the most part dependent on local financing for expansion. As a result of the risk involved in a limited number of outlets and the relatively small number of possible shares outstanding, the small companies will find it difficult to attract equity funds in the national capital markets and will depend upon the ingenuity of management to obtain equity funds locally.

Supermarket management must borrow on the most favorable terms possible in this narrow-profit industry. To do this, it will be necessary to maintain a satisfactory financial condition and operating record. Furthermore, management (especially of the smaller firms) should make certain that capable younger executives are available in the organization to take over the reins. This has been a weakness in many of the smaller firms and in part has contributed to the increase of mergers in the industry. Supermarkets have borrowed extensively for working funds, for expansion, equipment financing, and real estate acquisitions. It is not unusual for debt to be equal to net worth. There appears to be no letup in the need for funds in the immediate future; thus debt will remain heavy.

Management of supermarkets has been astute in its method of controlling assets through lease. While a concern is liable for lease payments over an extended period of years, the company actually uses assets that are financed over a long term by others. Supers have been forced to pioneer new locations with modern stores that require a substantial investment in equipment. Under the lease arrangement, the fixed assets used do not appear on the balance sheet, nor do the lease payments contracted for over a period of years appear as a liability. Inasmuch as supermarts are merchandising organizations that thrive on a large volume of fast-moving merchandise, the lease has proved an essential element in expansion. With growing need for cash to finance larger inventories and modernization, the lease method will be more essential in the future, especially during periods of tight money and high interest rates.

DETERRENTS TO SUPERMARKET GROWTH

Management must recognize certain limiting internal and external forces that restrict the supermarket growth; some concerns are particularly vulnerable.

Consider the first limitation, namely, the distribution cost cycle. According to Malcolm P. McNair:

> It seems to be characteristic of new types of distributive enterprises that in the first state of their development they gain a foothold primarily by means of low prices. In the second stage they "trade up" the quality of the merchandise carried, and in the third stage they compete by offering services. Companies in this third stage, unless they are managed with exceptional ability, not uncommonly encounter an increasing cost of doing business, a rising ratio of fixed investments to total investments and a decline in the rate of return on capital.[5]

At the time this concept was advanced, the large food chains had made substantial sales gains in the food store industry. But they had entered the third stage of the cycle, and their rate of growth was decreasing. The analysis in this text indicates that although the supermarket industry is relatively young in years and has shown considerable growth, it also appears to have entered the third stage of the distribution cost cycle. To date, supermarkets have operated in a progressive manner; they have demonstrated ability to experiment, to adapt, and to take advantage of changing trends. This has had a direct bearing on their development; but in this third stage, management must operate with exceptional ability if this industry is to continue expansion. There is the ever-increasing problem of attracting young men to this field who are managerial timber. Future skilled executives must be developed for an industry in the third stage of the distribution cost cycle. Currently, the competitive situation confronting the supermarkets, coupled with the basic nature and composition of the industry, indicate vigorous administration

---

[5] Malcolm P. McNair, *Expenses and Profits in the Chain Grocery Business* (Cambridge: Harvard Business School, Bureau of Business Research, 1931, Bulletin No. 84), p. 21.

in the near future. Those individual concerns under ineffective management in this third stage of the cost cycle will continue in the doldrums until management changes or the company expires.

Another limitation to the growth of this industry is that the small food stores cannot be completely eliminated. They fall by the wayside at a remarkable rate, and this trend will continue. But, owners of many small food stores are not aware always of their costs; they live in the rear of the premises, and perhaps the husband is employed elsewhere during the day. The everlasting hope for gain and independence keeps many small stores in business.

Machine vending, certain limited-line stores that are well entrenched, and the superette also will prevent the supermarket from completely dominating the food store industry. Strategically located superettes handling limited brands of convenience items will continue to play a role in food store sales. They have copied the techniques that made the supermarts low-cost operators. Many operate at an expense rate that compares favorably with that of a super. Membership in buying associations or cooperatives enables them to lower the cost of merchandise purchased and to realize other advantages such as cooperative advertising. These endeavors of the superette have tended to reduce the price advantage of the supermarket.

In time the pattern of food store retailing probably will be one in which the majority of the so-called convenience items needed for supplemental shopping will be handled by superettes or by machine vending. A small core of limited-line stores will handle special products. Small combination markets will become relatively insignificant volumewise. Strategically located supermarkets will dominate their respective trading areas as well as the food store industry. Gigantic supers, merchandising a wide line of junior department store products as well as foods, will be the core store dominating large shopping centers.

Another deterrent to extensive growth is the limitation of size of supermarkets. All stores cannot be gigantic operations since some consumers prefer the personal touch and friendly attitude on the part of the store personnel that cannot be obtained easily in a mammoth operation. Personalized management can lead to more community acceptance of the store, particularly if it is a member of a large chain.

In 1958 the supermarket transacted 57 per cent of total food store sales. Eventually the super will encounter market saturation at possibly 80 per cent of total food store volume. When this condition occurs, progress will be limited to population growth unless supermarket activities are channeled into other fields of retailing, wholesaling, food processing, and manufacture. With the vast distribution system that members of this industry have attained as the foundation, supers can invade these other areas successfully. Unless the government intervenes, this appears to be the future pattern.

The adaptable supermarket has added an increasing number of nonfood lines. This movement has been one of the industry's recent developments to increase sales. Here, too, there are limitations, but these have not been reached. The supermarkets' successful sales of these nonfood lines have forced drug, variety, and department stores to review their selling techniques. All three of these competitors in the nonfoods area are boosting the number of their outlets, embarking on modernization programs, and opening branches in the suburbs and in shopping centers. They have adopted self-service or simplified selling and have copied the display techniques of supermarkets. The chain members in these areas have been growing in size through horizontal and vertical integration. For example, many drug chains now produce pharmaceuticals, toiletries, and ice cream; many process films. At the retail level, these drug chains have broadened their product lines to include glassware, books, hardware, toys, jewelry, foodstuffs, and appliances. Where local regulations permit, packaged liquor has been dispensed. Department stores, with their new satellite units in outlying shopping centers, also handle increased lines of baked goods, frozen foods, and convenience food products such as completely prepared dinners for the busy shopper. Variety stores have broadened their lines in the impulse soft-goods area. The trend toward scrambled merchandising among all types of large retailers continues on the increase. In the near future there will be more stress on food items of the convenience type by the drug, department, and variety stores. Trends are under way to make all three of these resemble the supermarket more closely.

THE ILLUSIVENESS OF GOOD WILL

The supermarket is constantly in the public eye inasmuch as food shopping is done frequently. It is imperative that supermarket management recognize the importance of the good will that establishes a patronage attachment for trading at a particular store. No fundamental differences exist among supermarkets as to basic products, prices, and values, inasmuch as this field is so highly competitive. Any manager who believes that the only prerequisite for success is to provide good merchandise values at competitive prices is in error. Management must fashion a store image that is favorable in the eyes of the general public in order to gain a patronage following.

Store differentiation can be due in part to appearance, facilities, advertising, promotional devices, or special merchandising techniques, all of which have been stressed in this chapter. These are all part of the store's personality. But there is some illusive factor in the store image that is difficult to measure; generalizations about it are difficult to make because of the diverse nature of the industry and community differences. In the main, this illusive feature in good will for an individual concern and for the industry as well is a function of management's attitude toward the consumers, the suppliers, the employees, the governmental authorities, and the community in which it operates. How well management meets the expectations of these interests will be reflected in part in the store image and in the success of the venture. These preconceived standards of behavior on the part of the different groups are not necessarily in harmony with each other, nor are they always of the same importance to the welfare of the supermarket concern.

The supermarket is not an eleemosynary institution; it is operated primarily for the profit of the owners. But its operations are influenced by the public's attitude toward it. What has supermarket management done to generate a favorable image in the minds of these interest groups?

To the American consumer, the supermarket has lowered food costs and raised the plane of living. It has given the customer what is wanted at a lower cost. These are its most noteworthy achievements from the viewpoint of the consumer. Individual concerns that have not been completely consumer-oriented have suffered in the battle for survival in this competitive industry. While there are limits in placating the customers, conditions in this industry dictate that management must consider foremost in its decisions the wants and desires of the consumer so that it can return a satisfactory profit to the stockholders.

Supermarket management has shifted the balance of power away from the food manufacturer and in the direction of the retailer. As a result of this countervailing power, supers have tended to relegate the wholesaler more or less to a status of delivery agent for the manufacturer who performs the selling function but who cannot handle physical distribution of the merchandise as economically as the wholesaler. Manufacturers have been forced to give ground in all quarters. Their entire selling program has undergone change for the better by lowering distribution costs. Supermarket management must realize, however, that the functions of the manufacturers still are vital to the success of this industry despite all its integration practices. Many consumers prefer the national brands. Management must continue to work cooperatively with the suppliers in an endeavor to merchandise on a profitable basis all the products the consumer desires. Unless fair dealings exist between the supers and the manufacturers, new-product development will be retarded, and the supers will lose their "life blood" or added source of profit resulting from new items.

Management's relations with employees affect the store image. In order to attract and keep desirable personnel, management must offer workers steady employment, opportunities for training and advancement, satisfactory working conditions and hours, fringe benefits, and a competitive wage. These are all subject to differences in opinion between management and employees, but the differences should be resolved without resort to strikes so as not to engender bitterness that may be expressed by store personnel in daily contact with the customers. The relatively pleasant employee-employer relations that have characterized this industry must be maintained, and the markets must continue to function under a team effort.

Decisions of supermarket management that affect relationships with the community and the government should be summed up in the phrase, "Supermarkets Are Responsible Citizens." Obviously a supermarket cannot devote 100 sq ft of space for a charity cookie sale, but management must stay in tune with the expectations of the community. These differ by location, and management on the proper occasions should make its sidewalks available for charity drives, put signs in the windows for relief funds, and assist in blood banks and cancer drives. How active managers are in civic affairs will depend on the community attitude. Management must know what is expected of the market to make it a responsible citizen.

Still another problem of community relationships is the advisability of continuing a policy of "scrambled merchandising" which is detrimental to many limited-line stores and small combination markets near it. Similarly, other community members in the nonfood areas feel the impact of the supermarket. Management's drive to sell general merchandise that is easily displayed, attractively packaged, inexpensively priced, and impulsively purchased has been to the detriment of department, drug, variety, and hardware stores, to name but a few. While the battle of the market place occurs daily and no retailer has the assurance of guaranteed profits, the victorious supermarket should not disdain its rivals. An old saying should be remembered: "Don't rub salt into the wound."

To paraphrase from a childhood game, the supermarket currently is "King of the Hill." How long it remains on top is a function of the industry's skill in keeping a favorable image in the eyes of the general public whose wants must be served so that the cash register will continue to ring up larger profits. For the individual firm, success in this highly competitive industry will depend primarily upon management's ability to think creatively so as to be a leader in judging the wants and whims of the consumer. And if a competitor gains some marketing superiority, success will hinge further on management's ability to recognize quickly any disadvantage and to take action accordingly.

APPENDIX A

119 COST-CUTTING IDEAS

Management is confronted with the Herculean task of controlling, and if possible reducing, expenses of operation if the supermarket is to perform its merchandising activity at a profit. Recognizing this need, the magazine *Super Market Merchandising* devoted the majority of its April, 1958, issue to the problem of "How to Fight Costs and Win." One article from this section, "119 Cost-cutting Ideas," contained a reference list of pragmatic suggestions which appear to be of extreme value to the supermarket operator who faces the task of expense control at the firing line. This check list is classified according to operations, labor, warehouse and transportation, construction and maintenance, store departments, and back room.

Operations

1. Accident costs can be reduced by equipping each store with a small flash camera. Kept at a handy location, pictures of each customer accident can be taken immediately. Experience demonstrates that customers will not file exaggerated claims if they know a photo has been taken.

2. A certain degree of shrinkage can be controlled in the area of the direct vendor. A good policy is to instruct all vendors not to put merchandise on shelves, or mix merchandise with any stock on hand until the person in charge of the department has checked in the merchandise. When a vendor leaves, he must have any outgoing packages checked to see that no merchandise is carried out that is unaccounted for.

3. Have stores send in weekly cash reports instead of daily reports. This should save a lot of time for store managers as well as for bookkeepers.

4. Proper use of self-insurance applied to such things as collision, plate glass, holdups, and even fires, boilers, and cargos can save you considerable money. Explore its possibilities with qualified insurance agents or others who have had experience with it.

5. Every time you create a new form, you increase clerical costs because each piece of paper has to be handled by many people. Take time out to review the use of your forms and simplify them. It is a good idea to have a trial run of 60 to 90 days on every form that you introduce be-

fore making it a permanent part of the business. You may decide after two months that some of these forms are worthless, and you can save on further clerical expense.

6. To save paper work on price reduction reports, make use of pilot stores. Here you can get information that you can apply to all your other stores.

7. By sorting the checks yourself, you can reduce the bank's charges. This calls for putting the checks of one type in an envelope.

8. There is something in the Draft Plan to bring money in fast from your neighborhood transfer banks to the banks used by the main head-quarters disbursement bank. The bank informs headquarters of the total deposits to be made the next day. The money is made available at the headquarters disbursement bank. The bank informs headquarters of the total of drafts. This plan will lower the daily balance in the neighborhood banks, but the extra charge may be worth it, since it makes so much ready cash available at headquarters.

9. You can reduce charges on customer checks by sending them directly to the main depository bank rather than depositing them in the local transfer bank.

10. Are you sure it's worth the cost and effort to list every customer check on a separate tabulation, just in case checks are stolen? A study of this may reveal that you are recovering very little money over a long period of time. You may be burdening your managers with useless and time-consuming work.

11. If you are a small company, it may pay you to hire an engineering service to reduce your insurance rates. The bigger companies use their own men for this purpose.

12. Don't rely on a building alarm for warehouse control. Either have an ADT system or tie your alarm in with the local police department.

13. Pay store employees in cash. They prefer it. And you can save on the bank charges, which can go as high as 10 cents on each payroll check. This method is being used by a national chain, particularly in the bigger stores, where there is a full-time cashier on hand to help the manager. It is worth investigating to establish the proper procedures for preparing the payroll journals.

14. Study the advantages of leasing equipment, particularly equipment that becomes obsolete fast, such as: air conditioners, sprinklers, supervisors' cars, incinerators, tabulating machines, delivery equipment.

15. Have clerks keep a daily inventory check on standard items. It will save the buyer's time.

16. Keep paperwork where it belongs—in the central office. It costs less per hour there. Even weekly payrolls can be done more efficiently at headquarters.

17. Turn out copies (up to 10,000) of reports, bulletins, etc., by xerography. Equipment for this quick, inexpensive process is made up of three pieces: camera, copier, and fuser. It cuts out second typing from original copy to stencils and eliminates second proofreading.

18. Use newsprint or cheap wrapping paper in handling glassware, rather than the much more expensive kraft paper bags.

19. Check to see whether your company should be paying local taxes as a single corporate unit rather than as separate stores. You may be under unnecessary assessment.

20. Set up a salvage department to make daily or weekly pickups of waste and damaged goods from the stores. It's all good for resale.

21. Put up reminders to your checkers to look into the bottom shelf of the shopping cart.

22. If your managers are paying cash for store-door deliveries, it may be wise to relieve them of this burden. Over the month, the "cash pay-outs" can amount to hundreds.

23. To cut public liability insurance costs, it may be wiser to pay small claims yourself.

24. Use the "miscellaneous" key of your cash register to ring up tax on registers that have no tax key.

25. Have all store managers submit ideas for cost control before going ahead on them. Cost controls can become big expenses in themselves, especially if store managers start keeping detailed records without asking which ones the head office may require.

26. Stamp "paid by cash" clearly on the face of merchandise vouchers. In that way, if the voucher is lost or stolen, no one will be able to redeem it again.

27. Keep an alphabetical check list handy in each store of people known to be phony-check passers.

28. Don't keep stock on odd-sized bags that you seldom use. Store bag supplies in a place where they won't be damaged in any way.

Labor

29. Try using a job assignment card that outlines employees' duties by days. In this way the employee gets definite assignments and does not waste time each day waiting for his next assignment.

30. You can cut down on telephone expenses by following these rules: Don't allow employees to send or receive calls during working hours

(emergency calls excepted); equip only one phone with a dial; use a buzzer system for signaling; calls should be brief and to the point; install pay phones; do not tie up office personnel with details that can be handled by supervisors; check phone bills carefully.

31. Compute employee tax deductions in payroll work in a single tax table combining FICA and withholdings. You can obtain combined withholding tables from companies that supply accountants.

32. Want to reduce costs of inventory taking? One company starts inventory at 7 A.M. on a Monday morning, using regular store help on a quarterly basis. An administrative staff member is sent in to help the store crew. This gives both crew and administrators a better understanding of the store problems and leads to new suggestions for improving operations.

33. You can increase productivity in checking orders if, when using two-man teams, the first half of the items on the invoice are placed on one side of a four-wheel selector truck and the other half on the other side.

34. Check unemployment compensation claims periodically. You may be paying tax on dead claims.

35. List special prices alphabetically at the cash registers to help checkers with sale merchandise.

36. Cut down on unnecessary phone calls by having a central place for locating supervisors after the switchboard is closed. One company has each supervisor give his schedule to one key store in his district.

37. Use guide pictures to help clerks stock departments in new markets. Place photos of segments of top departments in other stores on shelves where you want the merchandise. Then send sufficient opening inventories to fill shelves. You'll save stocking time, layout time, and inventory time.

38. Have the company nurse make spot checks at the homes of men who are absent because of illness. Usually the man is really sick and will appreciate a call from the nurse. If not, a friendly talk with his boss will usually keep him from playing sick another time. Also, the calls will discourage other employees from trying the same ruse. If your company has no regular nurse, you can have your personnel office check with employees' doctors.

39. Check time cards regularly for employees who are late three or more times in a month. Have supervisors talk over with these men ways in which they can avoid being late.

40. Check previous employment records of all job applicants before you hire them, to make sure they are trustworthy. Some companies em-

ploy an investigation service to check prospective cashiers, managers, and others who will be handling large amounts of money.

41. When you fire an employee, keep a record in your central personnel office of your reasons for firing and of his social security number. Check this list whenever you hire a new man. This is particularly important where store managers hire their own personnel. A man who has been fired from one of your stores for dishonesty may look for work in another store in your chain.

42. Careful records of reasons for separating employees can lower your payments for unemployment compensation in many states. The amount you have to pay to the state for unemployment compensation usually is determined by the number of valid claims filed by former employees of yours. Thus, if you can show that you fired employees for reasons which were their own fault, such as dishonesty, your unemployment compensation payments will be lower. Many employers issue written warnings to workers and have the workers initial them, before they fire them. Then if you have to fire the workers, the warnings prove that you did so for good and just cause.

43. Punch employees' time cards each time you issue laundry to them, to make sure they return it. Issue laundry according to a regular schedule—so many fresh uniforms, aprons, towels, etc., for each classification of worker per week. Check all laundry against delivery sheets before the driver arrives.

44. To cut down on accidents, have store managers or department heads fill out an accident report each time a mishap occurs. In addition to having them fill in details of the accident, have them tell how the accident could have been prevented and what has been done to keep it from happening again.

45. Kroger appoints an employee in each store to serve as "Safety Promoter" for one or two months. Working under direction of the store manager, the "Safety Promoter" inspects the store and its equipment daily to remove safety hazards. At the end of his tour of duty, the job passes to another employee. Albers uses a similar system. A "Mr. Super Safety" or "Miss Super Safety" reports daily to the manager on safety conditions in each store.

46. Schedule part-time help only when and where it's really needed. Don't have part-timers standing around with time on their hands in off hours.

47. Set up a system of department numbers on pay checks so that checks for each department can easily be told apart from the others.

48. An easy way to eliminate extra help and overtime problems in

also pictures, shelf-guider, etc.

stocking new markets is this technique: Soon after the market has had its floors and shelving installed, and electricians, carpenters, and decorators are finished with their work, set your stocking crews to work. Let them work from master plans, filling in first one front-faced row of items and later depositing the balance on each line. As a gondola or section of shelving is completely stocked, huge sheets of clear plastic are draped over it to seal it off from the dust and dirt resulting from unfinished work. When the store is ready for opening, the covers are removed to reveal gleaming, dust-free stocks.

Warehousing and Transportation

49. For additional security measures, use seals on trucks making grocery deliveries to stores.

50. Unload and tally in small units when you check warehouse deliveries into the store. That way, if a difference shows up between the store receiver's count and the truck driver's billing count, you won't have to retally the whole load to find where the trouble is. Here's how to do it: Unload in lots, say, of 20 pieces. Mark the twentieth piece. Enter a "20" on your tally sheet. Any difference in count will show up immediately within the group of 20 pieces and can be cleared up in a few minutes.

51. When you order carload shipments from suppliers, specify the track over which it should be shipped to reach your spur of the railway. This will eliminate possible delays through misrouting. Some companies have a special warehouse assistant to study rail and trucking tariffs and routings.

52. An electronic scale in the dispatcher's office to register axle loads of outgoing trucks can save on traffic fines. If the axle load exceeds legal limits, the dispatcher can head off the truck and direct it to a dock for unloading before it gets out on the road.

53. To cut paper work in warehouse receiving, install a tape recorder in your warehouse tabulating office with a microphone at the receiving dock. As merchandise arrives, a clerk dictates receiving into the microphone. Another clerk in the tabulating department transcribes the receivings from the tape recorder. If the receiving dock and tabulating office are too far apart for a direct cable connection, a telephone with a special attachment may be used for dictating into the tape recorder. Transcribing the receivings on continuous forms further speeds the operation.

54. Some warehouses install two-way radios on lift trucks to maintain constant contact with the warehouse office. The radios eliminate a lot of delay and wear and tear on warehouse supervisors.

55. Have delivery truck drivers phone the warehouse dispatcher's

office from the gate for instructions on where to deliver their load. This system helps avoid delivery delays and traffic snarls.

56. To head off misrouting of orders going to different offices, use different-color mailing envelopes for each order destination.

57. Hold on to the cardboard cartons in which warehouse merchandise comes to the store. Then send them back for use a second time.

58. In warehouse orders, list items in any given line of goods in the same sequence as they turn up in the orders left by the service salesman.

59. Send pallets to local distributors who do not already use them. And encourage them to send palletized deliveries to your warehouse. If you sell the pallets at or near cost, your savings in warehouse efficiency will make up any loss many times over.

60. Price-mark as much of your merchandise as you can in the warehouse. This saves the time it takes for clerks in the stores to look up prices. It is recommended particularly for nonfoods.

61. Carry portable conveyors under trailers of your trucks. This avoids the necessity of having a complete conveyor system in small stores.

62. Use nets to separate orders for individual stores in your delivery trucks. They allow better use of space than rigid dividers.

63. Use hub mileage meters on trailers of delivery trucks. Tractors and trailers seldom travel the same distances, so you need separate mileage meters to tell you when the trailers should be serviced.

64. One chain has a store unloading system that cuts down time of unloading each truck from a half-hour to 5 minutes. The company's new markets are coming equipped with compartments exactly matching in size the standard 35-ft trailer. The compartments are tilted slightly, and the trailer backs into its "twin" compartment. Gravity pulls its merchandise down the slope on conveyor belts and pallets.

65. In warehouse receiving you can get increased labor productivity by separating the palletizing operation from the storing operation. By doing this and by providing the palletizing crew with pallet jacks, four-wheel trucks, or skids, you can reduce the number of men on the job by one-third.

66. One man working alone in palletizing groceries and moving the loaded pallet out of the car is nearly 38 per cent more productive per man-hour than a two-man team. You can gain economies by one man, providing you leave the car in the dock long enough and the one man does not have to unload extremely heavy merchandise.

Construction and Maintenance

67. Laundry bills can be cut down by following these procedures: Assign a responsible employee to head up laundry handling in the markets. Have employees sign a record form every time a uniform is issued. Have employees use partly soiled coats for messy work and change to clean uniforms once the work is completed.

68. To cut utility expenses, assign one person to oil all motors, as specified by the manufacturer; keep motors clean and drive belts tight; replace used bulbs; turn off lights when not in use; check filters in air conditioners and replace or clean when necessary; check burners in the heating units to see that they are firing properly; check water lines and water heaters against leaks.

69. Investigate whether or not capacitators can be installed as a means of cutting power cost, despite their rather high initial cost.

70. To protect shopping carts against breakdowns, observe the following rules: Don't use shopping carts in place of heavy-duty trucks. Don't use shopping carts for carry-out service. Make sure that the carts are properly maintained. For special jobs use special equipment.

71. Put in a clock thermostat control if you have air conditioning. It will shut the units off when your stores are not open.

72. Put up prominent notices in all stores, telling your employees not to throw water on fires starting in electrical equipment.

73. Post a notice near your garbage disposal machine, telling what should not be thrown in.

74. Channel all orders for equipment servicing through central purchasing at headquarters. These people have the service contacts and can get better prices than the store manager.

75. Check scales to see that they're properly calibrated. Make frequent test weights. Each overage costs money; each underweight can cost you a paying customer.

76. Keep up-to-date telephone numbers of your company's maintenance office or service firm posted conveniently. This keeps store personnel from putting off a maintenance call.

77. One way to keep down shopping cart losses is to point out what each one costs. Most shoppers value the carts at less than $5.00 each and are amazed to learn that they cost up to $50. They think twice before inadvertently stealing something that expensive. You can offer to sell carts to customers; put a price tag on them.

78. Cost-saving construction technique: Concrete wall panels are precast on the floor of the warehouse and tilted up into place by a crane.

Then reinforced concrete columns are poured between the wall panels.

79. Flexible plastic strips along the hinged edge of doors prevent crushed kiddies' fingers, which could mean expensive damage suits against you.

80. Establish a regular schedule for using a light meter to check intensity of light from the lamps in your stores, and for cleaning and replacing lamps.

81. Attach pull cords to light bulbs so that it won't be necessary to throw the main switch in order to turn off lights in individual areas of the store.

82. Throughout the day make frequent temperature checks on refrigeration equipment. Catch any defects before they get a chance to pile up spoiled goods. Know the defrost cycles of each piece of machinery, so that your temperature report will be a valid one. Make sure compressors are kept clean. Dirt makes extra wattage necessary.

83. Put up a complete diagram of the plumbing and electrical layout in each store, with "X marks the spot" indications for all the sewer clean-outs and fuse boxes.

84. A stainless steel moulding on each side of the gasket on walk-in freezer doors in stores will keep the gasket from pulling loose.

85. Make scale models of new stores before the real thing goes into the works. This way you can avoid "hindsight blues" over layout.

Store Departments

86. To handle quarters of beef you will save considerable labor time if you cut into wholesale pieces, trim, and then put into the cooler. That is faster than putting them into the cooler in quarters and then cutting them into wholesale cuts later.

87. When handling cartons of meat, cut the tops off, place in cooler, and work from the cartons. That proves at least 70 per cent faster than unpacking the cartons and hanging or shelving them in the cooler.

88. Decide what specific sizes of cellophane or other wraps you need, and keep only those sizes on hand. Where you can use second-quality paper instead of first (cheese, for example), do so. Cut down on overlap in sealing packages.

89. Use silver polish instead of steel wool to take price markings off cellophane-wrapped items in meat and delicatessen departments. It won't tear the wrapping.

90. Cut down on power-saw accidents by putting decals on the saws reading, "Turn off main switch before opening."

91. To avoid duplicate payment and to get greater efficiency in trans-

shipment, print and staple labels to crates of produce from local farmers.

92. In filling produce racks, two hands are better than one. The USDA estimates that 4 to 5 man-hours weekly can be saved if an employee takes items in both hands and places them simultaneously on the display. In a test, the two-handed technique reduced display filling time by as much as 14 to 38 per cent.

93. To cut unloading time, use a production-line setup in your back room. One man calls off items as they arrive, while a second checks them with the order sheet. The third man splits the case, and the fourth opens it on the conveyor, exposing tops of two layers of merchandise containers. Two more men stamp prices, and the goods are ready for the store shelves.

94. File special display signs under item headings and use them again when these items come up for another special; this saves you the cost of printing new signs each time.

95. Carton openers have a tendency to disappear like rabbits. You can cut down on carton-opener losses by selling them to clerks at wholesale prices.

96. Keep weekly records of produce "throw-outs" by items or poundage, or both. With a comparison record of waste to sales, you can correct your ordering.

97. You can facilitate deliveries on sale items by splitting them up—half in the week before the actual sale and half during the sale time.

98. Check your use of boards and trays and cellophane in meat-packaging departments. By using materials just 1 inch less in width, you can save.

99. Instruct meat department heads to inspect and weigh all products carefully upon receiving. You can cut down on short weights and poor quality this way.

100. Place elastic bands around chicken parts and fresh-cut whole birds before packaging to keep loose parts from tearing the wrapper.

101. Tie beef rib roasts and all kinds of rolled roasts with butcher's twine before wrapping, to prevent damage to the package from inside.

102. Place the sharp, bony side of pork loin roasts against the cardboard in the package, and use rubber bands around the outside to safeguard against tearing.

Back Room

103. Assign one man to the back room and do not allow him to leave this room unless someone replaces him.

104. Do not permit anybody to take anything out of the store through

the back door without a signed transfer or charge note, to be checked by the person assigned to the back room.

105. Do not permit a delivery man to take anything into the front of the store without permission of the back-room man. No boxes, bags, or other containers should leave the store without being checked thoroughly.

106. Give strict warning, just once, to any delivery man who is found to have taken something through the back door without first being checked. If there are any further violations, ask that another man take over his route.

107. Do not permit employees to take anything out of the store unless they go through the check-out stands. Never permit them to leave by the back entrance. See to it that all their purchases are paid for at the time they leave the store and never before.

108. Make frequent checks to see that back doors are locked.

109. Set a fixed time for deliveries, except in case of emergency. After the set time for deliveries, the manager should collect all keys to the back room and should not permit anyone to open these doors without his consent.

110. Check delivery man, particularly when he collects the empty bottles.

111. Lock in night stockers and cleaning crews for your stores.

112. Locate your receiving office for all merchandise in the back room.

113. Make it your store policy to limit access to the back room to authorized personnel only.

114. Keep a running record of "ins and outs." Check this record periodically by physical inventory.

115. If you have an outside service for protection against pilferage, extend it to surveillance of back-room operation.

116. Do not permit any open cases or damaged merchandise to be stored in the back room.

117. Do not permit employees to change clothes in the warehouse or back room, but see to it that they go to the employees' locker room.

118. When you notice that back-room losses are getting excessively large, hold a staff meeting and direct the attention of personnel to the fact that if the losses are traced to pilferage, they will come under the heading of stealing—with corresponding punishment.

119. Put two separate locks on the back-room door: one a daytime lock, and one a nighttime lock.

BIBLIOGRAPHY

The author owes a debt of gratitude to the editors, contributors, and staff writers of the magazines *Super Market Merchandising, Progressive Grocer,* and *Chain Store Age,* Grocery Executive and Supermarket Editions. Articles that appeared in these publications over the years have traced the creative thinking of the leaders of this industry. The yearly reports over the past decade of the Super Market Institute, *The Super Market Industry Speaks,* and of the *Progressive Grocer, Facts in Grocery Distribution,* also were of value. Statistics issued by the Topics Publishing Company in *What the Public Spends for Grocery Store Products* were essential in the analysis.

An alphabetized list of all sources of information used in this text is given below. Inasmuch as the footnotes were given in detail, only the names and publishers of the various periodicals are submitted here.

Advertising Agency, Moore Publishing Co., Inc., 48 W. 38th St., New York 18, N. Y.

Applebaum, William, and Moulton, Richard. *An Exploration into Reasons Why Supermarkets Add and Discontinue Items.* New York: McCall Corp., 1956.

Baking Industry. Clissold Publishing Co., 105 W. Adams St., Chicago 3, Ill.

Barker, Clare W., Anderson, Ira D., Butterworth, J. Donald. *Principles of Retailing.* New York: McGraw-Hill Book Co., Inc., 1956.

Barron's, Barron's Publishing Co., 50 Broadway, New York 4, N. Y.

Beckman, Theodore, and Nolen, H. C. *The Chain Store Problem.* New York: McGraw-Hill Book Co., Inc., 1938.

Boyd, Harper W., and Westfall, Ralph. *Marketing Research.* Homewood, Illinois: Richard D. Irwin, Inc., 1956.

Bureau of Agricultural Economics, U.S. Department of Agriculture, *Consumption of Food in the U.S.,* Agriculture Handbook No. 62, Government Printing Office, Washington, D.C., October, 1955.

Business Week. McGraw-Hill Publishing Co., Inc., 330 W. 42 St., New York 36, N. Y.

Chain Store Age, Grocery Executive Edition, Lebhar-Friedman Publications, Inc., 2 Park Ave., New York 16, N. Y.

Controllers Congress. *1954 Merchandise and Operating Results.* New York: National Retail Dry Goods Association, 1955.

Converse, Paul D., and Huegy, Harvey W. *The Elements of Marketing.* New York: Prentice-Hall, Inc., 1956.

Cooperative Merchandiser, Cooperative Food Distributors of America, 141 W. Jackson Blvd., Chicago 4, Ill.

Donohue, Al. An address given by this executive of Kidder Peabody and Company at the 20th Annual Meeting of the National Association of Food Chains in Washington, D.C., on December 5, 1953.

Edison Electric Institute, Edison Electric Institute, 750 Third Ave., New York 17, N. Y.

Electrical Merchandising, McGraw-Hill Publishing Co., Inc., 330 W. 42 St., New York 36, N. Y.

England, Wilbur B. *Operating Results of Food Chains in 1958.* Cambridge: Harvard Business School, Bulletin No. 156, 1959.

Facts in Grocery Distribution. New York: Progressive Grocer, 1950 to 1959.

Federal Trade Commission. *Chain Stores, Final Report on the Chain Store Investigation,* submitted to 74th Congress, 1st session. Senate Document 4. Government Printing Office, Washington, D.C., Dec. 14, 1934.

Federal Trade Commission. *Federal Trade Commission Economic Inquiry into Food Marketing—Interim Report,* Government Printing Office, Washington, D.C., June 30, 1959.

Food Business, Putman Publishing Co., 111 E. Delaware Pl., Chicago 11, Ill.

Food Field Reporter, Topics Publishing Co., 708 Third Ave., New York 17, N. Y.

Food Mart News, 333 N. Michigan Ave., Chicago 1, Ill.

Food Topics, Food Publications, Inc., 708 Third Ave., New York 17, N. Y.

Forbes, Forbes, Inc., 70 Fifth Ave., New York 11, N. Y.

Fortune, Time, Inc., 9 Rockefeller Plaza, New York 20, N. Y.

Frozen Food Industry. Philadelphia: Curtis Publishing Co., 1954.

Goodwin, Arthur E. *Markets Public and Private.* Seattle: Montgomery Printing Co., 1939.

Graham, Benjamin, and Dodd, David. *Security Analysis.* New York: McGraw-Hill Book Co., Inc., 1953.

Grimes, Don R. An interview with the assistant to the president, IGA, on July 10, 1957 at Chicago, Ill.

Guthmann, Harry G., and Dougall, Herbert E. *Corporate Financial Policy.* New York: Prentice-Hall, Inc., 1955.

Hardware Retailer, National Retail Hardware Association, 964 N. Pennsylvania Ave., Indianapolis 4, Ind.

Haring, Albert, and Yoder, Wallace O. *Trading Stamp Practice and Pricing Policy.* Bloomington: Indiana University, 1958.

Harvard Business Review, Soldiers' Field, Boston 63, Mass.

Hayward, Walter, and White, Percival. *Chain Stores.* New York: McGraw-Hill Book Co., Inc., 1922.

Here's How We Shop for Our Big Grocery Order. New York: Batten, Barton, Durstine & Osborne, 1949.

Home Testing Institute, Inc., *McCall's Food and Grocery Products Purchase Diary Study.* New York: McCall Corp., 1956.

IGA Grocergram, Independent Grocers' Alliance of America, 131 S. Wabash Ave., Chicago 3, Ill.

International Super Marketing, Red and White Corp., 300 W. Washington St., Chicago 6, Ill.

Journal of Marketing, Marketing Association, 27 E. Monroe St., Chicago 3, Ill.

Journal of Retailing, New York University School of Retailing, Washington Square, New York 3, N. Y.

Kintner, Earl W. Testimony given by the chairman of the Federal Trade Commission before a Subcommittee of the Select Committee on Small Business, United States Senate, 86th Congress, 1st session, July 2, 1959. These hearings are published as *Mergers and Unfair Competition in Food Marketing,* Government Printing Office, Washington, D.C., 1960.

Kleppner, Otto. *Advertising Procedure.* Englewood Cliffs, N. J.: Prentice-Hall, Inc., 1950.

Kohler, Eric. *Dictionary for Accountants.* New York: Prentice-Hall, Inc., 1952.

Kornblau, Curt. An address, "Facts about New Supers Opened in 1957," given by the Director of Research, Super Market Institute, at the annual convention in Cleveland, Ohio, in May, 1958.

Kornblau, Curt. *Facts and Figures About Non-Foods in Super Markets.* Chicago: Super Market Institute, 1959.

Kuznets, Simon. *Shares of Upper Income Groups in Income and Savings.* New York: National Bureau of Economic Research, Inc., 1953.

Lilly Digest, Eli Lilly and Company, Indianapolis, Ind., 1955.

Logan, John A. *Progress in Food Distribution.* Washington: National Association of Food Chains, 1957.

Market of the Sixties. New York: Time, Inc., 1960.

Mattei, G. L. A letter written by the district manager, William J. Burns International Detective Agency, to the Super Market Institute on January 22, 1958.

Maynard, Harold, and Beckman, Theodore. *Principles of Marketing*. New York: The Ronald Press Co., 1952.

McNamara, Harley V. An address, "Modern Trends in Food Retailing," given by the President of National Tea Company before the Chicago Federated Advertising Club on October 12, 1952.

Meat and Dairy Products, Standard and Poor's Industry Surveys, 1959. New York: Standard and Poor's Corp.

Meat Markets—Operating Results in 1954. New York: Dun & Bradstreet, Inc., 1954.

Merger Movement in Retail Food Distribution. Chicago: National Association of Retail Grocers, 1959.

Moody's Industrial Manual. New York: Moody's Investor Service.

Myers, Herman L., and Scott, Forrest. *The Rise of the Super Market*. U.S. Department of Agriculture, Bureau of Agricultural Economics, MTS-103. Government Printing Office, Washington, D.C., December, 1951.

McCloskey, Joseph, and Trefethen, Florence. *Operations Research for Management*. Baltimore: The Johns Hopkins Press, 1954.

McNair, Malcolm P. *Expenses and Profits in the Chain Grocery Business*. Cambridge: Harvard Business School, Bureau of Business Research, 1931.

Nargus Bulletin, National Association of Retail Grocers, 360 N. Michigan Ave., Chicago 1, Ill.

Nielsen Researcher, A. C. Nielsen Company, 2101 Howard St., Chicago, Ill.

1954 Furniture Operating Experiences. Chicago: National Retail Furniture Association, 1955.

1954 Operating Statistics. New York: American National Retail Jewelers Association, 1955.

1958 Survey of Super Market Shoppers, Their Buying Habits and Attitudes. Cincinnati: Burgoyne Grocery and Drug Index, Inc., 1959.

Nugent, William C. An address given November 12, 1957, to the Grocery Manufacturers of America, Inc., at New York, N. Y.

Nugent, William C. An address presented at the United States Wholesale Grocers' Convention, April 21, 1957, St. Louis, Mo.

Nystrom, Paul H. *Economics of Retailing*. New York: The Ronald Press Co., 1936.

Nystrom, Paul H. *Retail Store Operation*. New York: The Ronald Press Co., 1937.

Peckham, J. O. *Planning Your Marketing Operations for 1959*. Chicago: A. C. Nielsen Company, 1959.

Phillips, Charles F., and Duncan, Delbert J. *Marketing Principles and Methods*. Homewood, Illinois: Richard D. Irwin, 1956.

Printers' Ink, Printers' Ink Publishing Co., 205 E. 42nd St., New York 17, N. Y.

Progressive Grocer, Butterick Co., Inc., 161 Sixth Ave., New York 13, N. Y.

Sales Management, Sales Management, Inc., 386 Fourth Ave., New York 16, N. Y.

Shaffer, Henry. An address, "Essential Factors in Sound Financing," given by this executive of Shaffer Stores Co., at the 20th Annual Meeting of Food Chains in Washington, D.C., on December 5, 1953.

Standard Ratios for Retailing. New York: Dun & Bradstreet, Inc., 1936.

Super Market Industry Speaks. Chicago: Super Market Institute, 1949 to 1959.

Super Market Merchandising. Super Market Publishing Co., Inc., 67 W. 44th St., New York 36, N. Y.

Super Market News, Fairchild Publications, Inc., 7 E. 12th St., New York 3, N. Y.

Supermarket News Food Industries Financial Manual. New York: Fairchild Publications, Inc., 1957.

Super Markets in the United States. Philadelphia: Curtis Publishing Co., 1954.

Tarrant, Christ. An interview with the secretary, Grocerland Co-operative, Inc., in Chicago, Illinois, on June 20, 1957.

U.S. Bureau of the Census, *Census of Business, 1954*, Bulletin R-2-2, Government Printing Office, Washington, D.C., 1957.

U.S. Bureau of the Census, *1951 Supplement, Survey of Current Business*, Government Printing Office, Washington, D.C., 1959.

U.S. Bureau of the Census, *Census of Business, Retail Distribution, Part I.*, vol. 1, Government Printing Office, Washington, D.C., 1933.

U.S. Bureau of the Census, *Census of Business, Retail Trade, Parts I and II*, vols. 1 and 2, Government Printing Office, Washington, D. C., 1952.

U.S. Bureau of the Census, *Census of Business, Retail Trade*, No. R-2-2, Government Printing Office, Washington, D.C., 1957.

U.S. Bureau of the Census, *Census of Business, Selected Service Trades,* Government Printing Office, Washington, D.C., 1957.

U.S. Bureau of the Census, *Census of Business, Retail Trade Summary Statistics,* vol. 1, Government Printing Office, Washington, D.C., 1957.

U.S. Bureau of the Census, *Current Population Reports,* Government Printing Office, Washington, D.C., 1958.

U.S. Bureau of the Census, *Food Retailing—Retail Distribution,* M-93, Government Printing Office, Washington, D.C., 1934.

U.S. Bureau of the Census, *Number of Inhabitants, U.S. Summary 1950 Census of Population,* Government Printing Office, Washington, D.C., 1952.

U.S. Bureau of the Census, *Sixteenth Census of the U.S., 1940 Population,* vol. 1, Government Printing Office, Washington, D.C., 1942.

U.S. Bureau of the Census, *Statistical Abstract of the United States,* Government Printing Office, Washington, D.C., 1959.

U.S. Bureau of Labor Statistics, *Monthly Labor Review,* Government Printing Office, Washington, D.C., 1933.

U.S. Department of Commerce, *Confectionery Sales and Distribution.* Government Printing Office, Washington, D.C., 1957.

U.S. Department of Commerce, *Distribution Cost Studies Number 1, Louisville Grocery Survey, Part IIIA,* Government Printing Office, Washington, D.C., 1932.

United States v. *The Great A & P Tea Company.* U.S. Circuit Court of Appeals, 7th district, Docket 9221, Records & Briefs, vols. I and II.

Variety Store Merchandiser, Variety Store Merchandiser Publications, 419 Fourth Ave., New York 16, N. Y.

Voluntary and Cooperative Groups Magazine, Cook Publications, 114 E. 32 St., New York 16, N. Y.

What the Public Spends for Grocery Store Products. New York: Food Topics Publishing Co., 1950 to 1959.

Weiss, E. B. *Winning Chain Store Distribution for New Products.* New York: Doyle, Dane, Bernbach, Inc., 1956.

Zimmerman, M. M. *The Super Market.* New York: McGraw-Hill Book Co., Inc., 1955.

Zimmerman, M. M. *Super Market—Its Growth and Future.* New York: Super Market Merchandising Publishing Co., 1948.

Zimmerman, M. M. *Super Market Spectacular Exponent of Mass Distribution.* New York: Super Market Publishing Co., 1937.

INDEX

A & P (*see* Great Atlantic & Pacific Tea Co.)
ABC Stores, Inc., 17
ACF-Brill Motors Co. (*see* ACF-Wrigley Stores, Inc.)
ACF-Wrigley Stores, Inc., 29, 181
Administration expense, 102, 103, 110, 111
Advertising, cooperative, 106
  expenditures, 65–66, 105, 106, 111
  media, 105
Albers Supermarkets, Inc., 158, 162, 163, 168, 180
Alexander, Milton, 49, 69, 92, 214
Alpha Beta Food Markets, 15
Alt, Richard N., 49, 196
American House Grocers, 18
American Stores Co., integration, 179, 180
  operating statistics, 25, 70, 91, 150, 159, 172, 173, 174
Anderson, Ira D., 62
Ann Page, 171, 184
Applebaum, William, 26, 57, 63, 79
Armour & Co., 172
Ashton's Supermarket, 180
Automobile, impact, 35, 37–38
  registrations, 38

Back room expense, 116, 117
Bakery product stores, number, 189
  position, 197–198, 209–211
  sales, 192, 199, 200
Balance sheet, 123–125, 132, 146
Bank loans, 139–140
Barker, Clare W , 62
Bayless, A. J. Markets, Inc., 69, 70, 90, 91, 118, 150
Beckman, Theodore N., 68, 158
Beem, Eugene, 68

Big Bear, 18–21, 23–25, 121, 123, 154–155
Big Bear Markets of Michigan, Inc., 181, 182
Big business, 28–29, 225–228
Birdseye, Clarence, 40
Bohack, H. C., 213
Boyd, Harper W., 232
Brand policy, chain, 84, 184, 239
  packer, 84
  private, 84, 184
Breakeven analysis, 145–147
Brevit, S. L., 16, 154
Brown, A. A., 38
Budget Markets, Inc., 180
Budgeting procedure, 113
Buildings, 122–125, 128–130
Bunnell, Charles N., 17
Butterworth, J. Donald, 62
Buying, associations, 85–87
  committee, 78–83
  decisions to make or buy, 83–84
  new products, 77–78
  routine, 76–77

Capital Stores, Inc., 180
Cardinal Stores, Inc., 181
Carl's Markets, Inc., 180
Carney, Robert, 230
Carrolls', Ltd. Stores, 180
Carty Brothers, 15
Catherine Market, 12
Century Food Markets Co., 70, 91, 150
Chain Store Age, 72
Chapman Park Drive-in Market, 16
Charvat, Frank J., 41
Chattel mortgages, 142–143
Cheapy supermarket, appeal, 31, 37, 45, 57, 222
  operating statistics, 23–24

Cheapy supermarket (*Cont.*):
    opposition, 154–159
    origin, 11, 18–25
Clayton Act, 181, 227
Clovis, L. L., 195
Colonial Stores, Inc., integration, 173,
        179, 180
    operating statistics, 70, 90, 91, 127,
        149, 150
Combination markets, number, 189–
        191
    position, 195–197, 203–206, 208–
        212
    sales, 191–193, 199–202
Comish, Newel, 58
Community relations, 251–252
Competition, among supermarkets,
        224–225
    intertype, 195–197
Concession-type markets, 12–15
Confectionery stores, number, 189
    position, 207–209
    sales, 192, 199, 200
Consent Decree of 1920, 171, 172
Consigned merchandise, 87–88
Construction & maintenance cost, 116,
        117
Consumer buying habits, 46–50
Converse, Paul D., 169–195
Cost of sales, 75–88
Cost reduction, 116–117, 253–263
Costs (*see* Operating expense)
Council Oak Stores, 180
Country general store, number, 189–
        190
    position, 193–195, 205, 210
    sales, 192
Crawford, R. P., 14
Crystal Palace Market, 12–13
Cudahy Packing Co., 172
Cullen, Michael (*see* Kullen, King)
Current assets, 125–127

Daitch Crystal Dairies, Inc., 69, 70,
        91, 127, 150
Dale Supermarkets, 180
Davidson, William R., 68
Dawson, Roy O., 18, 121
Debentures, 140–142
Decentralization movement, 43–46
Decision making, 229–232

Delicatessen stores, 189, 192
Department of Justice, 184, 187
Devan's Food Stores, 180
Dipman, Carl W., 19, 25, 28, 45
Display techniques, 60–61, 240
Distribution, costs, 108, 111–112,
        117
    cycle, 246–247
Dixie Home Stores (*see* Winn-Dixie
        Stores, Inc.)
Dodd, David L., 141
Dollenger, Emil, 13
Dolly Madison International Foods,
        Ltd., 181
Donohue, Al, 126, 144
Dougall, Herbert E., 149
Drive-in markets, 15–16
Dun & Bradstreet, Inc., 26
Duncan, Delbert J., 194
Durrant, B. A., 195

Eagle-United Supermarkets, 129
Eavey's Supermarket, 63
Edins Food Stores, 181
Eisner Grocery Co., 180
England, Wilbur B., 55, 69, 110, 111,
        137
Equipment, costs, 55
    lease, 137
    requirements, 122, 123, 124, 127–
        128
Equity capital (*see* Ownership capi-
        tal)
Euclid and 46th Street Market, 12
Evans Grocery Co., 141, 142
Executive development, 241–243
Expense, budgeting, 112–114
    comparison other retailers, 101–107
    control, 112–117
    fixed, 115, 145–147, 236–237
    functional, 107–112
    individual concern, 91
    major items, 102–104
    reduction, 116–117
    relationships, 236–237
    standards, 114–115
    trends, 99–101

Faneuil Hall Market, 12
Federal Trade Commission, chain store
        report, 21, 23

Federal Trade Commission (*Cont.*)
  economic inquiry, 171, 174, 176,
    177, 179, 183, 186, 187
  enforcement, 179, 181, 227
Federated Department Stores, Inc.,
    62
Financing, borrowing, 137–144
  equity, 144
  growth, 243–245
  leasing, 131–133, 135–137
First National Stores, Inc., 25, 159, 173
Fisher Brothers Co., 70, 91, 127, 141,
    150
Flint, Lucius, 15
Food Center Stores, 180
Food Center Supermarkets, 180
Food Fair Stores, Inc., financing, 121,
    128, 142
  integration, 168, 172, 173, 179, 180,
    182
  operating statistics, 70, 90, 91, 121,
    150
Food Mart, Inc., 70, 91, 150
Food Topics, 64
Food stores, number, 188–191, 193–
    198
  sales, 191–198
Foodtown Stores, Inc., 181
Food Town study, 92, 200
Foster, H. M., 16, 153, 155, 157
Fruit & vegetable stores, number, 189
  position, 204–206
  sales, 192, 199–200
Furr's, 128

General & overhead expense, 109, 110,
    111, 116, 117
General Foods Corp., 40
Gibson, Edwin T., 40
Gilman, John R., 49, 61, 73, 101
Good will, 130, 249–252
Goodwin, Arthur E., 12
Graham, Benjamin, 141
Grand Union Co., Inc., integration,
    173, 178, 179, 180, 228
  operating statistics, 70, 91, 150
Great Atlantic & Pacific Tea Co., in-
    tegration, 83, 168, 171, 172,
    173, 176, 177, 178, 179, 184,
    187, 227
  nonfoods, 88

Great Atlantic & Pacific Tea Co.
    (*Cont.*):
  operating statistics, 23, 27, 123, 159,
    160, 173
  supermarket movement, 23, 25–26,
    90, 101, 158, 159–166, 167
Grimes, Don R., 86
Grocery stores, number, 189, 190
  position, 205, 210, 212–213
  sales, 192, 193, 199, 200
Gross margin, comparison, 93–95
  improvement, 96–98
  individual company, 91
  product lines, 92, 95–96
  specific products, 201–202
  trends, 89–93, 223
Growth, cycle, 223–225
  deterrents, 246–249
  financing, 243–245
Guthmann, Harry G., 149

Harb, Ray, 64
Haring, Albert, 67
Hartford, John A., 25, 160, 164
Harvard Business School Study of
    Food Chains, 54, 69, 95, 108,
    116, 119
Hayward, Walter, 14
Henke & Pillot, Inc., 17, 179
Hill, H. G. Stores, Inc., 181
Huegy, Harvey W., 169, 195
Humpty Dumpty Stores, 181

Illinois Valley Stores, 180
Indebtedness, 137–144, 149, 151
Independent Grocers Alliance of
    America, 4, 86, 87
Intangible assets, 130
Integration, food chains, 172–185
  horizontal, 169–172, 227
  vertical, 169–172
  with other retailers, 73, 227
Inventory, nonfoods (*see* Nonfood
    products)
  number of items, 68–69
  selection, 69
  turnover, 69–71, 134, 135
  vs. real estate, 133–135
Ireland, William S., 60

Jane Parker, 171, 184
Jewel Tea Co., Inc., 70, 76, 91, 150, 173, 179, 180
Jitney Jungle Stores, 181

Ketner-Milner Stores, Inc., 181
Kintner, Earl W., 183
Kleppner, Otto, 106
Kohler, Eric, 141
Kornblau, Curt, 130, 213, 215
Krambo Food Stores, Inc., 179
Kresge, S. S. Co., 62
Kroger Company
    integration, 14, 173, 177, 178, 179, 184, 227
    operating statistics, 70, 91, 150
    supermarket movement, 25, 26, 158, 159, 163
Kullen, King, 18–19, 21, 24, 25, 160
Kuznets, Simon, 33

Labor expense (*see* Payroll)
Lakewood Center, 45
Land, 122, 123, 124, 125, 128–130
Larrabee, C. B., 17, 20, 154
Lease
    equipment, 137
    fixed assets, 131–137
    new locations, 135–137
    vs. owning buildings, 132–133
Leaseback method, 136
Leasehold improvements, 130–131
Lebhar, Godfrey, 197
Lebow, Victor, 57, 58
Lexington Market, 12
Life, 50
Limited-line food store, 195–198
Lincoln Village, 44
Loblaw Groceterias Co., Ltd., 180
Loblaw, Inc., 180, 181
Location of supermarkets, 63–65
Logan, John A., 122, 129
Logan's Supermarkets, 180
Long-term indebtedness, 140–144
Los Angeles supermarkets, 11, 15–17, 153–154
Louisville Grocery Survey, 22
Lucky Stores, Inc., 70, 91, 150, 179, 181

Maker's Food Chain, 180
Mann, Everett, 145
Manufacturing and processing techniques, 35, 40–41
Marcus, Meyer, 121, 128
Margins (*see* Gross margin)
Market Basket, Inc., integration, 182
    operating statistics, 70, 90, 91, 149, 150
Market Basket Corp. (New York), 180
Market of the Sixties, 50–52
Market stores, 11, 15–17
Marketing research, 232–234
Mattei, G. L., 97
Maynard, Harold H., 68
McCall's Food and Grocery Products Diary Study, 48, 61, 63, 64
McCloskey, Joseph, 232
McNair, Malcolm P., 31, 69, 158, 195, 246
McNamara, Harley V., 122
Meat and seafood markets, number, 189, 190
    position, 202–204
    sales, 192, 199, 200
Merchandising, definition, 68
    display, 60–61
    new items, 77–78
    nonfoods, 71–73
    policies, 238–240
Montag's Supermarket Co., 180
Montgomery, Charlotte, 50
Moulton, Richard, 79
Mueller, Robert, 196
Myers, Herman L., 34

National Association of Food Chains, 122, 129
National Grocery Co., 73
National Recovery Act, 166
National Retail Dry Goods Association, 108
National Tea Co., building, 129
    costs, 122
    integration, 29, 178, 179, 180, 181, 227
    sales, 173
New products, 77–83
Nolen, H. C., 158

Nonfood products, impact, 216–219
  policies, 238–239
  purchases, 71–74
  sales, 213–219
  saturation, 248
Northwest Piggly Wiggly Co., 180
Notes payable, 140–141
Nugent, William C., 78, 79, 82
Nystrom, Paul H., 12, 166

Occupancy, 102, 103, 105
One-stop shopping, 46–49
Operating expenses (*see* Expenses)
Operating statements, 55, 56, 100, 124
Operations research, 232, 233, 234
Organization of supermarkets, 228–229
Otis, Robert M., 18, 121
Ownership capital, 144, 146

Parsons, Don, 61
Payroll, 55, 56, 102–104, 111, 116
Personnel, 103, 109, 241–243
Phillips, Charles F., 21, 22, 25, 30, 89, 194
Piggly Wiggly Stores, 11, 13–15, 29, 158, 180
Pike Place Market, 12
Population impact on supermarket, 41–43
Price, appeal, 57–58
  policies, 58–60
Printers' Ink, 153
Profit, comparison, 119–120
  Great Atlantic & Pacific Tea Co., 166
  individual company, 91
  on net worth, 133, 145–148
  on total assets, 133
  related to volume, fixed expense, and promotion, 230–237
  trends, 117–119
Progressive Grocer, 67, 96, 107, 108, 168, 208
Promotion, 65–68, 105, 236–237
Purity Stores, Ltd., 70, 91, 150

Rack jobber, 72, 87, 88, 214, 215, 219
Ralph's Grocery Co., 15
Rapp, Fred, Inc., 181

Ratio analysis, 148–150, 123–125
Reading Terminal Market, 12
Real estate expenses, 55, 56, 103, 105, 109, 111
Real estate mortgages, 143–144
Red and White Corp., 4, 64, 86
Refrigeration, 35, 38–40
Rent expense (*see* Occupancy)
Rental-purchase plan, 137
Research, 232–236
Richland, Arthur H., 138
Robinson-Patman Act, 106, 166
Roosevelt Field center, 45
Rowaldt, M. J., 153

Safeway Stores, Inc., integration, 14, 73, 173, 176, 177, 178, 179, 181, 184, 187
  operating statistics, 70, 91, 150
  supermarket movement, 158, 159
Salaries, 55, 56, 103–104, 109
Sales, food stores, 192–194
  percentage store area, 123
  policies, 57–74
  supermarket, 3
Saunders, Clarence, 13, 14
Schmalz, Carl N., 23
Schwegmann Brothers, Inc., 62, 73, 90
Scott, Forrest, 34
Scrambled merchandising, 31, 46, 49, 196–197, 251
Self-service, 61–62, 104, 116, 242
Selling operations, 53–74
Serv-U-Meat Markets, 181
Shaffer, Henry, 138
Shaffer Stores Co., 70, 90, 91, 118, 138, 150
Sherman Anti-trust Act, 171
Shirley Food Stores, 180
Shopping Bag Food Stores, 70, 91, 101, 150
Shopping, centers, 43–45
  facilities, 62–63
  habits, 46–50
Short-term indebtedness, 139–140
Slater, Charles, 197, 209
Small Business Administration, 140
Smith, C. F. Stores Co., 180
Smith, H. A. Markets, Inc., 180

Smith, V. B., 43
Southwest markets, 17–18
Smith's, George T. Basket, Inc., 180
Standards, establishment, 114
    measurement, 114–115
Stop and Shop, 180
Stop and Shop enterprise, 180
Store, expense, 109, 110, 111, 117
    image, 249
    operations, 107–112, 240–243
Straight-lease plan, 137
Subsidiary corporations, 136
Sunrise Supermarkets Corp., 70, 91, 150
Supermarket, decentralization, 45–46
    definition, 6–7
    development, 11–29
    impact, Chapters 10 and 11
    industry statistics, 3–6
    location, 5–6, 62–65
    operations (*see* functional areas
        such as advertising, buying, and
        selling)
Super Market Institute, 26–27, 80, 100,
        104, 105, 108, 111, 114, 115,
        119, 130, 214, 249
Super Market Merchandising, 27, 66,
        90, 99, 108, 118
Super Valu study, 92, 200
Supplies, 55, 56, 100, 111
Swift and Co., 172

Tanner Stores, 180
Tarlin, Lloyd B., 113
Tarrant, Chris, 73
Teutsch, Carl, 129
Thriftmart, Inc., 70, 91, 101, 150
Toilet Goods Association, 217
Tousley, R. D., 9, 197
Trade on equity, 149, 182

Trading stamps, 66–68, 106–107, 109
Transportation expense, 109, 110, 111,
    117
Trefethen, Florence, 232
Turnover (*see* Inventory)
Two Guys from Harrison, Inc., 73

Underhill, H. W., 129
Utilities, 55, 56, 100, 111

Value Markets, 180
Van de Kamp, Walter, 15, 16, 154
Voluntary Chain growth, 185–186
    integration, 185–186
    retail, 86–87
    wholesale, 86

Walgreen Drug Co., 62
Warehouse expense, 109, 110, 111,
    117
Weingarten, J., Inc., 17, 70, 91, 150
Weiss, E. B., 50, 77, 79
Westfall, Ralph, 232
Weston, George, Ltd., 180, 181, 184
White, Percival, 14
Wilt's Supermarket, 54, 56
Winn-Dixie Stores, Inc., 173, 178, 179,
    181, 182
Winn-Lovett Company (*see* Winn-
    Dixie Stores, Inc.)
Woolworth, F. W. Co., 62
Wrigley Stores Co. (*see* ACF-Wrigley
    Stores, Inc.)
Wyatt and Evans Food Stores, 179

Yoder, Wallace O., 67

Zimmerman, M. M., 18, 19, 21, 24, 25,
    27, 28, 57, 121, 122, 154, 156,
    157